Sex and Uncertainty in the Body of Christ

Gender, Theology and Spirituality

Series Editors
Lisa Isherwood, University of Winchester
Marcella Althaus-Reid, University of Edinburgh

Gender, Theology and Spirituality explores the notion that theology and spirituality are gendered activities. It offers the opportunity for analysis of that situation as well as provides space for alternative readings. In addition it questions the notion of gender itself and in so doing pushes the theological boundaries to more materialist and radical readings. The series opens the theological and spiritual floodgates through an honest engagement with embodied knowing and critical praxis.

Gender, Theology and Spirituality brings together international scholars from a range of theological areas who offer cutting edge insights and open up exciting and challenging possibilities and futures in theology.

Published:

Resurrecting Erotic Transgression: Subjecting Ambiguity in Theology
Anita Monro

Patriarchs, Prophets and Other Villains
Edited by Lisa Isherwood

Women and Reiki: Energetic/Holistic Healing in Practice
Judith Macpherson

Unconventional Wisdom
June Boyce-Tillman

Numen, Old Men: Contemporary Masculine Spiritualities and the Problem of Patriarchy
Joseph Gelfer

Ritual Making Women: Shaping Rites for Changing Lives
Jan Berry

Forthcoming titles:

For What Sin was She Slain? A Muslim Feminist Theology
Zayn R. Kassam

Our Cultic Foremothers: Sacred Sexuality and Sexual Hospitality in the Biblical and Related Exegetic Texts
Thalia Gur Klein

Through Eros to Agape: The Radical Embodiment of Faith
Timothy R. Koch

Baby, You are My Religion: Theory, Praxis and Possible Theology of Mid-20th Century Urban Butch Femme Community
Marie Cartier

Radical Otherness: A Socio/theological Investigation
Dave Harris and Lisa Isherwood

Catholics, Conflicts and Choices
Angela Coco

Telling the Stories of Han: A Korean, Feminist Theology of Subjectivity
Jeong-Sook Kim

Sex and Uncertainty in the Body of Christ

Intersex Conditions and Christian Theology

Susannah Cornwall

Routledge
Taylor & Francis Group

LONDON AND NEW YORK

First published 2010 by Equinox, an imprint of Acumen

Published 2014 by Routledge
2 Park Square, Milton Park, Abingdon, Oxon OX14 4RN
711 Third Avenue, New York, NY 10017, USA

Routledge is an imprint of the Taylor & Francis Group, an informa business

British Library Cataloguing-in-Publication Data

A catalogue record for this book is available from the British Library.

ISBN 13: 978-1-84553-668-8 (hbk)
ISBN 13: 978-1-84553-669-5 (hbk)

Library of Congress Cataloging-in-Publication Data
Cornwall, Susannah.
Sex and uncertainty in the body of Christ : intersex conditions and
Christian theology / Susannah Cornwall.
    p. cm. — (Gender, theology, and spirituality)
    Includes bibliographical references and index.
ISBN 978-1-84553-668-8 (hb) — ISBN 978-1-84553-669-5 (pbk.) 1.
Sex — Religious aspects — Christianity. I. Title. BT708.C665 2010
233'.5 — dc22

2009035240

Typeset by S.J.I. Services, New Delhi

CONTENTS

For Nathaniel, Charis, Charlie, Elias, Jack and Tirzah, the next generation; and in memory of my grandmother, Margaret Stephen, née Marshall, who had to choose between marriage and academia. (She chose marriage or I would not be here; but she lived to see a world where I, and other women, could choose both.)

Acknowledgements

I would like to thank everyone who has read, discussed and commented on parts of this manuscript and the thesis out of which it grew; thrown ideas around; suggested ideas for further reading or exploration; stepped in when my curiosity has outrun my proficiency in Hebrew and many other areas; or otherwise shared the doctoral journey. In particular, Rebecca Catto, Frances Clemson, Dom Coad, Anna Collar, Jenny Cornwall, Brutus Green, David Grumett, Cassie Hague, Mike Higton, Symon Hill, Emily Holden, Ingrid Holme, Dave Horrell, John Hughes, Cherryl Hunt, Louise Lawrence, Renato Lings, Alastair Logan, Sandra Lohmann Newall, Sarah Lorimer, Morwenna Ludlow, Mary Macneill, Stuart Macwilliam, Rebecca Mayes, David Moss, Noel Moules, Donald Murray, Andy Robertson, Christopher Southgate, Francesca Stavrakopoulou, Jacqui Stewart, Bee Taylor, Samuel Tongue, Jim Walters, Andrew Worthley, and Mark Wynn; and all the participants in the University of Exeter Department of Theology's graduate research seminars. Any mistaken notions contained here are mine, not theirs.

I am particularly grateful to my PhD supervisors – Rachel Muers, whose enthusiasm and dedication far exceed the call of duty, and Adrian Thatcher, who has remained supportive of my work and given invaluable encouragement and advice – and to my examiners – Marcella Althaus-Reid, whose dynamism and creativity have inspired me greatly and who is much missed, and Tim Gorringe, whose life is truthful and who always seems to know what I will do before I do it.

The PhD study out of which this book developed was funded by a scholarship given by the States of Jersey Department of Education, Sport and Culture, which allowed me the luxury of full-time study from 2004–2007.

Finally, to Jon Morgan, whose theological insights, and input on topics from the academic to the absurd, have been matched only by his patience in tidying up after me: God only knows what I'd be without you.

Exeter, 2009

Chapter 1

INTRODUCTION

> I am a creature of God, and ... I'm created, and intersexed people
> are created, no less than anyone else, in the image and likeness
> of God ... This is the way that we are, and ... what we've got here
> is not a walking, talking pathology, but a human being (Sally
> Gross, speaking in van Huyssteen 2003).

Traditionally, Christian theology has valued the integrity of the
body and the goodness of God reflected in creation, but has also
set much store by the apparent complementarity embedded in male
and female physiology. It has sometimes been threatened by
liminality, shifts in sexed and gendered identity, and non-marital
sexuality. Its unyielding norms of sexual morality have led to the
unnecessary exclusion and alienation of individuals from the
community of faith. Theology has both shaped and been shaped by
a culture which has tended to shun ambiguity and liminality
in favour of clearly demarcated categories of sex and gender.
Humans have all but divinized male-and-female sex in asserting
that it is all-encompassing – and, concomitantly, have been
suspicious of 'transgressive' sexual identities. However, prompted
by intersex and other marginal or contested sex-gender identities,
a deconstruction or querying of male and female as essential,
necessary or all-embracing human categories is possible. Human
bodies and human beings are different by virtue of more than sex.
In this book I show that theology should reflect an image of God
and of humanity more complex and diverse than an all-encompassing
male-female binary allows. Since ethics and praxis should be rooted
in theology, these, too, must reflect the diverse and non-binary
character of human sex.

Theologies stemming from other configurations of contested
and excluded bodies help to provide models for how intersex/DSD
might affect theologies in the future. Such theologies are explored
throughout the book. In this introductory chapter, however, I

outline the nature of intersex/DSD conditions and introduce the broad theological and ethical issues addressed in the book.[1]

Introducing Intersex/DSD

Human sex is more complex than a simple male-female binary where every individual is solely and unambiguously male or female. However, the common notion of the 'hermaphrodite' as an individual with a full set of both male and female organs is also inaccurate and misleading. Estimates suggest that at least 1 in 2,500 children in Europe and North America is born with an intersex/DSD condition – roughly the same prevalence as Down's syndrome or cystic fibrosis (Preves 2003: 2–3). All human foetuses start off with genital regions which appear identical, and typically, beginning at around seven weeks' gestation, the region gradually diverges along broadly male-related or broadly female-related lines (Preves 2003: 24–26). Because the difference between typically male-related and typically female-related genitals is actually a continuum rather than a binary, some genitals appear 'ambiguous', with a glans between the typical sizes for a clitoris or penis, or a genital opening which is only partially fused, so that the child cannot be readily identified male or female at birth. Other intersex/DSD conditions only become apparent later, perhaps at puberty when a girl does not begin to menstruate as expected. Across the various conditions, the external genitalia can appear typically male, typically female, in between, or mostly absent; internal genitalia and reproductive organs can include testes, ovaries, one testis and one ovary, or an ovotestis. Chromosomes can be XX, XY, XXY, XX/XY or a range of variations.

Doctors caring for genitally-ambiguous newborns have often advised parents to sidestep questions about the baby's sex from friends and relatives until further tests and karyotyping[2] have been

1. A glossary with more detailed information about specific conditions can be found at the end of this book.

2. Karyotyping involves arranging the chromosomes from a single cell and arranging them so that each numbered 'pair' of matching chromosomes is together. The chromosomes can thus be easily compared and examined for any unusual, extraneous or missing material. Karyotyping includes identifying the sex chromosomes, which are typically XX or XY but can vary. Where the external genitalia of an infant are ambiguous or missing, karyotyping is often carried out to give an indication of the child's sex – although basing sex on chromosomes alone can be problematic.

carried out and the child has been found to be male or female, or has been designated boy or girl. It is significant that the delay in waiting to be (or to make) certain has been deemed preferable to admitting that the sex is, for a time, unknown (Kessler 1998: 22; Preves 2003: 55). Parents thus not only 'bear the burden of the secret of their child's difference', but must also '[mask] the tension produced by the necessity of concealing this difference', in order to protect the social status quo (Feder 2006: 192). The eventual gender assignment has, in many cases, been reinforced by genital surgery. Surgery on an XX child with fused labia and a large clitoris might include clitoral reduction or recession, and surgery to open the vagina. Children with XY chromosomes and testes, but very small external genitalia, may have the penis and testes removed altogether and a rudimentary vaginal opening constructed in their place. Sometimes doctors have failed to explain to parents exactly why such operations are being done (Arana et al 2005), what is involved, or the fact that the child will often need a series of further procedures and/or hormone therapy throughout its life (Feder notes that parents of intersexed children whom she approached for interview expressed surprise and even suspicion that anyone wanted to hear their side of the story – Feder 2006: 193). Although this approach might stem from good motives, it also mitigates the capacity for informed consent on behalf of the parents and their ability to communicate with the child later about the medical condition. In the recent past it was common in Britain and North America for surgeries to be performed neonatally, but pressure from intersex/DSD groups has led to an increase in delayed or non-surgical treatment. Where early genital surgeries have been carried out in the past, it has generally been advised that corrected children should never be informed about any erstwhile ambiguity of sex.

Thea Hillman notes that the nebulous 'intersex community' is not homogenous:

> What many of us have in common are repeated genital displays, often from a young age. Many of us have had medical treatments done to us without our consent to make our sex anatomy conform to someone else's standards. Many of us suffer from intense shame due to treatments that sought to fix or hide our bodies. And many of us have experienced none of the above. (Hillman 2008: 149).

Although many people who received genital surgery as children have protested about their treatment (as I discuss in Chapter 2), not every individual who has had surgical intervention is unhappy with the outcome, and numerous people whose gender assignment was changed via surgery in childhood have grown up as contented and fulfilled individuals. Indeed, several support groups for people with intersex/DSD and their families have tended not to challenge established medical protocols of early surgery (Dreger and Herndon 2009: 205). The erstwhile Intersex Society of North America (ISNA) stressed in its guidance notes for parents of children with intersex/DSD conditions that not many children do change from their early gender assignment, and that children without intersex/DSD conditions might be just as likely to transition genders as they get older.[3] However, it is also possible, as a group of doctors working on studying outcomes suggest, that recurrent genital surgery 'may be associated with long term dissatisfaction with sexual function and an altered perception of body image', which 'may, itself, lead to a change in gender identity from female to male or vice versa' (Ahmed, Morrison and Hughes 2004: 848).

Existing Theological Work on Intersex/DSD

Although excellent sociological studies of intersex exist (e.g. Kessler 1998; Preves 2003), and considerations of why the treatment of intersex is *ethically* problematic exist (e.g. Dreger 1999; Sytsma 2006a), in-depth *theological* explorations of the topic have seldom occurred. Where theological engagement with intersex does exist, it has very often been done as an adjunct to reflection on transsexualism or homosexuality rather than in its own right.

An early engagement with intersex from the perspective of Christianity is made by Karen Lebacqz (1997). Crucially, Lebacqz maintains that just because a phenomenon like ambiguous genitals

3. 'Choosing a gender ... for your child is like choosing a gender for any child; you use what is known to make the gender assignment ... If your child grows to act gender 'atypical,' that is not because you have done anything wrong, and it does not mean your child is diseased or that you necessarily picked the wrong gender assignment; it just means your child is different from the statistical average, and the best thing you can do for him or her is to provide love and support for the child's individuality' (Consortium on the Management of Disorders of Sex Development 2006b: 49).

presents in a given child, it need not be accepted as a good thing. Provocatively, she asserts,

> We need not see all differences as God's mistakes, but we also need not see them all as God's will. The fact that children are born with ambiguous genitals may be incontrovertible evidence that there are not only two ways of being born, but that fact does not, alone, mean that we should allow every way of living that happens in nature (Lebacqz 1997: 224).

She asks whether, given the 'ostracism, rejection and ridicule' likely to be attached to life with unusual genitals, it is justifiable *not* to perform corrective surgery (Lebacqz 1997: 225). Although sympathetic to the argument that these issues are just as much social ones as ones attached to individual children, she also suspects that parents would be unwilling to allow their uncorrected intersexed children to undergo social suffering for the sake of making society more diverse and welcoming (though the testimonies of several families since 1997 show that this is not universally the case). Despite the fact that appropriate support will mitigate such suffering (Lebacqz 1997: 228–29), then, Lebacqz cannot unreservedly say that rejecting early surgery is the best path. Her essay contains helpful pointers to affinity between a politics of difference from intersex as compared to those grounded in disability and ethnicity, but I suspect it takes insufficient account of the ways in which theology itself has contributed to polarized gender norms in the West. Her suspicion that 'we cannot claim that it is necessarily God's will for people to grow up intersexed' (Lebacqz 1997: 225) is strongly belied in work by Mollenkott, Gross and others (discussed below), and means she cannot go far enough in an imaginative reconstruction of ethics grounded in sophisticated theological analysis.

Two later papers by Looy (2002) and Looy and Bouma (2005) give a useful psychological overview of the theological and ethical issues raised by intersex, including brief treatments of Bible verses such as Gen. 1. 26–31 and Mt. 19.12, but also lack close critical theological engagement. Their work, though admirably broad in scope, does not adequately question certain social assumptions about gender. For instance, they say,

> A person who is intersexed, whose brain has been organized to produce predispositions and preferences that do not nicely fit either of the available gender categories, is forced to fit a Procrustean

> bed that is either too long or too short; neither produces a good
> fit, but there is no bed of the right size available (Looy and
> Bouma 2005: 174).

This implies that *all* intersexed people have predispositions and
preferences which do not 'fit' gender categories, and thus feel
uncomfortable. In fact, as Koyama (2006), Liao (2007) and others
stress, plenty of intersexed people feel unremarkably male or female
even if their genitals appear unusual. By insisting that the
dichotomous gender system is 'a reasonably functional one', in which
'the vast majority of us are generally comfortable' (Looy and Bouma
2005: 174), Looy and Bouma also fail to acknowledge that
stereotypes about who is or is not oppressed by arbitrary standards
of conformity in gender and sex are unhelpful.

Looy and Bouma do conclude that it is hard to imagine that the
diversity of genders both across various species and among humans
(and the diversity of traits within genders among humans) all result
from sin or a fall. It is therefore also difficult to suppose, they
suggest,'that God's creational intent was monolithic females and
males' (Looy and Bouma 2005: 175). Similarly, Looy suggests,
'Rather than instinctively and unreflectively labelling intersexuality
as either sinful action, or an example of a broken creation, we should
at least ask whether intersexuality could be part of God's good
creation' (Looy 2002: 16). However, Looy and Bouma also comment,

> The mere observation that a phenomenon exists in nature does
> not by definition mean that it is part of God's intended good
> creation order. It may well reflect the consequences of the fall
> into sin ... We believe that sin has distorted both physical
> experiences and cultural expressions of gender. We believe that
> intersexed and transgendered persons exist in, and create for
> all of us, a tension between healthy diversity and the distortions
> of sin (Looy and Bouma 2005: 175-76).

But just as the existence of pain in creation does not automatically
render creation 'fallen', neither does the existence of non-binary
sex and gender. Looy and Bouma's position raises further questions
about where the 'line' might come between diversities which are
'healthy' and those which result from sin – and are thereby,
presumably, pathological – as well as *how* sin might have caused
(and continues to cause) distortions not factored into the original
creation. Their somewhat sweeping appeals to 'science' and

'experience' are not particularly persuasive. However, their main strength is to pose questions about how Christian communities 'might ... seek to minister with persons who are intersexed and transgendered' and 'recognize that gender assignments for such persons ... are tentative and might be subject to change' (Looy and Bouma 2005: 176), even if the answers are limited to a story about one pre-pubescent transgender boy who has been welcomed into a local church boys' club.

Two 2006 essays by Hester and Jung explore some ethical implications of the treatment of intersex/DSD in theological perspective. Hester explores the notion of healing, arguing that this is more than 'healing from' something. People with intersex/DSD conditions are involved with their own healing, their own rejection of oppressive socio-cultural narratives, just as much or more than the doctors who may set out to 'cure' them through eradicating their difference (Hester 2006). Jung's piece focuses mainly on critical analysis of a natural law-type objection to intersex/DSD, arguing that 'in a polymorphic model of human sexuality intersexuality would most probably be seen as morally normative' (Jung 2006: 298). Jung notes that many behaviours often rejected by the mainstream Christian tradition (such as homosexual activity, gender-bending and intentionally child-free marriages) would not necessarily be seen as problematic if the sexually dimorphic model on which so-called gender complementarity supervenes were disturbed. I expand this argument myself in Chapter 3. Jung also briefly critiques some inadequate Christian pastoral responses to intersex/DSD (Jung 2006: 303–304), but otherwise her essay largely provides useful background to the question of sexual polymorphism in the Roman Catholic tradition rather than specifically exploring intersex/DSD itself.

Unfortunately, Quero's 2008 essay on transgender, intersex, body fascism and incarnation addresses intersex in name alone, not engaging in any detail with its specificities. Quero does not appear to have read extensively on intersex/DSD, as evidenced by his reference to 'adrenal hyplasia' (as opposed to Congenital Adrenal Hyperplasia, the condition he seems to mean) (Quero 2008: 82); and his inclusion in his title of 'transgender/intersex bodies' is bothersome. Although transgender and intersex are by no means mutually exclusive categories, neither should they be conflated; Saraswati, a woman interviewed in Mortimer's 2002 film, says, 'It's ironic that the title of this programme is *Gender Trouble*, because there isn't any gender trouble for me or for many of my friends who have intersex conditions. It might be trouble for other people to accept our genders or how we see ourselves, but not for us' (Saraswati, speaking in Mortimer 2002). References to 'the common experience of transgender and intersex people' (Quero 2008: 90) risk conflating the two, particularly since Quero's essay focuses almost exclusively on transgender experience rather than the specific experience of intersexed people.

Quero is right that 'there is little, if any, room for transgender and intersex people' in many Christian churches (Quero 2008: 92); however, he does not go far enough to show why or how this affects intersexed people specifically. His examples and quotations, with the exception of one footnote, exclusively draw on transgender. He insists that he is advocating for the recognition that every human life is valuable beyond the dictums of heteronormativity, but by seeming to conflate transgender and intersex experience he risks failing to recognize the particularity of human experience and identity.

One theological work to have engaged more closely with intersex is Mollenkott's *Omnigender: A Trans-Religious Approach* (2001/2007).[4] Mollenkott holds that 'the binary gender construct ignores or contradicts factual reality' (Mollenkott 2007: 2), and that Christianity has oppressed people with intersex conditions just as it has those who are transgender, homosexual and bisexual. She asserts that 'God made no mistake by creating intersexuals. Therefore, their condition represents God's perfect will for them and for our culture' (Mollenkott 2007: 7), and that a more liberating and just system than the present binary one would be a paradigm of 'omnigender': God has chosen to embody Godself in multitudinous and various human gendered particularities (Mollenkott 2007: 17–18). Sex-gender segregation across society should end: sport, prisons, schools and public toilets should all be unisex. Mollenkott, like Gross (below), draws on readings of Genesis that appeal to a primary hermaphroditism in the original human, suggesting that sex (and genital) differentiation occurs only after the asexual creature has

4. The revised version of Mollenkott's book appeared after the bulk of my background work for this book had been done, and engages with much recent scholarship which I also cite but which was not part of the 2001 edition.

been divided. Thus 'intersexuals are not only part of God's original plan, they are *primarily* so!' (Mollenkott 2007: 98) and might be 'viewed as reminders of Original Perfection' (Mollenkott 2007: 99). Mollenkott's work is one of the only theological accounts of gender which fully acknowledges the reality of intersex.

However, *Omnigender* still has its shortcomings. By discussing intersex as a variant of transgender alongside transsexualism, cross-dressing, homosexuality, drag and so on, the book very explicitly renders it a comparable sexuality/gender-identity issue. In fact, many people do not understand their conditions in this way, and prefer to figure their intersex/DSD state as a *medical* condition rather than one which inevitably affects sex-gender identity. (It is for this reason that I suggest in Chapter 5 that it is also important to consider intersex through the lens of other variant body-states such as disability.) There is much helpful discussion of how intersex may be theologically understood as similar to these other states, but – as with Quero – little about what makes it different or distinctive (and Mollenkott admits that her background information on intersex is superficial [2007: 55]). Second, perhaps because the intersexed people whose stories Mollenkott cites are almost exclusively those who were vocal in the early, militant days of ISNA, there is no acknowledgement that not every intersexed person has an atypical or queer gender identity or considers a binary sex-gender system oppressive. This is unwittingly to treat intersexed people as many mainstream theologians have done, by lumping them in with other people whose sex-gender-sexuality configurations are deemed inevitably problematic – ironically, since Mollenkott actually wants to disrupt a pathological reading of intersex. Third, Mollenkott sometimes risks unproblematized anachronism when she suggests, for example, that the various cross-dressing nuns and saints in the Christian tradition were evidently transgender (Mollenkott 2007: 130–34). Fourth, although Mollenkott's endorsement of visions of a genderless or 'omnigender' future society is appealing in many respects, it seems to rely on an erasure of *all* distinct sex-gender identity and practice – as in the assertion that all children should be taught to urinate sitting down, rather than boys being taught to stand (Mollenkott 2007: 186), even if this may prove messier, less comfortable and less practical for those who *do* have the facility to stand. I do not feel that the implications of this amorphousness are sufficiently explored, nor that in order to make a less oppressive world all specificities of bodily difference need be elided. In fact, I believe just the opposite is true. Finally, Mollenkott's use of terminology is somewhat idiosyncratic, as when she seems to equate intersex with eunicism (Mollenkott 2007: 168), and in her practice of referring to an extremely wide range of people, including gay and lesbian people like herself, as transgender. Of course, Mollenkott is entitled to self-identify however she likes; but using a term commonly understood to mean something else may confuse or obscure the issues. So although I am grateful for the groundwork Mollenkott has done in this area, I hope in this volume to take it further, particularly with regard to the specificities of intersex as it differs from other kinds of bodiliness. There are certainly parallels in the ways and means by which intersexed and other people have been oppressed, but in challenging these we must not risk eroding their differences.

Gross' 1999 paper 'Intersexuality and Scripture' is the most important existing attempt to explore intersex in light of the Bible, and provides a perspicacious response to two texts which are, according to Gross, sometimes used as 'proof-texts' for rejecting intersex: Gen. 1.27 and Num. 5.3 (Gross 1999: 69). Gross reports that both verses have been used in conversation with her to argue that God created each person either male or female with nothing in between, and that intersexed people do not therefore satisfy the biblical criterion of humanity (Gross 1999: 70). Such deeply hurtful remarks are, however, unjustifiable, both ethically and – says Gross – textually. She argues in more detail the point noted by Mollenkott, that 'there is a rabbinical gloss on Gen. 1.27 which suggests that "Adam", at least, most certainly did not have a clear and unequivocal gender identity, and indeed that Adam was a hermaphrodite' (Gross 1999: 70). This is based on a grammatical shift in the Hebrew which, says Gross, 'suggests that to use the verse in support of a razor-sharp division of humankind between male and female is perhaps misguided' (Gross 1999: 71). The suggestion that Adam's androgynous nature predated Adam's sinful nature is important, holds Gross, for it may imply that sexual differentiation, not hermaphroditism, is 'fallen' (Gross 1999: 74).

In the 2003 documentary *The 3rd Sex*, made for the South African Broadcasting Corporation, Gross describes the vast change in attitude toward her when she realized in her 40s that the masculine gender in which she had been brought up and lived her life did not do justice to her full personal identity. Gross, at the time a Roman Catholic priest, was keen to take a 'life audit' to explore personal identity issues, surrounding her Jewish heritage as well as sex and gender, in preparation for possible appointment to priorships within the Dominican Order. She realized in the process that her sex of rearing did not tell the whole truth about her (in van Huyssteen 2003). Gross says,

> This was at the time when, in the Church of England, there was fierce debate about the ordination of women, and there was a lot of publicity about this, and [the head of the Order] was fearful. If the news about my own situation came out, it would be claimed that here was a Roman Catholic woman priest ... It was quite clear that he connected it with ... sexual abuse ... He was almost determined to see this as a perverse moral choice (Gross speaking in van Huyssteen 2003).

Gross consulted the head of the Order in England and was honest about her intersex/DSD condition, but says she was perceived as 'dangerous' and a 'monster'. When Gross did decide to live full-time in a feminine gender identity – without surgery – she says she faced opposition. Gross was not allowed to return to the priestly life. In 1994 she was told by the head of the Dominicans that Pope John Paul II had issued a rescript annulling her vows (van Huyssteen 2003). As well as being barred from priestly duties, she was no longer even allowed to receive communion. Gross comments that she felt utterly bereft, that the roots of her faith had been excised and denied the necessary nourishment of fellowship. She says, 'The loss of [my] faith was something which was forced. It was ... smothered because I am intersexed' (Gross speaking in van Huyssteen 2003).

Gross' desire to live an identity which she felt did less violence to her body (van Huyssteen 2003) meant that she was perceived to be moving away from an 'unambiguous' masculine life. This was despite the fact that Gross remained celibate and her body was as it had always been (Coan 2000a, 2000b, 2000c). It was made to seem that Gross had been masquerading as something she was not, when in fact she merely sought to be honest about what she was. Gross could not be allowed to decide what was an authentic outward expression of her body and psychology without, apparently, compromising her vocation and putting herself beyond speakability and conceptual legitimacy. This was particularly problematic, of course, given the male-only catchment of the Roman Catholic priesthood, and is an example of how essentialist male-female demarcations falter when faced with a body or identity which pushes their boundaries.

Theological Themes: Justice, Speakability, Dubious 'Goods'

In Christian theology, God, unlike humans, is 'officially' not sexed or gendered; masculine and feminine human genders are both held to echo aspects of God. It would be naïve to suppose that masculine imagery for God is not still privileged in many quarters,[5] but this is less universal than it used to be. However, within much mainstream Christian thought, to be made in the image of this God, even where *God* is genderless, is to be made either male or female, for male-and-female as a group description has come to be the all-encompassing conceptual arena in which social meaning is inscribed. We can just about think God beyond maleness, but, by and large, we cannot think ourselves beyond male and female. However, as the historian of intersex/DSD Alice Dreger asserts, 'The discovery of a "hermaphroditic" body raises doubts not just about the particular body in question, but about all bodies. The questioned body forces us to ask exactly what it is – if anything – that makes the rest of us unquestionable' (Dreger 1998: 6). Similarly, in Judith Butler's model (a valuable resource when considering the 'real' versus 'constructed' nature of bodies and bodily identities),

> It is the exception, the strange, that gives us the clue as to how the mundane and taken-for-granted world of sexual meanings is constituted. Only from a self-consciously denaturalized position can we see how the appearance of naturalness is itself constituted (Butler 1990: 110).

As self-evident as a binary biological model of sex might appear, it is already influenced by cultural assumptions about bodies, sexes and genders.

5. Ruether comments, 'Christianity has never said that God was literally male, but it has assumed that God represents pre-eminently the qualities of rationality and sovereign power. Since it is men that were assumed to be rational, and women less so or not at all, and men who exercised public power, normally denied to women, the male metaphor was seen as appropriate for God, while female metaphors for God came to be regarded as inappropriate and even "pagan"' (Ruether 1998: 82–83).

In her discussion of the prophetic-liberating tradition (which calls for justice for the oppressed, and equal worth to be given to all people whatever their sex), Ruether notes that it is 'a plumb line of truth and untruth, justice and injustice that has to be constantly adapted to changing social contexts and circumstances' (Ruether 1983: 23). I follow Ruether in believing that the 'plumb-line' of justice at the heart of theology must not be allowed to calcify so that it is not flexible or adaptable according to other tenets of human knowledge. To maintain that every human being is exactly and ineluctably male or female and that this entails a specific path of gendered and sexual orientation, and that any human being who cannot or will not follow this trajectory is more sinful, flawed or fallen than any other human, is unjustifiable in light of what scientific evidence tells us.

As Ruether notes, prophetic language, when used by religious people to stabilize and justify existing social structures, can be 'deformed in the interests of the status quo. It becomes a language to sacralize dominant authorities' (Ruether 1983: 24). Where settled, blood-related, normally male-led households are considered the ideal for stable, flourishing societies, and where the leaders of such households are likely to find it easier to climb the ladders of other social and cultural movements – including churches – it is far more difficult for the less privileged members of such societies to publicly question the incontrovertibility of the 'goods' – like heterosexuality – which come under the innocuous heading 'family values'. This is particularly significant since such 'goods' are already what is at stake when corrective surgery on genitally-ambiguous children with intersex/DSD conditions happens. However, such surgery may be no more justifiable than prescriptive heteronormativity in other areas of discourse, either ethically or ideologically. For example, the paradigm of early surgical intervention for intersex conditions, often beginning neonatally, has been criticized for making medically non-pathological bodies into social 'emergencies'. One paediatric urologist makes a startling claim: 'After stillbirth, genital anomaly is the most serious problem with a baby, as it threatens the whole fabric of the personality and life of the person' (Hutson 1992, cited at http://www.isna.org/agenda). As Amy Bloom comments, such an assertion implies that it is 'only slightly worse to be dead than intersexed' (Bloom 2002: 102).

Genital anomaly is portrayed here as more serious and, significantly, more *threatening*, than any other medical condition which might present itself at birth: more serious than severe brain damage, heart or lung defects, or a damaged spinal cord. But what exactly is it about the body which cannot easily be fitted into the expected male or female categories which is so threatening that such young children should have to undergo the trauma of surgery? While it would be extremely misleading to suggest that intersex/DSD conditions never carry concomitant medical issues which require immediate attention and close monitoring, the nature of these is often such that the medically urgent and the socially urgent do not coincide. Early surgery on the genitals is controversial exactly because it is rare for this to be medically necessary in infancy. Many neonatal surgeries carried out on atypical genitals are elective, non-essential ones. Much surgery could be delayed until at least the years immediately before puberty, when, whilst still a minor, the child would be old enough to know about their condition, and to understand the reasons for the specific proposed procedure, as well as to express their own sex and/or gender identity; some surgery could occur even later, when the individual is ready to become sexually active.

Why, then, does non-essential genital cosmetic surgery in infancy and childhood still occur? As a growing number of critics have suggested, it is possible that what is really hidden within pressures to perform early surgery is a desire that the bodies of people with intersex/DSD conditions not be visibly ambiguous for long enough to draw attention to the arbitrary nature of the apparently self-evident male/female binary. Gross asserts that, through intersex/DSD, 'What is being threatened is not the infant's health, but the infant's culture' (speaking in van Huyssteen 2003): a culture where either/or male and female sex and gender are 'just so'. In short, argues Holmes, 'Interventions made on the bodies of intersexed infants and children are proxy treatments of parental anxiety' (Holmes 2002: 165). She suggests that 'it is a function of power, rather than a statement of fact, to attribute the source of crisis to the birth of the intersexed child. The crisis in the clinic ought instead to be understood as a failure of the discourses of personhood in which expectant parents and their attendants invest' (Holmes 2008: 170). Grabham suggests that ethnicity is also an important consideration here, arguing that intersex surgeries tend to perpetuate certain genital forms that favour 'whiteness'. Surgeons' ideals of what genitals 'should' look like, the mythical genitals they have in mind when 'correcting' ambiguous genitalia, are just as much raced as gendered, being grounded in the white norms of surgeons in Europe and North America (Grabham 2008).

A consideration of the phenomenon of operating on intersexed children in order to 'correct' their disparate genitalia, therefore, must also be a catalyst for a broader consideration of the nature of hegemony and exclusion. For Butler, where femininity is viewed not simply as the inverse but actually as the absence of something, it cannot be described in its own right; it becomes unrepresentable, a 'sex that cannot be thought, a linguistic absence and opacity' (Butler 1990: 9). This notion of unrepresentability is even more compelling when applied to people with intersex/DSD conditions. Intersexed bodies as a category discrete from explicitly male and female ones have rarely been allowed to persist, at least in Western culture. Doctors have the power to 'disappear' genitals deemed unacceptable, rendering intersexed anatomies as unremarkable as possible. Doctors' positions are privileged ones, with concomitant authority to pronounce what bodies should and should not look like, and which bodies do or do not meet the accepted standards.[6] Similarly, theology has also found itself in a position of privilege, and has asserted its authority over bodies and their sexes, as, for instance, pronouncing which bodies may undertake certain roles within the Church, or delimiting which bodies may be joined in marriage. It is for this reason that, although intersex and homosexuality are quite different, some of the work done by homosexual and queer theologians in questioning sexual norms is also of importance in considering intersex (as I explore in Chapter 6).[7]

6. It might be countered that doctors do not *decide* which bodies are acceptable, but simply *respond* to the taxonomies already concretized in society. However, as Kessler notes, although culture does demand gender, the whole process is a circularity: 'If culture demands gender, physicians will produce it, and … when physicians produce it, the fact that gender is "demanded" will be hidden from everyone' (Kessler 1998: 75).

7. A comprehensive examination of the ongoing hermeneutical debates surrounding homosexuality in theology and biblical studies is beyond the scope of this book. However, I work from the premises that same-sex erotic activity and relationships are no more inherently sinful or 'fallen' than their heterosexual counterparts; that the biblical texts discussing homosexuality

It is therefore encouraging to see an increasing theological engagement with intersex in responses to homosexuality, as in Hare's recent essay (Hare 2007). Hare, a priest also trained in gynaecology and obstetrics, uses intersex to open a space of questioning around homosexuality for those whose default position is that everyone is unproblematically male or female and their gender and sexuality should supervene on this (Hare 2007: 98–99). He summarizes,

> The existence of intersexuality confounds the tidy categories that some Christian ethicists and church leaders work with and challenges us all to think more deeply about the God-given nature of our sexuality ... The condition of intersexuality ... draws our attention to the complexity and diversity involved in the development of human sexuality (Hare 2007: 99).

Nixon suggests there are three main reasons why churches are often reluctant to heed minority sexual voices: the 'broad methodological issues involving the use of human experience in the making of theology'; concerns about 'accessing or translating human experience acquired through other academic disciplines and methods'; and, crucially, 'an embarrassed reluctance to listen to alternative stories about sex ... because of the substantial investment in hetero-patriarchy among powerful parts of church and society' (Nixon 2008: 613). The last of these is particularly important, particularly given that intersexed voices may be excluded on the grounds of sexed 'deviance' even if the individuals concerned do not consider their condition a sexual matter at all.

In this book, then, I set out to render intersex representable and speakable within a theological framework, and query the strands within Christian theology which privilege clearly-sexed, heteronormative configurations of sexes, sexualities and genders to the exclusion of people whose bodies or identities do not 'fit'. This reflects back into all manner of theological assertion about the meaning and significance of gender: it becomes far more difficult to unproblematically assert that women should not be ordained, or

are not necessarily prohibiting the same-sex relationships possible in our own culture; and that there are questions to be asked surrounding whether biblical mandates about sexual activity, as with other moral injunctions, must or should be taken as normative for today.

be made bishops, if we can no longer be quite so certain of what a woman actually is.

Dreger, in undertaking an historical study into hermaphroditism and its figuring in the context of broader categories of sex, was shocked to discover the ongoing problems and culture of shame still facing some of those who had undergone surgery for intersex. In an epilogue to *Hermaphrodites and the Medical Invention of Sex*, she describes the continued physical and psychological pain of some intersexed people, and says, 'Ethical behavior means recognizing and respecting the imperatives embedded in stories of suffering' (Dreger 1998: 170). This is a crucial reminder to theologians from beyond our own discipline. Just as it cannot be ethically justifiable to say that women's rights are a sideline or a secondary issue in Christianity, because millions of women and girl children continue to be killed and injured specifically because they are female (Soskice 1996: 24–25), so it cannot be ethically justifiable to endorse, tacitly or otherwise, the violation of the bodies of those with intersex/ DSD conditions simply because they are intersexed. Ruether argued in the 1980s that 'whatever diminishes or denies the full humanity of women must be presumed not to reflect the divine or an authentic relation to the divine ... or to be the message or work of an authentic redeemer or a community of redemption' (Ruether 1983: 15). The same goes for intersex/DSD and non-binary gender identities. If our theologies of sex and embodiment are to be rooted in praxis, the stories recounted by intersexed people demand our critical and compassionate ethical responses too.

Vocabulary and Terminology

People with intersex/DSD conditions use a range of terminology for their states: 'epicene' (Chris in Harper 2007: 152); 'intersex variations' (Morris 2004); 'intersexuality' (Beck 2001); simply 'IS' (Talley 2005). The recent convention of scholars, such as Dreger and Kessler, has been to refer to 'intersex conditions', describing those who have them as 'intersexed', and using 'intersex' to refer to the issue in general. Although the term 'condition' may be seen as having pejorative associations (see e.g. Preves 2003: 44), it is preferable to terminology used in the past, particularly in medical literature, such as 'disease', 'disorder' or being 'sexually unfinished' (Money and Ehrhardt 1972: 5; Money 1980: 21). 'Intersexuality' and 'intersexualism', terms used by some other writers, are problematic because they sound so much like 'homosexuality', 'bisexuality' and 'transsexualism' that it is tempting to consider all of these in the same breath, whereas some intersexed people are keen to distance themselves from the LGBT movement. For example, Mairi MacDonald of the United Kingdom Intersex Association says, 'In general, we are distrustful of those who wrongly presume that their experiences are similar to ours. We tend to view suggestions of alliances built on this basis as invasive and attempting to appropriate our experiences for agendas other than our own' (MacDonald 2000).[8] 'Intersexinity' as a term analogous to 'masculinity' and 'femininity' has been mooted (Looy and Bouma 2005: 167) – but since many intersexed people argue that intersex in itself does not compromise the ability to express a masculine or feminine *gender* identity, the necessity for such a term is debatable.

In 2005, ISNA, one of the largest and most influential intersex support and advocacy groups, began to use the term 'DSD', Disorders of Sex Development, in place of 'intersex conditions', in communication and discourse surrounding medical reform. This has been continued by ISNA's successor organization, Accord Alliance. It was felt that DSD was a less emotionally charged term than intersex and would be better received by the doctors and parents whom ISNA aimed to educate. I explore the issues surrounding this terminology in greater detail in Chapter 2. My decision not to use 'DSD' exclusively throughout this book is not to ignore warnings about the limitations of intersex terminology. I have chosen to use 'intersex' or 'intersex/DSD' for several reasons. First, at the time of writing, 'intersex' continues to be the more widespread term among support groups and in related discourses. There is still much debate among those with intersex/DSD conditions about whether or not 'disorder' is an inevitably unhelpful or stigmatizing term. The 2006 publications from the Consortium on the Management of Disorders of Sex Development (2006a; 2006b)

---

8. Similarly, the website of the AIS Support Group UK states, 'We are not happy with the recent tendency of certain trans groups/people to promote *transgender* as a term to encompass, for example, transsexuality, transvestitism *and intersex*. We object to other organisations/individuals putting us in categories without consulting us, especially categories that imply that intersexed people, of necessity, have gender identity issues' (http://www.medhelp.org/www/ais/).

both contain acknowledgements that some of the intersexed people interviewed for the DSD Guidelines project do not support the term DSD (Consortium on the Management of Disorders of Sex Development 2006b: ii). Whilst I acknowledge Bo Laurent and Accord Alliance's reasons for endorsing it, the language of 'disorder' still seems to fail to disrupt adequately medical-social paradigms of normalized sex and gender.

My other major reason for retaining 'intersex' is that I discuss intersex/DSD not only in the medical context in which DSD is arguably more useful, but also in its broader context. One of the strengths as well as weaknesses of the term 'intersex' is that it has been used so broadly. As such, it has been taken on and invested in as an identity by many people who have wanted to question established norms of sex and gender. Since I, too, attempt to explore and query these norms, it seems appropriate to acknowledge the social as well as physiological-medical aspects of intersex. Where I use 'intersex/DSD', I do so acknowledging its visual clumsiness. However, the very presence of the unsightly slash in this construction is important, illustrating tension as a visual reminder of the uncertainty of the term and its resonances. It demonstrates the imperfection and incompletion of either term alone, and precludes reading and accepting the term easily or unthinkingly. Much more than either/or, intersex/DSD is at once both and neither, a perpetually-debatable term for a perpetually-debated group of phenomena. This construction, then, might be figured as an instance of what Iain Morland calls 'narrative ambivalence':

> Taking seriously narrative ambivalence means acknowledging that arguments made in "postmodern times" for medical reform do not get their ethical force from univocal, incontestable statements about what is the right thing to do. On the contrary, postmodern ethical statements productively destabilize such categorical, didactic claims to authority ... An ethical account of intersexuality is one that through narrative ambivalence continually queries its own mastery (Morland 2006: 330).

In general parlance, 'male' and 'female' tend to be used as shorthand for 'masculine' and 'feminine'. However, the existence of transgender reminds us that not everyone who presents as a man is necessarily male. Moreover, as I show in Chapter 2, definitions of what actually renders someone male or female have changed over time and are not necessarily as unwavering as we might suppose. A transgender woman who interacts socially in a feminine role may, in fact, still produce sperm (that is, male gametes), although there may be nothing in her appearance to suggest she is not female. We tend to base our assumptions about sex on secondary signals such as dress, build, and voice register, which concretize into beliefs about individuals' 'cultural genitals' (Herdt 1994b; Morland 2001a: 528); that is, the genitals (and, by association, gametes) they are *assumed* to have although it is not considered generally polite to look inside their underwear to find out.

In this book, therefore, I endeavour to use the terms 'male' and 'female' *only* in reference to sex, rather than as shorthand for 'man' and 'woman' (which I use as cultural gendered terms, rather than sexed ones). On this account, a woman may or may not be female. I am aware that the very act of distinguishing sex and gender has been effectively questioned – in, for instance, Butler 1990: 23–33. The whole structure of gender relies upon an appearance of internal coherence between sex, gender and sexuality, but in fact the labels are never finished and are being continually redefined – it is society itself which sustains the myth of the finished norms. However, I maintain a clear distinction between sexed and gendered terms because this helps draw attention to the many instances where sex is assumed and often then taken up and made compulsory, despite the fact that an individual's sex may not 'match' what is supposed.

Methodology

The PhD thesis on which this book is based was grounded in library-based research. My two main sources of literature were non-theological works on intersex from sociology and history, and theological works on the topics of transgender, disability and queer theology. This use of existing material was conscious and necessary; given the scope of the project, carrying out empirical work and interviews would have left too little time for analysis. During my research I made contact with self-identified intersexed people largely through internet forums and discussion boards. Several intersex groups did not wish to pass on my details to their members, since the purpose of the group was for peer support rather than research, and they were understandably wary of allowing non-intersexed people to participate. I have thus made extensive use of previously-published intersex/DSD testimonies (such as those in Dreger 1999), and of television interviews with, and documentaries about, Max Beck, Ilizane Broks, Kristi Bruce, Howard Devore, Mani Mitchell, Angela Moreno, Sally Gross, Louise Thompson and others. I am, however, acutely aware of the problems associated with drawing on previously-published interviews and statements: not least, the issue of self-selection, the fact that those who have made their stories public, particularly those unhappy with current or recent protocols, are not necessarily representative of a majority of people with intersex/DSD conditions. Where interviews are presented as part of television films or newspaper articles, there is always the risk that a particular spin has been put on the words of the interviewees. First-hand statements or self-publications, such as blogs, might appear more 'direct', but an element of self-censorship (or tempering one's words to make them suitable for a particular perceived audience or context) is inevitable. The testimonies of those people with intersex/DSD conditions cited herein must therefore not be viewed as overarching or characteristic of all people with similar conditions.

Representing intersexed individuals, and working toward a theology from intersex/DSD, is problematic if done, as here, by a non-intersexed person. However, this does not mean that thinking with intersex/DSD as a non-intersexed person is entirely inappropriate. In fact, whilst it would be reprehensible to colonize the standpoint of an intersexed person as my own, it is crucial that those who are not intersexed consider and participate in discourse about it along with those who are. To say that only someone from a particular group can speak about or reflect on that group risks ghettoizing particular issues, so that they are always pushed to the edges, left as minority concerns rather than those which conceivably impact upon and implicate everyone. This point is made convincingly by Alice Dreger, a non-intersexed activist for intersex/DSD issues, who has written of her opposition to the notion that identity politics can only be done by individuals who claim the specific, given identity (Dreger 2006b). It is crucial, as far as possible, to reflect on intersexed people's *own* reflections and testimonies concerning their lives and experiences; but *my* own reflection on intersex/DSD also necessitates a self-critical evaluation of my assumptions and the ways in which my background affects the manner in which I view it. The existence of intersexed people can help to query the perceived norms of physiology and gender which seem to undergird much mainstream theology (not just that concerned with 'sex' issues), but I should be asking them *on my own behalf.* They should prompt me to re-examine my own assumptions and situation as a non-intersexed person. In her study of Christian feminism among black and white women, Susan Brooks Thistlethwaite remarks,

> Gustavo Gutiérrez once said that he is suspicious of anyone who is not in the liberation struggle for themselves. I am not in this exploration of the difference race makes *for* black women; nor am I in it *on behalf* of black women. I want to know *for myself* what is being hidden and carried along unexamined in the class and race solidarity of white women (Thistlethwaite 1990: 46).

My non-intersexed experiences are mine to own in a way that those of people with intersex/DSD conditions are not. Throughout the book I have done my utmost to consider Emi Koyama's 'Suggested Guidelines for Non-Intersex Individuals Writing About Intersexuality and Intersex People' (Koyama 2003a).[9]

I follow Marcella Althaus-Reid in believing that mainstream Western theology largely rests upon 'a heterosexual construction of reality, which organizes not only categories of approved social and divine interactions but of economic ones too' (Althaus-Reid 2000: 2). It is necessary to employ a hermeneutic of suspicion in order to explore which voices have been marginalized and what they have been trying to say. As such, I am keen to embrace Althaus-Reid's rejection of 'androcentric' methodology (Althaus-Reid 2000: 5). This rejection entails an acceptance that subjective testimony and personal experiences – including sexual experiences – are legitimate sources for theological reflection. It is sometimes necessary to make theology 'indecent' (Althaus-Reid 2000: 5) in order to reveal what is naturalized hegemony.

Despite the problems associated with classic Liberation Theologies, particularly that of Enrique Dussel, as explored by Althaus-Reid and others (in Althaus-Reid 2006a), I retain throughout

9. These include: recognizing intersexed people themselves as experts on what it is to be intersexed; reading texts by non-intersexed doctors and academics critically; acknowledging that 'intersex people are no more responsible for dismantling gender roles and compulsory heterosexuality than anyone else is' (Koyama 2003a: 32); not conflating intersex and LGBT experience; not reducing intersexed people to their conditions; focusing on what intersex says about my own and society's perspectives; and recognizing the multiplicity and diversity of intersexed people. See Koyama 2003a: 32–33.

the book Dussel's suspicion of Totality, of all-encompassing ontologies which leave no space for otherness beyond their internal system (Dussel 1978: 20). Dussel comments, 'Just as dead as totalized flesh is divinized totality because it believes itself to be God; it is the idol. It is that Totality that Otherness breaks into' (Dussel 1978: 29). Although Dussel himself would not necessarily have recognized it as such, I assert that a heteronormative, male-and-female binary sex system is indeed a divinized totality held to be all-encompassing; as such, it must be exposed as the golden calf that it is. Totalities are closed and absolutized through a process of fetishization (Dussel 1985: 95). Either/or male-and-female sex has itself been fetishized. Humans have believed that to describe human beings as male and female made in the image of God means that *only* recognized patterns of male and female are made in the image of God. As David F. Ford comments, 'Above all, [theology's] alliance with ontology conspires against doing justice to an ethics which resists the assimilation of the other person to oneself and one's overview' (Ford 1999: 50).

In the following chapter I give an outline of how intersex has been treated and understood at different points in history, in order better to understand its relationship to socio-cultural norms of sex and gender, and to begin to see how theological attitudes to sex and gender have both influenced and been influenced by these.

Chapter 2

REFLECTING AND REPRODUCING: THE HISTORY OF INTERSEX

> The presupposition that there are two sexes is a theoretical
> presupposition and the models must be constructed so as to
> fulfil that theoretical claim. We might think of models more clearly
> as tools with which to think about the world. We need such
> tools for a variety of reasons, not the least of which is that the
> world has too much going on in it and we need to make choices
> about which particular features we should be looking at. Just
> that recognition alone, however, gives a different slant to what
> it is that science does. So the theory is describing the model, not
> the world (Crasnow 2001: 143).

Human sex has not always been understood (and still is not
understood in every human culture)[1] as an obvious and immovable

1. This project cannot explore in detail attitudes to intersex in non-European
and North American societies, but work done by Serena Nanda, Gilbert Herdt
and Will Roscoe is illuminating in the consideration of liminal or 'third'
gender roles for intersexed, transgender or transvestite and homosexual people,
such as the Native American *berdaches* and Indian *hijras* (Roscoe 1994; Nanda
2002). Herdt discusses societal attitudes toward people with 5-ARD in
communities in the Dominican Republic and Papua New Guinea where it is
comparatively common, and explores the extent to which intermediate *sex* is
accommodated even within strictly bi-gendered societies (Herdt 1994a, 1994b,
1994c). However, as Anne Fausto-Sterling notes, Herdt has been criticized for
projecting 'assumptions that reflect his own culture' (Fausto-Sterling 2000:
18) and failing to reflect critically enough on Western models of sexuality
and gender. Commenting on her own engagements with Roscoe's work,
Morgan Holmes adds that he, too, 'continually focuses his attention specifically
on anality and mode of dress as though those were the most salient and
important features of the *berdache* when, in fact, it is likely that those features
take on a central importance only in a history of Euro-American colonization'
(Holmes 2004). Nanda, in her discussion of *hijras* (that is, castrated males who
dress and behave as women) in Hinduism, notes that the concept of a third
gender goes back to at least the eighth century BCE in India, but that members
of the intermediate gender were traditionally considered at least partially
defective males because of their lack of procreative capacity (Nanda 2002:

binary. The either/or two-sex model of human sex in which the early corrective surgery paradigm is grounded is a strikingly recent one, and early and secretive surgery has been done as much to bolster the model as to promote the well-being of the individuals who undergo it. The 'goodness' of maintaining the model has, in fact, become confused with the 'goodness' of unambiguous genitals themselves. This has occurred in theological as well as social contexts; theology is therefore responsible for engaging with and critiquing the ethically problematic consequences of the recent and ongoing treatment of intersex/DSD.

Inadequate Models?

The model of two human sexes, male and female, with no overlap or exception, is a clear and useful way of making sense of a world which, as Sharon Crasnow asserts, often seems to have too much going on in it (cf. Feder 2006: 191). However, the existence of intersex/DSD, and of people who are transgender or who otherwise do not appear to fit every aspect of this model, suggests that it is inadequate. Any model is only ever a line of best fit, stretched by unusual cases. It might be tempting to suspect that the more visible and prevalent intersex/DSD is, the more convincingly it subverts concretized gender binaries: Professor of Biology and Gender Studies, Anne Fausto-Sterling, has faced criticism for work in which, it is argued, she implied that intersex was statistically more common than it actually is (Sax 2002).[2] In a 2001 interview, Fausto-Sterling suggested, 'We should lighten up on those who fall in between [male and female] because there are a lot of them' (Sax 2002; Dreifus 2001: 3) – which implies, deliberately or not, that *frequency itself* should be a motivation for taking intersex/DSD seriously. However, as Georgia Warnke says,

138). For an ethics-based overview of approaches to intersex/DSD in Asia, see Warne and Bhatia 2006.

2. Sax's criticism is based on the fact that Fausto-Sterling (2000) uses figures of about 1.7% of births being of 'intersexed' children – rather than the more conservative estimate of 0.04% (or 1 in 2,500) births used by other scholars, such as Preves (Preves 2003: 2-3). Fausto-Sterling's figures are higher because they include statistics for conditions which are not always classed as intersex conditions (such as Turner's syndrome, hypospadias and MRKH), though interestingly they may now be included under the umbrella DSD.

The relevant question is not whether cases of ambiguous or unacceptable genitalia occur often enough to undermine the biological basis for dividing populations into two sexes. The relevant question is rather what genital surgery says about the categories of sex themselves: are they written into nature or are they insisted on by cultural and historical conceptions of gendered forms and practices? (Warnke 2001: 129).

In her seminal work *Purity and Danger*, Mary Douglas says,

Culture ... mediates the experience of individuals. It provides in advance some basic categories, a positive pattern in which ideas and values are tidily ordered ... But its public character makes its categories more rigid ... They cannot so easily be subject to revision. Yet they cannot neglect the challenge of aberrant forms. Any system of classification must give rise to anomalies, and any given culture must confront events which seem to deny its assumptions. It cannot ignore the anomalies which its scheme produces, except at risk of forfeiting confidence (Douglas 1966: 38–39).

Douglas sets out five possible ways in which societies might deal with anomalous or ambiguous events, like the births of unusual-looking children:

1. Re-classifying them so that they are no longer anomalous (like the Nuer people who reckon that 'monstrous' children are really baby hippopotamuses accidentally born into human families, and so 'return' them to the river).
2. Eradicating anomalous forms (by killing or abandoning atypical children or animals).
3. Avoiding contact with anomalous things wherever possible.
4. Categorizing them as 'dangerous' rather than 'anxiety-provoking', in order to buttress the 'normal' and keep it above contradiction.
5. Incorporating them into myth and story as windows onto other, usually inaccessible, levels of existence (Douglas 1966: 39–40).

There is evidence that intersex/DSD has been treated in each of these ways at various points, but the early surgery paradigm seems rooted particularly in the first, the second and to some extent the fourth approaches. Asserting that a child is 'really' one gender or another but is 'unfinished' smacks of the first strategy, and carrying out early genital surgery to conceal or remove genital atypicality of the second. Either way, the fact that medicine responds at all to intersex/DSD demonstrates a confrontation of events which seem to deny its assumptions: in this case, the assumption that there are only two legitimate sex configurations.

Butler comments that a poststructuralist reading of Douglas might 'understand the limits of the body as the boundaries of the socially hegemonic' (Butler 1990: 131). This is important in beginning to contextualize the ways in which intersex/DSD has been equated with 'transgressive' identities and activities such as homosexuality, one significant reason why it has incited suspicion in some Christians. In this chapter I give space to the testimonies of people who have undergone corrective surgery, in order to keep these at the forefront of considering intersex/DSD even as they stand in distinction from my own position in this history of sexed 'meaning'.

The Pre-Modern Period: Anatomy, Appearance and A Priori *Beliefs*

Throughout history there has been a fine line between the consideration of 'hermaphroditic' bodies as miracle (roughly, Douglas' fifth approach to anomaly) and as monstrosity. Importantly, as Thomas Laqueur contends in *Making Sex: Body and Gender from the Greeks to Freud*, the ways in which even male-female sex difference has been figured at given times in history have been 'largely unconstrained by what was actually known about this or that bit of anatomy, this or that physiological process', and 'derive instead from the rhetorical exigencies of the moment' (Laqueur 1990: 243). He says,

> The history of the representation of the anatomical differences between man and woman is … extraordinarily independent of the actual structures of these organs or of what was known about them. Ideology, not accuracy of observation, determined how they were seen and which differences would matter (Laqueur 1990: 88).

In other words, beliefs about anatomical difference reflect existing beliefs about the cosmic and social order, and are part of what reproduces them. Although we might now like to suppose that our knowledge of sex and gender relies solely on rigorous scientific observation, actually, as Crasnow implies, what is observed is always affected by what one is looking for in the first place. The 'evident' differences between male and female bodies which make them mutually exclusive and discrete are only so evident because of particular meanings attached to specific characteristics *a priori*. A tall, broad, muscular man may be characterized as particularly masculine and a small, slim woman as particularly feminine; but there are also tall, broad, muscular women and small, slim men. There are men with fatty breast tissue and women without it. As Warnke says, arguing that most characteristics are always and ineluctably 'sexed' (that is, linked to one particular sex) makes as little sense as deeming certain characteristics irreducibly and incontrovertibly 'raced' (Warnke 2001).[3] This does not mean there may not be a clustering of particular characteristics – individuals who produce more oestrogen and progesterone are likely to have a broadly different distribution of body fat from those who produce androgens – but it does mean acknowledging the self-reinforcing quality of such clusterings (if slenderness is considered a 'feminine' quality, this is likely to prompt more women to keep their bodies slim, which then buttresses slenderness as 'characteristic' of women).

Part of what has continued to inform particular binary models of human sex has been the belief – reinforced by some strands of Christian theology – that sex must coincide with gender, where masculine and feminine characteristics are deemed to complement and complete each other. However, the idea that there are two (and only two) *different* sexes is a strikingly recent one. Laqueur

3. Warnke says, 'The concept of race does not hold up as a scientifically viable way of grouping human beings. It does not identify a cluster of genes at the biological level that could serve to sever human beings into neatly separable groups. It does not help identify discrete packages of color and morphology that could separate groups. It is muddled and asymmetrical in its groupings of individuals by ancestry. Finally, while genetic predispositions to certain diseases might provide a more useful way of grouping individuals, at least for medical purposes, such groupings deviate from ordinary uses of the term "race" ... [Intersex] surgery raises the question of what our categories of sex are meant to refer to: chromosomes or anatomy? Moreover, if they can refer to either depending on the decisions of teams of doctors, how different, really, are the categories of sex and race? Is assigning a female sex to an infant with one Y chromosome any more securely based in "nature" than assigning a black race to a pinkish infant with one-sixteenth African-American heritage?' (Warnke 2001: 126, 128). This has also been explored in some detail by Alison Stone in *Luce Irigaray and the Philosophy of Sexual Difference*; Stone explores the charge of biological essentialism often levelled at Irigaray, and essentialism's problematization by intersex (A. Stone 2006, especially 113-19).

argues that, throughout the Graeco-Roman era, for example, beliefs about gender meant that it made sense for male bodies and female bodies to be figured as sharing in a *single* sex – though to different degrees. In the Hippocratic model, sex was figured as a continuum with (unequivocal) male and female at either end and hermaphrodites in between. Aristotle viewed the sexes as more distinct, and the hermaphrodite as an individual who was authentically one sex but who also possessed 'extra' material of the other sex, perhaps from an abortive twin (Dreger 1998: 30). Removing this 'surplus' matter, Aristotle believed, would reveal a perfect individual of one sex or the other. Laqueur believes that the Hippocratic and Aristotelian representations are both instances of a 'one sex' model, viewing male and female as, respectively, more and less perfect reflections of a single larger human state, where females are merely incomplete males.

Later theorists amplified this 'one sex' view, figuring female reproductive organs as inverse or inferior versions of male organs; Galen believed women must produce sperm, for they had 'testes' and sexual urges, as men did (Laqueur 1990: 40). Female gonads were figured as male-gonads-but-less-so (Laqueur 1990: 40); females could not have a sex or sexuality actively, specifically or distinctly their own, but only a pale imitation of males'. Laqueur expands,

> Claims that the vagina was an internal penis or that the womb was a female scrotum should ... be understood as images in the flesh of truths far better secured elsewhere. They are another way of saying, with Aristotle, that woman is to man as a wooden triangle is to a brazen one ... Anatomy in the context of sexual difference was a representational strategy that illuminated a more stable extracorporeal reality (Laqueur 1990: 35).

Right up until the seventeenth century, in fact, argues Laqueur, sex remained a *sociological* rather than an *ontological* category (Laqueur 1990: 8).[4] He holds that the major conceptual divide occurred in the eighteenth century, when 'a biology of cosmic hierarchy gave way to a biology of incommensurability, anchored in the body, in which

4. Laqueur says, 'In ... pre-Enlightenment texts, and even some later ones, *sex*, or the body, must be taken as the epiphenomenon, while *gender*, what we would take to be a cultural category, was primary or "real" ... To be a man or a woman was to hold a social rank, a place in society, to assume a cultural role, not to *be* organically one or the other of two incommensurable sexes' (Laqueur 1990: 8).

the relationship of men to women ... was not given as one of equality or inequality but rather of difference' (Laqueur 1990: 207).

For Laqueur, then, cultural discourses shape how individual and social experience is understood. In the Graeco-Roman period, biological maleness and femaleness were mapped onto already-socially-sanctioned 'gender' significations. The main focus was on the maintenance of status, as reinforced through correct gender functions; the genitals merely facilitated these. The births of children who appeared as if they would be infertile in adulthood (because of ambiguous or missing genitalia) interfered with the way in which biological reproduction helped to perpetuate the reproduction of particular social norms. Aristotle thus attributed hermaphroditic births to a disruption in *order* rather than in *nature* – a traversing of the socially, as well as cosmically, desirable. It was believed that females could spontaneously reproduce without male influence – but that such births would be of monstrous, soulless children, since it was the male sperm which was held to provide the 'spiritual', rational matter. As hermaphroditic children were thought to be the result of parthenogenesis, they threatened gender boundaries twice: through the absence of the male element in their generation; and in and through their own unusual bodies.

The one-sex model might also be read as having influenced, if indirectly, some much later theological sexual anthropologies, such as those of Aquinas (who could argue that, since women were lesser versions of men, women were also less perfect mirrors of the image of God) and of Karl Barth. Although Barth appears to stress the *difference* of men and women, as we will see in Chapter 3, and thus appears to have a strongly two-sex model, a shortcoming in his theological sexual anthropology is his failure to conceptualize women other than as a necessary concomitant of men. Women are not therefore *truly* 'other' to men for Barth, but exist only in relation to men, the necessary facilitators and repositories of masculine 'completeness'. Arguably, then, the supposed 'otherness' of women in Barth's model is nothing but men reflected back at themselves. This is important, because much fear or distaste at bodies which do not 'fit' social norms also stems from a failure to make space for otherness which is not simply self-reflective.

Sharon Preves notes that, in the twelfth century, it was believed that the uterus had three separate chambers and that the sex of the child conceived would depend on the chamber in which it was implanted: one chamber for male children, one for females, and one for hermaphrodites (Preves 2003: 34). This belief meant that 'hermaphroditism was conceptualized as a natural, if not expected, state' (Preves 2003: 34). Nature was not equated with a male-female either/or binary, despite the relative infrequency of births of hermaphroditic children. During this period the Church thus allowed hermaphrodites to choose whether to live as men or women depending on which 'organ' the individual felt to be more 'active'. Crucially, however, once the decision had been made and the individual had attempted sexual activity in one role, they could not transition to the other lest the situation should appear to endorse homosexuality. This point is crucial, for it betrays the extent to which the concern was to eradicate the 'unnatural' *appearance* of particular acts or lifestyles; even in cases of genital ambiguity, the party line was that once a *role* had been chosen it could not be altered. But it is essential to recognize that this was always a pragmatic and arbitrary demarcation, based on bolstering *a priori* beliefs about natural human activity, and foreshadowing Kessler's assertion that 'gender is marked by the obviousness of an organ and not its existence' (Kessler 1998: 99).

The Sixteenth – Nineteenth Centuries: Regulation, Classification, Taxonomy

During the early modern period, hermaphroditic bodies became potent symbols for the vulnerable, shaken body politic, and thus regained an almost mythic significance. Ruth Gilbert argues that the issues raised by the existence of hermaphroditic bodies highlighted questions about the very nature of order and knowledge hammered out during the era (Gilbert 2002: 1). Private conduct and private existence began to become public property, regulated by professionals, to an extent that they had not been before. In the sixteenth century, says Gilbert, interest in hermaphroditic bodies shifted from their spiritual connotations – as cosmic harbingers of good or ill fortune – to the mere discernable facts of their physicality. Previously, hermaphrodites had been associated with the mythical image of the androgyne, a perfect unity of male and female in one being (Gilbert 2002: 10).

The sixteenth century also saw concerns about clarifying hermaphrodites' status for economic reasons; because, for instance, of inheritance laws: 'If the hermaphrodite could inherit property s/he paradoxically entered into a social and economic system which could not recognize his/her existence' (Gilbert 2002: 42). There was a new importance ascribed to dress at this time, too, which Gilbert links with the rise of the market economy, where clothes signified identity and status, literally making the man/or woman (Gilbert 2002: 79). This may have heightened suspicions about people who appeared to dress deceptively.

In the eighteenth century, the female-related genitalia acquired specific labels – ovaries were no longer simply called 'gonads' or 'female testes' – suggesting a shift to figuring femaleness as more than a washed-out version of maleness. Dreger, focusing on the medical treatments of hermaphrodites in England and France during the late nineteenth and early twentieth centuries, suggests that the explosion of interest in hermaphrodites as such in this period may have been due to new evidence that established gender/sex roles were not the only ones, and that there was not necessarily a single 'type' of male and female. The rise of feminism and gradual move to more widespread acceptance of overt homosexuality, as well as ethnographic and anthropological studies of sexual patterns in other cultures, led to an atmosphere of exploration (Dreger 1998: 26) – even if there was a tendency to depict those from other cultures as 'divine savages', romantically portrayed as possessing simple, unrestricted attitudes to sexuality (Herdt 1994b: 36). Although hermaphrodites had been figured as 'monstrous' at various points, the new medical interest in them in the taxonomic climate of the nineteenth century led to a situation where 'the teratological was stripped of its wonder and made merely pathological' (Dreger 1998: 35). European doctors and scientists, claims Dreger, wanted to understand hermaphroditism so that they could work out how to eradicate it – to avoid the possibility of unwitting homosexual relationships, as well as to prevent conflicts between an individual's 'true' and 'lived' sexes. However, there also seems to have been a conscious concern to promote the well-being of hermaphrodites themselves – brought into focus by the case in France of Alexina/Abel (alias Herculine) Barbin, recounted by Dreger and others,[5] well-known via the popular media of the day.

5. The story was also published with an introduction by Foucault as *Herculine Barbin: Being the Recently Discovered Memoirs of a Nineteenth-Century French Hermaphrodite* (Barbin 1980). Barbin had been brought up as a girl in all-girls'

Nineteenth-and twentieth-century advances in endocrinology, and understandings of the divergence of male-related and female-related anatomy in the six-week foetus and beyond, eventually led to a solid naturalization of what Laqueur calls the 'two-sex' model. He argues that it was changes in *cultural* assumptions about what 'male' and 'female' actually meant which led to a new spin being put on the significance of hormones and foetal divergence, rather than hormones and foetal divergence *per se* changing attitudes about sex (Laqueur 1990: 88, 243). 'Advances' in knowledge of anatomy, in Laqueur's account, could not of themselves have led to a paradigm shift in conceptions of sex and gender until discourse had shifted sufficiently. Scientific discoveries about physiology had always to be figured in the context of what was known, *a priori*, about men and women; to reduce men and women to actually *being* their physiology was a startlingly recent development. Thus unambiguous sex was also not 'scientifically' self-evident.

The acceptance of the two-sex model led to the conclusion that if the sexes were fundamentally different, not just stages on the same road as in one-sex or continuum-type models, then everyone must belong to one or the other. In 1876, the German pathologist Theodor Klebs formulated a taxonomy which divided hermaphrodites into three categories based on gonads: 'true hermaphrodites' (with one testis and one ovary), 'male pseudohermaphrodites' (with testes), and 'female pseudohermaphrodites' (with ovaries) (Preves 2003: 27–29). Far fewer people were classed as hermaphrodites than before (Dreger 1998: 146). Klebs' use of the 'pseudo' prefix emphasized the idea that *true* sex was actually defined by gonads alone: the girl with Androgen Insensitivity Syndrome *appeared* hermaphroditic but was *really* male. The rarity of 'true hermaphrodites' in Klebs' model reinforced the view that, almost without exception, everyone fitted into one or other of the two 'true' sexes. This may have led to a heightened suspicion of hermaphrodites and an increased sense of their bodies as

schools, and experienced sexual attraction to her classmates. She also had a sexual relationship with a woman. Later, Barbin was forcibly reclassified as a man, and eventually committed suicide as a result of the consequent loneliness and alienation. Butler suspects that Foucault over-romanticizes Herculine's story and portrays her as non-sexual rather than homosexual (Butler 1990: 99), and argues that, rather than 'freely confusing' sex as Foucault claims, surely Herculine's actions are not really free, still taking place as they do within a discourse of power (Butler 1990: 100).

pathological rather than just natural but unusual. Klebs, sited well and truly in what Dreger terms the 'age of gonads' (Dreger 1998: 30), bolstered its taxonomy. Dreger notes that doctors at this time got only as far as seeing hermaphrodites as *exceptions* to the male/ female model, rather than asking whether the doubt 'extended far beyond the individual case to the endeavour as a whole' (Dreger 1998: 83). William Blair Bell, in 1915, was the first twentieth-century doctor seriously to challenge the gonad-only model of sex, saying that secondary sexual characteristics should also be considered (Dreger 1998: 163–64). However, the language of 'pseudo-hermaphroditism' persisted well into the late twentieth century, albeit alongside other terms including 'intersexuality' and 'ambisexuality' (Ashley 1962: 225–39).

The Twentieth Century: Money, Reimer and the Early Surgery Paradigm

During the first part of the twentieth century, particularly after transsexual surgery began to be performed, and in light of advances in urology and endocrinology (Preves 2003: 51), the emphasis shifted – in contrast with the attitudes evident during Dreger's 'age of gonads' – from *discovery* of sex to *assignment* of sex. Doctors accepted that individuals' 'true sex' could not be reduced simply and unequivocally to gonads, nor to chromosomes, genitalia, gender identity or sexual orientation, but was a mixture of all these.

From the mid-twentieth century, children who were given treatment for salt-wasting Congenital Adrenal Hyperplasia sometimes received genital surgery as well, if they had any degree of genital ambiguity. It is important to emphasize that some intersex/DSD conditions do carry with them concomitant health complications affecting more than simply the genitals or reproductive system, and it would, of course, be reprehensible and tragic if these were not properly addressed and treated. For example, there have been links made with increased cancer risks in the testes of girls with AIS if left in their bodies, though the risk of cancer before puberty is small, and the removal of the testes means the child will need to take hormone replacement throughout her life. What appeared to take place in the 1950s was a quantum leap, from (justifiably) treating the medical complications attached to CAH to (more dubiously) treating the unusual genitals themselves as the medical issue. Ambiguous genitals came to be called 'diseased' or 'disordered', rendering the body itself somehow deviant. Much of the rationale behind early corrective surgery was in order that the children concerned should be able to grow up as 'normally' as possible, and segue unremarkably into ordinary masculine and feminine (and heterosexual) adult gender roles.

The majority of corrective surgery before the 1950s was done on intersexed adults who had autonomously sought medical advice about their physiology, often as a result of discovering after embarking on sexual relationships that their anatomies did not 'work' for conventional sexual intercourse, or after investigative enquiries about absent menstruation. This was made possible by advances in sex-change surgery on adult transsexuals. During the 1950s the first paediatric endocrinology unit was founded at Johns Hopkins University in Baltimore, and hormone and chromosomal analysis to work out intersexed children's genetic make-up became customary. The unit's staff came to include John Money (1921–2006), the clinical psychologist now notorious in intersex circles for his involvement in the seminal 'John/Joan' (David Reimer) study.

Reimer was born a boy called Bruce, with an identical twin brother, Brian, in Canada in 1965. The boys suffered from phimosis in infancy, and were scheduled for circumcision when they were eight months old. Bruce's circumcision with an electric cauterizing machine went wrong and his penis was badly burned (Colapinto 2001: 12). In early 1967, his parents saw a television programme in which John Money was discussing the possibility of gender reassignment, and contacted him. Money believed that Bruce was still young enough to be reassigned as a girl, and arranged for his testes and the remains of his penis to be removed (Colapinto 2001: 53). The Reimers, on Money's advice, renamed Bruce 'Brenda' and brought him up as a girl. Each year the family travelled to Baltimore so the twins could be monitored by Money at Johns Hopkins University; Brian provided a perfect 'control' to test Money's thesis that gender identity relied on upbringing as much as biological factors. Although the monitoring focused mainly on Brenda, Money also worked with Brian, trying to imprint appropriate sex/gender roles on each child. The twins later said that this included making them act out sexual positions in order to learn 'correct' sexual behaviours for males and for females (Colapinto 2001: 86–87). Money reported in books and papers that Brenda was doing well in her new gender assignment, that she had feminine qualities and was very different from her brother (Colapinto 2001: 68–69). The case was central to the argument of Money and Ehrhardt's 1972 book *Man and Woman, Boy and Girl*. Its alleged success was a catalyst for increased early surgery and gender reassignment on intersexed children.

However, it subsequently transpired that Brenda had never been happy as a girl, had disliked dresses and 'feminine' activities, always stood to urinate despite the fact that her post-surgery anatomy made this all but impossible, and had always had a sense that there was something different about her although she had never been told about her reassignment. She fell behind her classmates academically and had very few friends (Colapinto 2001: 116–17). Her mother later said,

> Brenda wasn't happy as a girl, no matter what I tried to do for her, no matter how I tried to instruct her, she was very rebellious, she was very masculine and I could not persuade her to do anything feminine. Brenda had almost no ... friends growing up ... She was a very lonely, lonely girl (Janet Reimer speaking in Cohen 2000).

Brenda had resisted Money's injunctions to take female hormones and to have vaginoplasty (Colapinto 2001: 129–30, 133). She did eventually did begin to take the hormones, but hated the breasts that grew as a result. When she was 14, a psychiatrist advised Brenda's parents to tell her the truth about her gender reassignment. After her father did so, Brenda immediately began wearing male clothing and living as a boy, choosing to take the name David, after 'the guy who was facing up to a giant eight feet tall' (Reimer quoted in Colapinto 2001: 182). David stopped taking female hormones, began taking testosterone, had his breasts removed, and underwent surgery to create a prosthetic penis and testes. Money never reported on this aspect of the case although he was aware that it had occurred (Colapinto 2001: 202–203).

In 1990 David married Jane Fontane and adopted her children. It was not until 1997 that Milton Diamond and Keith Sigmundson (who had been a consultant psychiatrist on the case for a number of years) published a paper reporting that the 'successful' reassignment of Bruce as Brenda had been a resounding failure (Diamond and Sigmundson 1997a). David met Diamond and learned that many intersexed children had been operated on and reassigned on the strength of his own case (Colapinto 2001: 209). He said in 2000, 'By me not saying anything the medical community was under the impression that my case was a success story and I was shocked when I heard' (in Cohen 2000). Colapinto's book about David, using his real name and citing transcripts from the young Brenda's interviews with Money and other psychiatrists (which had been returned to David in 1998 – Colapinto 2001: ix), was published in 2000. David suffered from depression throughout adulthood and made several attempts to take his own life. Sadly, in 2004, he committed suicide; it is believed that he was having financial difficulties after having been made redundant. He was also said to have been affected by problems in his marriage, and by the death of his brother Brian from a prescription drug overdose. However, Colapinto has suggested that too little attention had been given to the lasting effects of the unusual circumstances of David's childhood and adolescence (Colapinto 2004).

John Money was interested not only in sexology, the science of sex, but also in what he called sexosophy, 'the philosophy of sex and eroticism' (Money 1980: 43). As with the Reimer case, Money and his colleagues asserted that gender identity was most plastic before about 18 months of age (though partly so until 4½–5 years – Money 1980: 33), and that if 'corrective' surgery on intersexed genitals was done before this time, and the child raised unambiguously in the new gender role, he or she would have no gender problems throughout childhood, adolescence and adulthood. Juvenile gender identity, held Money, was based on a range of influences, including, most significantly, one's 'optimum gender of rearing': the signals given by parents and other carers through their treatment of one as a girl or boy (Dreger and Herndon 2009: 202). Prenatal and pubertal hormones also had an influence, through influencing post-adolescent morphology and eroticism (Money and Ehrhardt 1972: 3; Money 1980: 22–26), but adult gender identity, too, largely followed what had been 'fixed' by upbringing. Money tried to demonstrate nurture's primacy through studies involving 'matched pairs', 'pairs ... of individuals who are intersexually concordant for prenatal etiology and diagnosis, but discordant for sex of assignment and rearing' (Money 1988: 30). Bruce/Brenda and Brian Reimer, though not intersexed, provided the ultimate 'matched pair', and this case 'was certainly used as very strong evidence that children are a blank slate ... and that we can impose a gender identity on a newborn' (Reiner speaking in Cohen 2000).

Money has been criticized for apparent inconsistencies in his theory, for his strong privileging of the social followed by what appears to be 'a quite crude recourse to the primacy of the biological body' (Hird and Germon 2001: 169). However, Money did not claim that genitals in themselves magically produced a particular gender identity/role; rather, he believed, they were markers prompting particular treatment by parents and other caregivers, which would reinforce the child's sense of its own gender (Money 1981: 382, 387). Money believed it was crucial for young children to receive unambiguous gender messages, particularly if (as with intersexed children) there was any doubt about their sex – and that surgery would reinforce this. He believed parents would be incapable of treating uncorrected children unambiguously, claiming that intersexed children who did not receive surgery would be 'handicapped by a sense of shame and mortification' (Money and Ehrhardt 1972: 15), swing between identifying as boy or girl, and suffer immense cognitive dissonance; he believed most human beings could not tolerate 'such a biographical inconsistency' (Money and Ehrhardt 1972: 15). Of course, this has been hotly debated ever since; but as J. David Hester comments,

> The claim that non-medical and non-surgical intervention would result in social and psychological damage is, at heart, a value judgment premised upon several naturalized presumptions. These include the presumption that the binary sex-gender system is self-evident, that variations therefrom are pathological variations in need of repair, that physiological variability of the genitals results in psychosocial stigmatization that patients cannot overcome without medical help, and that it is the role of the physician to to ensure psychosocial adjustment through medical and surgical intervention (Hester 2006: 50).

Part of the justification for early surgery by Money and his associates was also that, since genital surgery was so traumatic, the earlier it occurred, the less chance there was of the child remembering it. This rationale, along with the argument that small children heal better and scar less, has been reiterated by many doctors since (as by those interviewed by Karkazis – see 2008: 156–60; see also Crawford *et al* 2009: 414). Performing surgery before a child begins to form long-term memories does not necessarily preclude distress caused in early childhood, however; Elizabeth Weil says,

> According to [Cheryl] Chase's notes ... her mother maintained that the clitoridectomy had not impacted her daughter's life. "When you came home," Cathleen Sullivan told Chase about her return from hospital after surgery, "there seemed to be no effect at all. Oh, yes, wait a minute. Yes, there was one thing. You stopped speaking. I guess you didn't speak for about six months. Then one day you started talking again. You had known quite a lot of words at 17 months, but you forgot them all" (Weil 2006).

Moreover, as many commentators have noted, it is highly likely that multiple follow-up surgeries will need to take place later on (see e.g. Karkazis 2008: 173).

It is ironic that it was Money's insistence on surgical intervention which became so influential and repeated, given that he also asserted, 'In human beings it need scarcely be said that erotosexualism exists as much between the ears, in the cerebral cortex, as between the groins, in the genitalia' (Money 1981: 381). However, through the 1960s, many doctors followed Money's rationale that early surgery prevented later psychological upset (see e.g. Ashley 1962: 288). By 1972, largely on the basis of the alleged success of the Reimer case (Kipnis and Diamond 1998), early surgery had become so commonplace that Money and Ehrhardt were largely preaching to the converted when they chided,

> When physicians fail to schedule first-stage corrective genital surgery for a hermaphroditic infant, it usually means that they have covertly postponed a fixed commitment to the sex or rearing because they do not feel secure in committing themselves to one decision or the other. The experts' uncertainty is rapidly conveyed to the parents whose own equivocation is then covertly transmitted to the child, as contagiously as though it were rubella (Money and Ehrhardt 1972: 15).

Money's insistence on cohesive genitals to promote consistent gender bolstered the notion that a boy with no penis would be better off made to look like a girl, and that his feminine upbringing would overcome his XY chromosomal make-up. This led to some boy children, typical in every respect but for a small penis or extreme hypospadias, having their testes and penis removed and a rudimentary vaginal opening created. Corrective surgery for intersex was not unheard-of before Money's reassignment of the non-intersexed Reimer, but it was the alleged resounding triumph of the case which led to Money's views on early surgery becoming accepted practice in the vast majority of units.

Although many intersex/DSD conditions were not threatening to the physiological health of the children concerned, surgery for atypical genitalia (even where there were no associated health complications) came to be done as soon as possible after birth. There was little regard for implications for sexual pleasure in adulthood, such as genital pain or insensitivity, and inability to orgasm (Kessler 1998: 56). Some genitals were called 'satisfactory' even when the clitoris had been completely removed (Kessler 1998: 55). Dreger noted in 1998, 'A constructed "vagina" does not have ... to be self-lubricating or even to be at all sensitive to count as "functional" ... Intersexuality doctors often talk about vaginas in intersex children as the absence of something, as a space, a place to put a penis' (Dreger 1998: 184). In short, the standards of success used were strikingly sexist, painting real boys as aggressively powerful and real girls as passive, both physically and psychologically (Dreger and Herndon 2009: 204). As very little follow-up work was done before the late 1990s, the procedures tended to be assessed on their aesthetic success by surgeons, such as the appearance of a clitoris or the ability of a vagina to be penetrated by a penis (Preves 2003: 56), rather than their later sensual success by the patients themselves. The emphasis on cosmetic outcomes can still be seen even in very recent studies such as that by Crawford *et al* (2009: 415). The San Francisco Human Rights Commission's report on its investigation into the medical 'normalizing' of intersexed people notes,

> The definition of a "successful outcome" differs greatly between medical providers and patients. Questions in follow-up studies tend to focus on heterosexual sexual behavior as being the standard for success, as opposed to fertility or pleasure. It is more common to ask a patient if she or he is married than to ask if that patient has a pleasing sexual life, is able to procreate, or has the ability to achieve orgasm (Arana 2005: 19).

Most children through the 1980s and 1990s were assigned girls, as it was harder to build a penis than to hollow out a vagina (Preves 2003: 55). Those with large clitorises typically had them cut back or removed altogether. Any child whose genitals at birth did not fit the accepted medical measurements (under 0.9cm for a clitoris, over 2.4cm for a penis) (Preves 2003: 55) was likely to be adjusted – without their consent, but also often without that of their parents. Helena Harmon-Smith, the adoptive mother of a child born with one testis, one ovary and a penis, and who was a genetic mosaic, was advised by doctors that he should have the testis removed as it was likely to be malignant. Loathe to agree to the removal of healthy tissue, Harmon-Smith consented only to a biopsy. However, without her permission, the surgeon went ahead and entirely removed the testis:

> When the surgeon returned from the operating room, he said the gonad was diseased. He had cut it off. Harmon-Smith pestered the doctor for the pathology report for more than a month. Once she got it, "the first thing I read was 'normal, healthy testicle." My heart stopped. I just cried," she says (Lehrman 1999).

The 1990s Onwards: Politics, Protest and Calls for Change

The Rise of Support and Advocacy Groups

In the 1990s, the revelation that Reimer's reassignment as Brenda had, in fact, been unsuccessful, and that Money had continued to laud it in books and papers nonetheless, led to Money's discrediting (Colapinto 1997, 2001, 2004; Cohen 2000; Cohen and Sweigart 2001). Moreover, many people who had had genital surgery as children began to protest about their treatment. Support and advocacy groups run by and for intersexed people had also begun to be formed: Cheryl Chase [Bo Laurent] founded the Intersex Society of North America in 1993, with a far more political bent (Turner 1999: 457) than other groups. Preves comments that support groups were crucial in allowing people to access information about their conditions which may not have been forthcoming from the medical profession, providing role-models of people with similar conditions, and being a site for new, positive outworkings of selfhood (Preves 2003: 126–33). Some individuals associated with ISNA in particular carried out political protest (Beck 1996). Such public, visible action, as well as the information and advice shared in support groups, led to some parents insisting on delaying surgery and hormone therapy until their children could express consent or understanding of their own conditions and gender identities.

This was a crucial move, for many adults with intersex/DSD conditions have claimed that it was the results of the surgery and other medical intervention they underwent as young children that left them literally and metaphorically scarred and marked out, rather than their original physical conditions which, if left unaltered until pre-pubescence or later, may not have stigmatized them to the same extent. Howard Devore, a clinical psychotherapist who has worked extensively with intersexed children and their families, and is opposed to early genital surgery after he himself was treated for extreme hypospadias (Gale and Soomekh 2000; Consortium on the Management of Disorders of Sex Development 2006b: 109), says,

> The doctors insist that you can't let a child go to school with ambiguous genitals, but the genitals they created were certainly strange-looking ... There was no reason for some of the work that they did on me outside of arrogance or incompetence ... If they had just left my urinary meatus ... where it was, at the base of my penis right by the scrotum, I could have avoided at least 12 of those surgeries (Devore 1999: 80–81).

Part of the ongoing debate has highlighted the fact that *not* intervening to surgically alter genitals also has its disadvantages. Many doctors still follow the convention that surgery must be early, and that children whose bodies do not fit must be corrected (see, for example, Christie Steinmann in van Huyssteen 2003; Pinsky, Erickson and Schimke 1999: 51; Hrabovszky and Hutson 2002: 93; Crawford et al 2009: 415). However, ISNA stressed that a range of treatment including counselling is necessary and appropriate for intersexed individuals. Non-surgical intervention is very different from total non-intervention.

ISNA existed from 1993 until 2008, founded via a letter from Cheryl Chase [Bo Laurent] to the editor of *The Sciences* in response to Fausto-Sterling's 'The Five Sexes' (Fausto-Sterling 1993) which had been published in the same journal. Chase wrote,

> As an intersexual I found Anne Fausto-Sterling's article ... of intense personal interest. Her willingness to question medical dogma on intersexuality is unique and refreshing. I understand that she has not had the chance to meet with any 'corrected' intersexuals; I think I can provide some perspective on the

experience ... I encourage intersexuals and people close to them to write to us at the Intersex Society of North America ... where we are assembling a support group and documenting our lives (Chase 1993: 25).

Even in this earliest letter, Chase criticized the lack of follow-up studies on corrected patients, the narrowness of cultural concepts of sexual normality, the primacy of the penis in making assignments, and the continued use of terms such as 'male pseudohermaphrodite' – 'a heritage of Victorian medicine – and without prognosticative value' (Chase 1993: 25). ISNA's early activities included picketing the Annual Meeting of the American Academy of Pediatricians in Boston (under the name 'Hermaphrodites With Attitude', also the name of the organization's erstwhile newsletter), and the production of the short film *Hermaphrodites Speak!*

By 2008, however, things had changed. ISNA was no longer effectively accomplishing what Chase [Laurent] believed was important. The 'farewell message' on ISNA's blog explains,

In the current environment, there is a strong need for an organization to assume the role of a convenor of stakeholders across the health care system and DSD communities. It's the primary gap between today's status quo and the wide-spread implementation of the new standard of care we envision. Unfortunately, ISNA is considerably hamstrung in being able to fulfil this role. Although it has been very successful in recent years in creating collaborative relationships ... there is concern among many healthcare professionals, parents, and mainstream healthcare system funders that ISNA's views are biased or that an association with ISNA will be frowned upon by colleagues and peers. And there is widespread misinformation about ISNA's positions (http://www.isna.org/farewell_message).

Consequently, Accord Alliance was founded in March 2008, its mission 'to promote comprehensive and integrated approaches to care that enhance the health and well-being of people and families affected by disorders of sex development ... by fostering collaboration among all stakeholders' (www.accordalliance.org).

In the twenty-first century support groups continue to be particularly important loci of acceptance and empowerment – and, as J. David Hester says, 'Unquestioning acceptance of intersexed bodies as normal and natural seems to be a powerful means of "healing" ... Intersex people whose bodies diverge from the gender ideal nevertheless find "health" through integration into the community and acceptance of their own bodies' (Hester 2006: 52). Karen Lebacqz noted in 1997 that internet-based groups were likely to become more and more important to the organization and networking of people with intersex conditions, since they traverse geographical boundaries and allow people who may be a tiny minority in their locale to find one another and generate a new politics of difference (Lebacqz 1997: 229). This has undoubtedly proven to be the case; although many of the largest and best-known support groups are still based in North America, web-based discussion forums allow members from all over the world to communicate and share information. However, it should be acknowledged that this may unwittingly exclude older people, those on low incomes, or those who for other reasons do not have internet access.

Controversial Nomenclature: Intersex versus DSD and Beyond

Accord Alliance founder Bo Laurent favours using the terminology of DSD rather than intersex. This is controversial among activists and support group members, some of whom have stated that they were not properly consulted about the proposed change of nomenclature. An entry on the website of the UK Androgen Insensitivity Society Support Group asserts that 'the DSD initiative was almost entirely a US-based enterprise ... Patient support/ advocacy groups outside the USA were not consulted and had no input' (http://www.aissg.org/21_overview.htm#Terminology). Curtis Hinkle argues that, since most of the people working to bring about the new DSD terminology were not themselves intersexed, this was yet another instance of non-intersexed hegemony being imposed on intersexed people (http://intersexpride.blogspot.com, entries for 29 February 2008 and 4 May 2008).

Elizabeth Reis, however, whilst acknowledging the limitations of the medical conference where the consensus statement on DSD terminology was formulated, comments, 'The conference was itself pathbreaking, specifically because intersex adults [Bo Laurent and Barbara Thomas] were included in the policy-making process at all' (Reis 2007: 538). Moreover, Bo Laurent argues that, among medics, 'disorder' is actually a normalizing term rather than a stigmatizing one. There are a range of conditions, including endocrine conditions, to which doctors refer as 'disorders'.

Including the conditions that used to be known as intersex conditions among these actually helps doctors consider them as possibilities among a range of others, rather than as something completely different and strange (Laurent 2008). She says, "Disorder' is a word commonly used in medicine. The causes of atypical sex anatomy include genetic disorders and endocrine disorders. Use of the word 'disorder' in the new nomenclature makes clear that DSDs are similar in many ways to other, more familiar disorders' (Chase 2006).

Laurent believes this is crucial for ensuring that people with DSDs can access proper and appropriate healthcare. She cites the case of Max Beck, a well-known intersex activist energetically involved in ISNA. Tragically, Beck died of metastasized vaginal cancer in 2008, leaving behind his wife and two young children. Laurent believes part of the reason for this is that Beck's doctors did not understand the particular health issues of someone with his condition. The terminology 'intersex', having been so closely identified with sex, has, says Laurent, not encouraged medics to treat the whole person who may have additional health complications as a by-product of their condition. Feder concurs, critiquing the historical conflation of intersex with homosexuality and saying that 'we must confront the surprising fact that doctors and activists alike have focused on matters of gender and genitalia at the expense of the ordinary health concerns of affected individuals' (Feder 2009: 226–27). As Iain Morland suggests (though not in support of 'DSD'), calling for psychological support and counselling as the primary mode of responding to intersex may in fact 'serve to discredit intersexed individuals by implying that their difficulties can be cured by just a friendly chat and a little positive thinking' (Morland 2006: 324), rather than acknowledging their real medical needs. Using 'DSD' instead gives medical credence to the conditions, and because it speaks a language doctors understand, should facilitate better healthcare provision (Laurent 2008).

Moreover, says Laurent, 'intersex' is very much seen as an identity-based position rather than a medical one. Because many early intersex activists spoke out about their sex and gender identity issues, the term 'intersex' became conflated with such issues. It is problematic to use an essentially identity-based term for an infant or young child: it would be rather like calling a child 'heterosexual' or 'homosexual' before they had had a chance to express such an identity for themselves. Reis comments,

> Some parents ... were uncomfortable with the intersex label for
> their affected children. To them, *intersex* meant a third gender,
> something in-between male and female. They wanted to see their
> newborn babies as girls or boys, not as intersex ... Some parents
> found the label as frightening, off-putting, and freakish as
> *hermaphrodite* ... Others have associated the word *intersex* with
> sexuality, eroticism, or sexual orientation and have had trouble
> reconciling their child's anatomical condition with thoughts of
> his/her future sexual activities (Reis 2007: 537).

Saying that the child *has* a DSD rather than that the child *is* intersexed
sidesteps this problem and also avoids identifying the child entirely
by their condition, suggests Laurent (Chase 2006; Laurent 2008).
The term 'intersex' might also be supposed to identify a *kind* of
person, whereas 'DSD' might encourage focus on specific individuals
and their specific conditions (Feder and Karkazis 2008: 34).

Although this might appear more respectful of the patient as a
whole person, however, it could also be read the other way; Curtis
Hinkle of Organisation Intersex International (OII) says,

> The medical approach focuses on parts of a person and defines
> the intersex child as a disparate combination of chromosomes,
> genitalia, hormones, gonads and internal reproductive anatomy.
> This is dehumanizing. The child is not welcomed into the world
> as a complete, totally intact, part of the whole tapestry of nature
> (Hinkle at http://www.intersexpride.blogspot.com/, entry for
> 27 April 2008).

Other intersex activists have noted that intersex is not necessarily
inherently or exclusively an identity-politics term; Emi Koyama
of Intersex Initiative says, 'While some intersex people do
reclaim "intersex" as part of their identity, most regard it as a
medical condition, or just a unique physical state' (http://www.
intersexinitiative.org/articles/intersex-faq.html).

Koyama, who supports the use of 'DSD' with some reservations,
argues that the term 'intersex' was 'wrong from the beginning',
since, she says, most intersexed people do not consider their bodies
to be *between* male and female bodies: they simply consider
themselves as male or female with a specific birth condition (Koyama
2006). Koyama acknowledges that the 'disorder' element of DSD
has negative connotations, but believes that the term still has the
potential to be embraced by individuals with these conditions and
their families. She is keen to draw links between the intersex/DSD

movement's methodologies and those of the radical disability rights movement, whereby 'disability is not simply a characteristic of one's body, but the product of social institutions that divide human bodies into normal and abnormal, privileging certain bodies over others' (Koyama 2006). She also recognizes the problematic elements of the fact that, by using the DSD terminology, the movement appears to be ceasing its critique of the medical model and 'embracing its former enemy', and taking a step back from querying sex-gender discourses in favour of a less identity-based approach (Koyama 2006). However, she says, 'I'd like to think of the shift not as the embracement of the medical model, but a commitment to the political strategy that seeks to radically redefine and re-read it' (Koyama 2006). Moreover, as Feder and Karkazis argue,

> The new nomenclature brings with it the possibility of focusing on genuine medical needs while – and this must be the ongoing challenge – understanding different anatomies that are symptomatic of these conditions as mere variations. Viewed in this way, the change in nomenclature offers the possibility that intersex conditions can be transformed from "disorders like no other" to "disorders like many others," and so must be treated both clinically and ethically in ways that are consistent with other medical conditions (Feder and Karkazis 2008: 35).

Of course, even more specific terminology is preferable; Lee et al say, 'Ideally, a system based on descriptive terms (e.g. androgen insensitivity syndrome) should be used wherever possible' (Lee et al 2006: e489).

Sherri Groveman Morris, founder of the US branch of AISSG and a former ISNA board member, writes in a letter to the *Archive of Diseases in Childhood*,

> It would ... be regrettable if the term "Disorder of Sex Development" were to be adopted even in a clinical setting for other than an interim period until a more appropriate term is adopted ... It is ... important that as we look forward, intersex support and advocacy groups don't abandon the term "intersex" even as they may work in tandem with the medical community to adopt a new nomenclature. "intersex" is a term which gives meaning and purpose to, and reflects the courage and determination of, a community which has dedicated itself – often at considerable personal risk – to seeking improvements in care and widespread awareness and acceptance (Morris 2006a).

Intersex activist Lynnell Stephani Long adds, in a letter to the same journal,

> When I first heard the term DSD ... I felt betrayed. But gradually I realized how using the term DSD could better help kids born Intersex ... I don't expect every Intersex Activist to embrace the term DSD. It does feel like a slap in the face. But ... if meeting doctors at their own level by using simple medical terminology like DSD will help them to better understand how to do a better job for children born Intersex then I am all for it (Long 2006).

The controversy rages on, and yet further alternative terms have been proposed. Milton Diamond advocates 'variations of sex development' (Diamond 2008), and Reis suggests 'divergences of sex development', since 'disorders of sex development', she says, does not move far enough from granting the medical establishment disproportionate power to name and demarcate (Reis 2007: 541). However, although both of these are ostensibly less stigmatizing, if they do not contain language that doctors understand, arguably they will not open the doors that Laurent and Accord Alliance hope, and will therefore not improve the healthcare and support given to children and their families (Feder 2009: 225). For further recent discussions of the terminology see Feder and Karkazis 2008, Karkazis 2008, Dreger and Herndon 2009, and Feder 2009.

'Good enough' Genitals: The Use of Moral Language for Intersex

If the ethical problems stemming from early corrective surgery are manifold, it is interesting that a fairly moralistic set of terminology is also attached to intersex and to genitals themselves. Surgery cannot 'fix' intersex/DSD: it cannot make a person produce different gametes, or change their chromosomes. Morgan Holmes says, 'By its own diagnostic standards ... the medical procedures meant to fix intersex are actually only imperfect measures to render it invisible' (Holmes 2002: 174). However, what is deemed normal is never an objective or *a priori* decision, but is shaped by what else is going on in a given society or culture. This is important, because sex in much theological discourse has come to be figured as somehow 'prior' to gender. It is for this reason, for example, that many Christians deem sex reassignment surgery for transsexuals to be illegitimate, because it is perceived to be putting more store by an individual's gender identity than by their 'irreducible', 'undeniable' 'biological' sex. Sexual acts deemed undesirable may include those figured as 'unnatural' because they do not lead to procreation (as in a natural law mindset), but, too, might be those which do not reinforce particular human social hierarchies (Moore 2001: 142–43). These vary from society to society, and are rarely openly acknowledged.

'Self-evident' patterns of maleness and femaleness still largely reside in assumptions about the 'goodness' of clear gender and access to particular gendered privileges. In the early modern period, says Gilbert, 'Reactions to sexual indeterminacy revealed anxieties about collective rather than individual well-being, about cultural rather than personal identity' (Gilbert 2002: 7). Not much, it seems, has changed. The medical criteria used for 'success' in surgery on intersexed children are still based – particularly where the kinds of reforms proposed by ISNA and Accord Alliance have not yet been implemented – on how the 'finished' genitals will measure up, as Karkazis explores in detail (Karkazis 2008, especially Chapters 4 and 5). The genitals must 'work' for heterosexual penetration. South African urologist Christie Steinmann is not alone in believing that it is usually best to 'make it [the intersexed child] a girl if you can, because you don't know if you are going to have good enough penile growth after puberty to have … [a] good enough penis to have sexual intercourse' (in van Huyssteen 2003). Such an attitude appears to confirm Anne Fausto-Sterling's suspicion that many intersex doctors work on the principle that 'females are imperfect by nature, and if this child cannot be a perfect or near-perfect male, then being an imperfect female is the best choice' (Fausto-Sterling 1997: 221). Suzanne Kessler, in discussing surgical protocols surrounding micropenis, says, 'In the case of the undersized phallus, what is ambiguous is not whether this is a penis but whether it is 'good enough' to remain one' (Kessler 1998: 19–20). Robert A. Crouch discusses the notion that a 'good' clitoris and vagina must be small enough and large enough respectively; that a clitoris should be modest-looking and a vagina should be able to admit a penis. Crouch says, 'Looming in the background of all this is a moralistic and gendered cultural script that views women as passive recipients during sex … and not themselves agents of sexual desire and feeling' (Crouch 1998: 374). A surgeon can argue that a clitoris is less essential to a girl with Congenital Adrenal Hyperplasia if he believes that she 'should' orgasm vaginally (or that her orgasm is not important at all). Several scholars have noted doctors' use of language such as 'embarrassing', 'objectionable', 'disturbing' and 'grotesque' for larger-than-average clitorises (see e.g. Karkazis 2008: 146–47, 151); but, as Kessler asks, 'If the clitoris is troubling, offending and embarrassing, who exactly is troubled, offended or embarrassed and why?' (Kessler 1998: 36).

When slippage into lazy metaphor occurs and a 'good' penis comes to mean something other than what it seems – not only one which can penetrate a vagina, or urinate from its tip (questionable as these goods are), but one which thereby reinforces social mores in which men, *to be marked out as men*, must be able to penetrate vaginas and urinate through the tips of their penises – then 'natural' and socially-determined goods are conflated. Despite the fact that, for many intersexed people who have undergone clitorectomy and vaginoplasty, to be penetrated by a penis is unlikely to bring about any pleasurable sensation, and fertility is usually not an option, this criterion of 'goodness', supervening on 'normality', has been well and truly hammered home. Louise Thompson, a woman in her mid-20s with ovotestes, commented prior to undergoing repeat vaginoplasty, 'It'll make me feel whole as a person, but at the minute I don't really know where I am, because there's not a lot I can do … If I get married I basically can't have sex at the minute, so I don't really feel whole' (in Godwin 2004). The extent to which Louise's surgery was 'freely sought' is unclear, but she evidently felt she was *not* free to be 'whole' without it – despite the observation by reformist clinicians that 'surgical correction of a vaginal anomaly does not correct the patient's self-image' (MacDougall and Creighton 2004: 123). Doctors have, it is said, sometimes refused vaginoplasty or other treatment to enhance sexual function to adult women who sought it themselves but were not 'legally married or involved in a monogamous heterosexual relationship' (Preves 2003: 57). Although there are good grounds for delaying many genital surgeries until intersexed individuals are ready to be sexually active, decisions about when this time has come should not be limited by external views about only marital heterosexual intercourse being legitimate. Nor should they reinforce norms whereby girls, in particular, are robbed of autonomy over their own bodies and sexualities because of fears that a large clitoris equals an annexing of male anatomy (Karkazis 2008: 147–48), or else sexual excess, insatiability, promiscuity and a propensity for masturbation (all of which have often been demonized theologically). Karkazis notes that doctors and parents alike have been anxious to ensure that girl children are given vaginas large enough for penetration by a penis, but comments, 'A vagina perceived as abnormal or inadequate ... locates the problem in the female's genitalia, not in conceptualizations of what counts as sex' (Karkazis 2008: 154–55). Theology must particularly consider the extent to which its own assertions about gender roles, marriage and sexuality have reinforced the notion that penetrative consummation is essential to marriage and to 'being whole', and that heterosexual marriage is the only legitimate arena for sexual activity.

Saying that 'males have a penis and females have a vagina' falls short, then, because the penis and vagina are not each other's 'opposites' at all. Advanced observations of foetal development now make it plain that if the penis has an equivalent female structure at all it is the clitoris, the 'opposite' of the vaginal opening being the raphe, the line running down the scrotum (showing where the original opening has fused). How often are the clitoris and raphe appealed to as markers of sex, by either doctors or churchpeople? Yet to contrast the penis and vagina is based in an outmoded Aristotelian biology whereby the female anatomy, and particularly the genital anatomy, is figured as the inverse of the male anatomy. In this reading, the vagina is literally a penis turned inside-out, so it makes some kind of sense to contrast them. By continuing to do so even in light of what we now know, however, we perpetuate a false picture which – as it happens – conveniently suits a heteronormative, procreational agenda. Seizing on penises as markers of male men and vaginas as markers of female women maps neatly onto a model which says that to be real, even Godly men and women, these particular body parts must be used to act out a particular element of sexual congress in order to allow the generation of offspring. This coincides with the obsession on penetration evident in much Church reflection on sexuality; adultery and consummation both require penetration of a vagina by a penis. A theologically broadened conception of desirable or legitimate eroticisms could benefit not only intersexed and transsexual people but also others whose particular erogenous treasures are deemed illegitimate within a narrow conception of appropriate sexual expression and enjoyment.

Although Church statements on intersex itself, particularly in light of the ethical problems posed by the early surgery paradigm, have been all but non-existent, reports on transsexualism have usually betrayed a conservative attitude to human sex and gender and have suggested that variations from these are disorders requiring psychological treatment. Some churches in the USA seem particularly loath to embrace intersex/DSD, given a somewhat blanket association of intersex with homosexuality and (thus) immorality. ISNA's *Handbook for Parents* tellingly contains a section entitled 'What to tell people who may think DSDs are sinful' (Consortium on the Management of Disorders of Sex Development 2006b: 42–43). Chuck Colson, whose daily commentary on Christian living is aired on over 1,000 radio stations across the United States, asserts:

> The Bible teaches that the Fall into sin affected biology itself –
> that nature is now marred and distorted from its original
> perfection. This truth gives us a basis for fighting evil, for working
> to alleviate disease and deformity – including helping those
> unfortunate children born with genital deformities ... Scripture
> tells us how God created us before the Fall, and how He intended
> us to live: as males and females, reflecting His own image.
> We take our standards and identity from His revelation of our
> original nature (Colson 1996).

As I show in the following chapters, however, even a 'Bible-based' theological anthropology is already more complicated than this. Christopher Southgate and others have demonstrated that the existence of pain and suffering in the non-human creation cannot simplistically be attributed to the results of human sin, since evolutionary biology suggests that predation and cruelty existed on earth well before *homo sapiens* did (Southgate 2003; Southgate, Negus and Robinson 2003; Southgate 2008). The 'marring' and 'distortion' of nature, therefore, seems to be rooted in something other than solely human behaviour. This matters in terms of understanding the place of variation in nature: Tim Gorringe has argued that for God to eradicate all sickness and suffering would compromise the free nature of the universe in a way that would preclude free will – so God could not eradicate all mutation without erasing that which works for good as well as ill (Gorringe 2001). Congenital disability, for example, is part and parcel of the random mutations which have led to the rise of all life: God did not specifically intend disability, but disability is a result of the way in which God's world functions freely. So *even if* we accept a Colson-type account whereby intersex/DSD-related 'genital deformities' have no place in a perfect world (which is, of course, highly contentious), we cannot pin this 'evil' on human activity, nor unproblematically argue that any deviation from male-and-female is also a deviation from a pre-Fall state.

'Why all the unsolicited attention?': Corrective Surgery and Stigmatization

As we have seen, part of the rationale behind secretive early corrective surgery is to avoid trauma for the child who might otherwise be bullied or suffer depression because they are different. However, it has been argued that corrective surgery has drawn more attention than the anatomy itself to the atypicality of people with intersex/DSD conditions (Morris 2004: 27). Iain Morland says, 'When I was about eleven, in the school locker-room ... I was teased *not* because of intersex characteristics that remained after surgery but specifically because of scars *caused* by surgery' (Morland 2009: 301). Whilst some individuals have reclaimed their scars as sites of subversive, queer identity (Roen 2008: 48), others resent them. Catherine Harper remarks that although Martha Coventry's clitoris 'was not diseased or misplaced' when it was removed, but 'just larger than deemed appropriate for a girl of six', the 'stitched-up stump' left in its place 'must be inappropriate to any body' (Harper 2007: 75). Surgery implies that some human bodies, and specifically some human sexes, are more valid than others, and that 'fixing' those perceived as less valid is an appropriate human project. However, among Preves' interviewees in *Intersex and Identity*, feelings of shame about their bodies were strongest for those who had had recurrent surgical corrections or medical examinations (Preves 2003: 63). Repeated touching, scrutinizing or manipulating of their genitalia was construed by some individuals as abuse. Fausto-Sterling notes,

> One method of measuring penile growth and function in intersex boys involved the doctor masturbating the boy to achieve erection. Young girls who receive vaginal surgery suffer similarly invasive practices ... Medicine's focus on creating the proper genitals, meant to prevent psychological suffering, clearly contributes to it (Fausto-Sterling 2000: 86).

This is confirmed by the memories of some who underwent such treatment. One woman reports that, during an examination at the age of nine,

> I was lying on the table, spread-legged, with my feet in stirrups. The nurse came over to me and insisted upon holding my hand ... This was a nice gesture but I ... thought it unnecessary – unnecessary until the moment arrived when Dr. Jones broke my hymen, that is. The pain shot through my body like a bullet searing my flesh. I was utterly shocked. No one had warned me of what was about to happen (Fran at http://home.vicnet.net.au/~aissg/fran.htm).

Some individuals who began to speak publicly about intersex in the mid-1990s felt the gender assigned in infancy did not fit with what they now knew of themselves. Others resented the fact that their capacity for orgasm or pleasurable sexual activity had been removed for the sake of making their genitals look less unusual (Morris 2004: 26), or to allow vaginal penetration (Kessler 1998: 56). Perhaps most problematically, such surgery almost invariably took place without the patients' consent, either because they were very young at the time or because (in later or repeat operations as older children and adolescents) they had simply not been asked:

> At the age of 13, I was scheduled for surgery. I was not allowed to accept myself; I was told what is normal and how I should be. I was never told that I was viable; or that who I was is all I had to be ... My body was altered to meet social values, but my values were never discussed. My puberty was focused on vaginal function before I had a chance to care (Morris 2004: 25).

> They didn't mention the part where they were going to slice off my clitoris. All of it. I guess the doctors assumed I was as horrified by my outsized clit as they were, and there was no need to discuss it with me (Moreno 1999: 138).

> Part of my left upper arm was pressed into genital duty here [to make a vagina], which bothered me greatly when I came out of surgery. I wish I'd been consulted or at least informed. Of course, why would I need to be informed? The objective was to make the hermaphrodite fuckable (Triea 1999: 143).

Although Justine Marut Schober, a doctor who has been involved with intersex/DSD surgeries, claims that 'surgeons have always given parents of minors the right to accept or refuse medical advice on behalf of their children' (Schober 1998: 394), testimonials suggest that, in fact, parents have often not known exactly what they were agreeing to.

Some people who underwent paediatric surgery for intersex/DSD report being traumatized by childhoods where curious doctors and medical students poked and prodded at their genitals, adding to their belief that, if all this was necessary, they must have been hideous and monstrous as they were (Preves 2003: 74):

> My doctors made a traumatizing hospitalization even more traumatizing by putting me on show for parades of earnest young residents with "you're-a-freak-but-we're-compassionate" grins on their faces. This, all without nurses or my parents anywhere around ... I know now from my parents that the pediatric endocrinologists repeatedly advised them that I did not need to know the truth (Moreno 1999: 138).

> The amount of medical resources that were brought to bear against a 14-year-old intersexed kid are pretty amazing, considering that life-saving surgery and treatments are routinely denied people ... Why all the unsolicited attention? (Triea 1999: 141).

Doctors involved in intersex surgeries on older patients in the early days often argued that 'the full nature of the anomaly should not be revealed ... as extensive explanation may suggest to the intelligent person the nature of his defect and may cause great distress' (Ashley 1962: 289). It is significant that the essay by an undergraduate medical student which took second place in a 1995 medical ethics essay contest recommended that the doctors of women with AIS should not tell them that they are genetically male, commenting, 'Physicians who withhold information from AIS patients are not actually lying: they are only deceiving' (Natarajan 1996: 569–70). Natarajan claimed that the Kantian categorical imperative to treat humans as ends in themselves meant that doctors should not risk confusing or disturbing AIS patients with information about their true state, and that this overrode the Kantian imperative of truth-telling (Natarajan 1996: 570). However, some intersexed people have said that the realization that they had not been told the truth about themselves in childhood – and that their parents had been co-opted into 'collaborating in a web of white lies, ellipses and mystifications' (Kessler 1998: 22) – was far more damaging than knowing their true condition would have been:

> It is … disorienting when you have always considered yourself loved and cared for to discover that your parents and doctors have lied and left you to your own devices to discover [the] truth … Learning the truth about being intersexed can be temporarily traumatic. But not knowing the truth culminates in experiences that are almost universally tragic (Groveman 1998: 358).

> [The endocrinologist] … told me that the so-called ovaries that were removed at 14 were not ovaries at all, but were underdeveloped testes … I was tremendously relieved after he told me everything, because the truth was manageable. This was *my* diagnosis, my body, my life, and I had been told nothing but a pack of lies. I was furious with my parents (Barbara, speaking in Mortimer 2002).

> I was devastated. Not that I was intersex, but that I had been lied to (Melissa, in Toomey 2001).

The encouragement to keep their intersex conditions secret further exacerbated intersexed individuals' sense of isolation (Preves 2003: 77). Children who did know the reasons for their repeated hospitalizations were not generally encouraged to discuss them. The responses to Natarajan's ethics essay from people with AIS expressed dismay that deception was still being suggested as an appropriate course of action, noting that secrecy in their own lives had 'crippled' them. Groveman, writing as the US representative for the AIS Support Group, said,

> Natarajan is correct: learning the truth about AIS is traumatic. But learning the truth alone and scared in the stacks of a library is shockingly inhumane. When physicians and parents abdicate their responsibility to speak the truth they not only allow this to happen, they virtually ensure that it will. It is almost inevitable that the patient will learn the truth. The real question is how and when we want her to do so. When I discovered I had AIS the pieces finally fit together. But what fell apart was my relationship with both my family and physicians. It was not learning about chromosomes or testes that caused enduring trauma, it was discovering that I had been told lies. I avoided all medical care for the next 18 years. I have severe osteoporosis as a result of a lack of medical attention. This is what lies produce (Groveman 1996: 1829).

People with intersex/DSD conditions have also spoken out against being made objects of research first and persons second:

I was nine years old when I had to have medical photos taken at [Johns Hopkins]. My mother tried to joke with me that I was posing for Playboy. I failed to see the humor. I had to stand naked in front of a white wall with height markings etched on it … Then I had to lie down on a table while the photographer zoomed in on my spread legs and exposed genitalia. My mother had to assist in spreading apart the lips of my vagina so they could get an even more graphic view. I was so embarrassed. I was so ashamed (Fran at http://home.vicnet.net.au/~aissg/fran.htm).

Before the operation, I had I don't know how many doctors and people come in to look at the freak. And I was taken into a teaching theatre, not sedated, and the surgeon who was going to do the operation on me actually did it and explained it to everybody (Mitchell, speaking in Chase 1996).

The worst thing is being put in a prone position, half-naked, [and] told to spread your legs while five or six other people look in your crotch and probe. That definitely had a direct effect on my sexuality. It is embarrassing. It is shameful. It's painful (Gaby, in Preves 2003: 67).

Since corrective surgery in infancy usually necessitates further surgery at puberty, the justification that carrying it out early will get it 'over and done with' is a somewhat misleading one. Several people with intersex/DSD conditions have spoken about the physical and emotional discomfort associated with repeat surgeries, which some have in fact refused to have done. Kristi Bruce says,

The first couple of months that I was a [bicycle] messenger, I was in so much pain that I could hardly sit down on the seat, because the vaginoplasty is so fucking disgusting and so barbaric … The … inner part of the intestine is starting to come out … And I was told … that I would probably have to wear a maxi-pad for the rest of my life (Bruce, speaking in Gale and Soomekh 2000).

Outing the Outcomes: Follow-Up Studies and Access to Information

A major problem since intersex/DSD surgeries became common in the 1960s was a lack of follow-up reports about patients' ongoing physiological and psychological outcomes. In Kessler's 1998 study, *Lessons from the Intersexed*, she claimed that many doctors still acknowledged that their attitudes to intersex were largely dictated by Money and Ehrhardt's 1972 book (Kessler 1998: 13) – confirmed by even more recent medical papers such as that by Hrabovszky and Hutson, which sends the reader straight back to *Man and Woman, Boy and Girl* (Hrabovszky and Hutson 2002: 101, n. 124). This stems, in part, from the wide prevalence of early surgeries and the comparative dearth of non-corrected adults with whom outcome comparisons could be made (Creighton and Liao 2004: 659). Other perceived problems included the bias introduced by the self-selecting nature of intersex/DSD adults who might volunteer for more *ad hoc* follow-up studies (Crawford et al 2009: 414; cf. Creighton and Liao 2004: 659). A lack of access to information about their medical histories was felt by some people to disempower them further, and to erode their capacity to take ownership of their past experiences. Thanks in large part to pressure from intersex groups, since the mid-1990s there has been accelerated coverage of intersex/DSD outcomes in clinical and psychological journals, with Sarah Creighton, Catherine Minto, Lih-Mei Liao and their colleagues being particularly outspoken in their claims that intersex/DSD treatment needs thorough review and excellent follow-up, and that many surgeries should at least be deferred. Johns Hopkins University also embarked on a series of follow-up studies on adults with such conditions as AIS, CAH and micropenis who had been through the Gender Identity Clinic as children since the 1940s, comparing outcomes for those who had and had not had surgery. These studies began to appear in 2000. (For a fuller overview of changes in standards of care since 2000, see Harper 2007: 81–6, and for an example of a recent interdisciplinary medical textbook for intersex/DSD informed by new paradigms see Balen et al 2004.) However, unfortunately, claims Katrina Roen, even where newer protocols are acknowledged, certain clinicians merely 'gesture towards the fact that some challenges have arisen, and then they dismiss those challenges within a sentence or two, going on to reiterate and reinforce the dominant clinical practice' (Roen 2008: 49).

Intersex/DSD activists have stressed that research and follow-up must major on counselling, support and education for intersexed people and their families, not just on finding more and 'better' surgical techniques (which some doctors feel sure will lead to better outcomes – see e.g. Karkazis 2008: 157; Roen 2008: 51). Cheryl Chase [Bo Laurent] is particularly opposed to claims that advances in surgery alone will eventually solve all the problems surrounding intersex/DSD. Chase [Laurent] says the attitude seems to be that, because surgical techniques are far more sophisticated than they used to be, this 'relieves surgeons indefinitely of the responsibility of listening to any former patient' (Chase 1998a: 387) – as though any problems created in the past were simply a result of inadequate techniques, rather than a possible side-effect of the entire process. She criticizes some of the newer techniques for actually creating more problems than they solve. For instance, clitoroplasty or clitoral recession for cases of clitoromegaly (i.e. a large clitoris), where the clitoris is reduced and/or 'hidden' by repositioning ligaments, can actually affect sexual sensation more than the seemingly-harsh clitorectomy which used to be common (Chase 1998a: 388). Subsequent studies have shown that even so-called 'nerve-sparing' surgery on the clitoris can damage sensation and capacity for orgasm (Liao and Boyle 2004: 460). Although cosmetically 'successful', such surgery makes sexual pleasure (the retention of which might be used as a criterion of success by patients themselves) even more elusive. (For a recent overview of clinical studies on clitoral and vaginal surgery and its outcomes, see Karkazis 2008: 163–68.)

Since many people with intersex/DSD conditions have had trouble accessing their medical records or being given accurate information about their conditions, this has exacerbated the sense of secrecy and shame surrounding their diagnoses (as well as fear that the unknown condition might be much more frightening than it turns out to be: Sherri Morris describes her relief upon discovering that her AIS was a 'known quantity' – Morris 2006b: 6). Preves suggests that if children with intersex/DSD conditions were given age-appropriate information as soon as they could understand it, this would avoid a dramatic and potentially distressing moment of revelation later on (Preves 2003: 108). It would also reduce the feeling of powerlessness in some children to own or describe their bodies: Morgan Holmes, for example, reports that, after her own genital surgery at the age of seven, she could not articulate what had happened to her because she had no vocabulary for the name or function of the tissue that had been removed (Holmes 1998: 223). Melissa, a participant in Mortimer's *Gender Trouble* film, says,

> At four I was taken into hospital. I was, [to] all intents and purposes, perfectly healthy – didn't feel ill, so I was quite worried and terrified … I woke up in a lot of pain, didn't know what was happening. Nobody would tell me, they just said "It's for your

own good when you're older", and that was it. It was excruciatingly painful, and I went from being a ... happy ... normal child to being quite shy and ... worried after that, of what was going to happen to me, because nobody would talk to me (Melissa, speaking in Mortimer 2002).

There continues to be debate within the medical profession about the extent to which full disclosure during intersex treatment might help or hinder the psychological well-being of the intersexed person (Alderson, Madill and Balen 2004: 82–83), and about whether failing to carry out surgery is really any less harmful overall than carrying it out. However, as Chase [Laurent] stresses, ISNA's suggested programme of treatment for intersexed people 'includes diagnosis, sex assignment, peer and professional counseling, and offers cosmetic surgery to patients who are mature enough to make an informed decision ... [It] cannot be characterized as "do nothing"' (Chase 2003: 240).

People with intersex/DSD conditions, and their parents, by no means always spurn medical intervention, but one of the largest changes since the mid-1990s is that they are now more likely to demand autonomy and full disclosure in medical treatment, and 'have realized that ... they need not be treated as fundamentally unacceptable or flawed' (Dreger 1998: 173). They are slowly becoming more likely to meet openness and disclosure from doctors when they do seek information or advice about intersex. Accord Alliance aims to improve this even further, through working to ensure that every hospital has an ethically sound protocol for working with DSD patients and their families, ensuring they are dealt with by interdisciplinary teams expertly trained in the newest and best standards of care for DSD. Interestingly, several medical practitioners interviewed by Karkazis suggest that shifts in their practice have occurred as part of an ongoing trajectory rather than as a direct result of pressure from intersex activists. Activists themselves tend to refute this (Karkazis 2008: 266).

Reconstructing Perfection: The 'Restitution Narrative'

Describing her experience at a ceremony in 2000 where Cheryl Chase [Bo Laurent] was honoured for intersex activism work, Karkazis notes her own discomfort at claims by Surina Khan of the International Gay and Lesbian Human Rights Commission that early genital surgery equals 'torture' or 'intersex genital mutilation'. Karkazis says, 'Although I am deeply sympathetic to intersex adults' criticisms of their medical care, Khan's comments present a disturbing image of half-crazed doctors running down hospital corridors wielding knives – one that clashes with my knowledge of clinicians working in the field of intersexuality, whose intentions are more benevolent' (Karkazis 2008: 2). Indeed, Karkazis' 2008 volume, *Fixing Sex: Intersex, Medical Authority and Lived Experience*, is an attempt to show the multiplicity of motives and attitudes to treatment protocols held by doctors, patients and families. Many doctors involved in paediatric genital surgery have received only rudimentary training in the complexities of gender identity and may have little or no sense that there are other possible options than making boys or girls (Karkazis 2008: 93). Karkazis claims that a physician's usual role of observation, diagnosis and treatment is severely stretched by having to make a decision about intersex/ DSD which 'involves the very personhood of the patient' (Karkazis 2008: 94). Moreover, where the wellbeing of young children is concerned,

> Clinicians and parents typically share the same goal, though their opinions on how to attain it may be diametrically opposed: to use the best medical technologies available to adapt the infant to life within the binary gender model; living as much as possible as a "normal" male or female (Karkazis 2008: 97).

Despite the negative testimonies of many people, then, it should be borne in mind that surgery to alter unusual genitals has occurred out of good motives as well as what might appear to be dubious ones. Medicine's and surgery's propensity to tidy away the atypical has usually stemmed from an endeavour to improve lives, not consciously to enforce a repressive and damaging quasi-normality. This stems in part from what Alice Dreger calls the 'restitution narrative' (Dreger 2004; 1998: 185), whereby doctors and families work together to bring about what they genuinely feel is in the child's best interests (to give the child the 'good' of 'passing' unremarkably in a given sex/gender) and to buff up what they *already believe* to be a near-perfect specimen. Dreger, whose 1998 book *Hermaphrodites and the Medical Invention of Sex* aimed to 'expose' the morally reprehensible nature of non-disclosure and unwarranted early surgical intervention in the treatment of genitally-atypical children, explores in a 2006 article why the 'concealment-centred' model of intersex/DSD treatment did not begin to crumble immediately on exposure. She concludes that the medical treatment of intersex/DSD people has not changed more, and more quickly, because it is not, after all, so distant from other medical treatments, so its 'revelation' is not as shocking as might have been expected. She has come to believe that it is, in fact, fairly commonplace for doctors treating other paediatric conditions to withhold information from children and their parents 'under the guise of bearing the burden of knowledge for them' (Dreger 2006: 76). Moreover, she has realized that the unwillingness of some medical professionals to move away from early surgeries for intersex/DSD is based in a genuine belief that early intervention is a way to show forth the perfection of an already near-perfect child, not to 'fix' a monstrous abomination:

> Whereas I used to think that [the] push to "normalize" signaled a rejection of the "abnormal" child, I am now more inclined to think that those pushing see it (paradoxically) as loving acceptance of the child ... The parent (and pediatric surgeon) sees the child as essentially perfect, and wants the often-cloddish and boorish world to see the same, so she "reconstructs" the child to normality ... I think I failed to understand how much parents and surgeons *believed* in the restitution narrative they spoke. They really think they are *restoring* the child to the normality they've come to see within that child ... In 1998 I thought doctors treating intersex had put themselves in an awkward position – wanting to help patients while unintentionally hurting them. Now I realize what I am calling them to is a much more awkward position. I'm asking them to put down their tools of "correction" when in their minds that would signal abandoning the child, rather than accepting her (Dreger 2006a: 77–78).

Kessler notes that the terminology used by physicians who do surgery on intersexed children is generally that of 'reconstruction' rather than 'construction' – the implication being that they reconstitute what should have been there (and, in some sense, *has* been there) all along rather than beginning from scratch (Kessler 1998: 23). Sally Gross concurs that surgeons do not perform intersex surgeries 'with malice aforethought' (speaking in van Huyssteen 2003). Doctors are generally not malevolently trying to wield power by imposing particular treatments or outcomes on people with intersex/DSD conditions (Kessler 1998: 36). Doctors are taught to improve their patients' lives (Preves 2001: 545), and the vast majority endeavour to do so; even if the outcomes are sometimes questionable, 'Medicine is often driven by hopes, desires and even fantasies of abolishing disease and ameliorating life' (Karkazis 2008: 175). Even Money believed that a major reason for reassigning most intersexed children as girls was to try to spare them the multiple surgeries that would be necessary to create a fully functional penis (Money 1988: 41).

It is not as simple, then, as a medical profession which conspires to wield power over unwitting victims; as Iain Morland notes, discourses about surgical intervention and its critique always happen from multiple narrative sites (see Chapter 3). However, doctors, too, stand in the prevailing culture of ideas not easily shifted (Kessler 1998: 36; Karkazis 2008: 96). When they consider early genital surgery self-evidently restorative (Holmes 2002: 162), doctors are already investing heavily in what appears to be a societal consensus. This is particularly important given the continual development of prenatal hormone therapy for CAH, and the development of gene therapies to reverse AIS in the womb, along with the ability to diagnose these conditions early enough that the parents can choose whether to continue with the pregnancy (Holmes 2002: 176–77), which mean that certain intersex/DSD conditions may come to be all but eradicated.[6] Sharon Sytsma, for instance, has discussed in detail the ethics of using the drug dexamethasone to prevent the virilization of female foetuses in mothers whose children are considered at an elevated risk for having CAH (Sytsma 2006b), even though such treatment will only help a small proportion of foetuses and may damage more. Parents of intersexed children, too, stand within a particular socio-cultural *habitus* which often leads them to want the easiest, most 'normal' path for them; parents do not create such conventions, but rather channel them (Feder 2006: 191–92). But as

6. As with certain disabilities which can be diagnosed *in utero*, however, the choice to abort intersex/DSD foetuses may be seen by some as ethically reprehensible, leading to a two-tier society where those already born who have these conditions come to be even more marginalized and undervalued. Discussing prenatal tests and postnatal therapy for intersex/DSD, Holmes says, 'Their shared weakness is the twin assumption that our children are ours to make of what we will, and that we ought to will what is least complicated' (Holmes 2002: 177).

Holmes asks, 'If some parents are resistant [to genital surgery on their intersexed children], does this not suggest that there may be less rigidity in the supposed demand for "acceptable appearance" than clinicians think?' (Holmes 2002: 163). The good motives of doctors require redirection rather than subsuming.

In this light, language such as 'incomplete' or 'unfinished' for intersexed genitals begins to sound less sinister: it stems from a genuine conviction, believes Dreger, that the intersexed individual's journey to fulfilment and signification has been unavoidably truncated by a failure to achieve full sexual differentiation, but that medicine can *help* the individual concerned to 'get there'. Where unambiguous sex identity is held by both parents and doctors to be a necessity *in order that intersexed children become persons*, says Holmes, 'there is little reason for clinicians and parents to be in conflict over how to proceed or what to withhold; it is obvious to the adult stakeholders that to withhold surgical 'correction' is to forestall unnecessarily the development of the child's identity' (Holmes 2008: 173). Of course, the issue is that notions of perfection and legitimacy are always already muddied even in the good motives of those who want to polish up intersex/DSD persons' perfection. And as we have seen throughout this chapter, the notion that the 'goodness' of a two-sex, two-gender world is self-evident (and always has been) is misleading at best. Surgery is profoundly bound-up with replicating and reproducing social narratives; Holmes says,

> From a clinical perspective, the desire to "manage" (i.e. to treat) the intersexed child's body through surgical and medical means is the volitional discourse that precedes the "I" that the child will become. That is, where in typical births a simple pronouncement of sex is all that is required for the discursive constitution of the subject to be established, when an intersexed infant is born, technical intervention must occur prior to the pronouncement of sex (Holmes 2008: 174).

In this account, what medical intervention is truly communicating is that intersexed persons whose ambiguity is allowed to persist are not actually persons at all.

Some Conclusions

Some people with intersex/DSD conditions argue that doctors have done harm by intervening to operate on ambiguous genitals, but some doctors retort that at least as much harm, though not necessarily identical harm, might have been done by not operating. For example, they say, children may suffer changing-room bullying, or find it difficult to formulate an unequivocal sex identity. It is ironic, though, that one of the reasons doctors give for resisting changing their approach to intersex/DSD is that it would be irresponsible to embark on an experimental, unproven course of action like not carrying out early surgeries, when actually, early surgery itself has carried many of the same risks. Creighton and Liao comment,

> Sex assignment by genital surgery also represents an experiment involving invasive, risky and irreversible intervention. We are unsure how the absence of rigorous evaluation of the intended outcome could ever have been justified in interventions with such grave consequences, but overconfidence in the past has left the current generation of clinicians and patients floundering with uncertainties (Creighton and Liao 2004: 663).

In cases of intersex/DSD, any harm-of-non-intervention will very often be social or psychological rather than strictly physiological; this does not render it any less significant, but it does mean that doctors are always already taking on the bolstering of broader goods than simply physical ones. Doctors (and parents) reflect and reproduce social norms about what constitutes correct or appropriate bodiliness. Ethically, then, what is at stake in assessing the legitimacy of early versus late (or no) surgical intervention is the awkward question of which goods 'trump' other goods, and which goods deserve to be sacrificed or compromised. The ethical problems attached to performing irreversible surgery in sexually sensitive areas without the fully informed consent of the patient are obviously manifold; the ethical problems attached to *not* doing this surgery must also not be downplayed, but whilst surgery left undone can always be done (at least in the six or seven years between infancy and early puberty, after which therapy for some conditions may become more complex because of hormonal changes), surgery once done cannot be undone.

Theological concerns surrounding protection and care for those considered vulnerable, such as those with particular impairments, are highly relevant in considering intersex/DSD. To erase all impairment would mean cancelling out much diversity and multiplicity as well as much pain and discomfort; erasing all intersex/DSD, even if it were possible, would carry the same double-edged consequence. Theologies based in a desire to protect the vulnerable and query heteronormative ideologies have important tools for addressing some of the injustices done to bodies and identities through secretive corrective surgery. However, this is, of course, complicated by the perpetuation in some theological strands of male-and-female, clearly-sexed, heterosexual norms. It is exactly where people's bodily and gender configurations do *not* easily chime with theologically-sanctioned 'ideals' that theology most needs to engage in dialogue and reflection. For this reason, in the following chapters I turn to theologies from three areas often considered peripheral or marginal in order to find theological resources for 'speaking with' intersex.

Chapter 3

RELINQUISHING AND RELATING: INTERSEX/DSD AND MARGINAL BODIES IN THE BODY OF CHRIST[1]

The resurrection of Christ's body is a generative event for the Spirit's incarnation in the church. These two events are inseparable, and the connection between them is the human body – Christ's incarnation, his resurrected body, and the body of Christ, the church. The body is the necessary link because humans do not merely have bodies. Rather ... it is more appropriate to say that humanity is "bodiliness" and therefore that the body is the only suitable vessel for humanity's reconciliation with God (McCarthy Matzko 1996: 102-103).

Just as hermaphroditic bodies in seventeenth-century England were sometimes used to symbolize the country's uncertain political future in the aftermath of the Civil War (Gilbert 2002: 53-5), so in the theological tradition bodies have often been made repositories of signification for a community's overall integrity or wellness. Bodies deemed weak or deviant have thereby threatened not only their own status, but that of every group and community with which they are associated. The actions, activities and conditions of given bodies are always already figured in relation to communities. A suspicion of untameable, recalcitrant fleshliness in some strands of the Christian tradition, particularly after Augustine, associated physicality – and specific carnal urges like those for food or sex – with fallenness and animality, rather than the rationality and dispassionate reason which humans supposedly shared with God. Some of the most irreducibly *bodily* things about bodies, particularly anything which seemed uncontrollable or irrational, were thereby quashed and demonized.

---

1. Portions of this chapter appear in 'The *Kenosis* of Unambiguous Sex in the Body of Christ: Intersex, Theology and Existing "for the Other"' (Cornwall 2008a).

In this chapter I consider the status of human bodies with intersex/DSD conditions in their similarity with and difference from other human bodies, and particularly their status as held within the Body of Christ. The context for the whole chapter is Paul's figuring of the Church as Christ's Body with its many parts in 1 Cor. 12.12, 18–20, and 24–27.

The Hidden God Mediated Through Flesh-Taking:[2] *Bodies Human and Divine*

To be Human is to be Embodied

'The biological is never left behind by transcendence. The body is not the antithesis of the spiritual but its organ. We should not contrast the spiritual with the material, nor should we regard the spiritual and the biological as being on altogether different levels. Rather, we should speak of transfiguration: the material infused with the spiritual, the body becoming the form of inter-subjectivity' (Hull 2003a: 23).

Why do bodies matter so much? The cosmos-shattering event of Christ's incarnation, death and resurrection in a human body, and the existence of stories such as the healing of the woman with a flow of blood in Mk 5, demonstrate that having a body and encountering other bodies is crucial to how God interacts with humans. Through his dealings with the haemorrhaging woman, says Elisabeth Moltmann-Wendel, Jesus 'experiences the truth about himself and his body, which is a human body, but full of divine powers, of life-giving energies which he can communicate to others … God is there in bodies and their energies, alive and active' (Moltmann-Wendel 1994: x). Moreover, every single piece of speech and thought and assertion that humans have ever had or made about God has been mediated by humans' location in finite, physical bodies. Everything we know as humans, we know as bodies. Jürgen Moltmann remarks that 'hope for "the resurrection of the body" permits no disdain and debasement of bodily life and sensory experiences; it affirms them profoundly' (Moltmann 1996: 66). Bodies have limits, and thus serve as reminders about particularity and specificity (Rogers 1999: 238). They are crucial to human interactions with God, and to human interactions with other humans, which always already is interaction with God; Tim Gorringe notes that

2. Gorringe 2004: 127.

'the hidden God is mediated only through flesh taking and through encounter with the Other' (Gorringe 2004: 127).

Intersexed bodies might be held to be imperfect, damaged, or in some respects incomplete (they have this in common with impaired bodies, as I argue in Chapter 5). Sally Gross reports being told by Christian acquaintances that her baptism was not valid since, as she did not fall into either of the categories 'determinately male' or 'determinately female', she also did not fall into the category 'human', and was therefore not 'the kind of thing which could have been baptized validly' (Gross 1999: 70; see also Holmes 2008: 173). If bodies with intersex/DSD conditions are held to be imperfect or 'fallen', it might also be expected that they will be 'healed' in the new creation: that ambiguous genitals will differentiate and overgrown clitorises be rendered neat and small. However, such assumptions already make huge leaps of faith about the nature of bodily resurrection, and of the continuity between present and future configurations of human bodies. Moreoever, they already presume that some configurations of human bodiliness are more perfect than others, but for reasons which are somewhat arbitrary if the 'givenness' of heteronormativity and procreativity are queried.

This chapter considers specifically what individual, given human bodies might mean in the context of wider Christian body-communities, where the individual and the community both participate in constructing each other; what it might mean for the Body of Christ to be comprised by members who remain impaired, unusually sexed, weak, ugly, or grotesque, even in the blossoming of the new creation; and how pain and imperfection might be figured so that there can be a continuity between bodies as they are now and bodies in the age to come. I argue that bodies both signify the other bodies around them (as part of a community) and are signified by them, as well as remaining profoundly particular in their material substance. I argue that humans take the wider body into their own bodies and thereby become what is signified.

The End of Male-and-Female: Gal. 3.26–28

Most relevantly to our particular concerns surrounding intersex/DSD, beliefs surrounding the cosmic significance of the human body have been influential in the formation and ardent maintenance of a male-and-female binary within much theological anthropology. The assertion in Gal. 3.28 that in Christ there is no longer male and female is seldom taken to be literally true, because of all the apparently overwhelming evidence to the contrary; God made humans male and female, and in God's own image (Gen. 1.27), two clauses sometimes taken to lead to one and the same conclusion. Patricia Beattie Jung notes that the Genesis verses have been so strongly emphasized within the Roman Catholic tradition in particular because not only do they link male-and-femaleness with imaging God, thus constituting (as stressed in a 2004 Vatican document) 'the immutable basis of all Christian anthropology' (Jung 2006: 301; Vatican Congregation for the Doctrine of the Faith 2004: 5), but they are also appealed to by the Markan and Matthean Jesus in his response to questions about divorce – suggesting they are somehow foundational. Sexual difference as male-and-female, then, at least in Roman Catholicism, is not only biological and psychological but also ontological (Jung 2006: 302). However, as Aušra Pazeraite notes, 'the Vatican *Letter* confuses human sexual differences with gender' (Pazeraite 2008: 106). Moreover, as I discussed in Chapter 1, Sally Gross argues that it is possible to read Gen. 1.27 as suggesting an equivocal or even hermaphroditic identity for the first human (Gross 1999: 70), and that it may therefore be reasonable to assert that symbolically it is sexual differentiation rather than hermaphroditism which falls short of perfection (Gross 1999: 74). As I explore below, in relation to the work of Iain Morland, it may be that clear sex-gender differentiation, rather than ambiguity, is what will be erased in the new humanity.

The most usual interpretation of Gal. 3.28 – based not just in Gen. 1.27, but in everyday experience of human intercourse which usually seems unremarkably two-sexed – is that its meaning for the Christian community is a sociological, not biological one. For example, Elisabeth Schüssler Fiorenza says,

> Gal. 3.28c does not assert that there are no longer men and women in Christ, but that patriarchal marriage – and sexual relationships between male and female – is no longer constitutive of the new community in Christ. Irrespective of their procreative capacities and of the social roles connected with them, persons will be full members of the Christian movement in and through baptism (Schüssler Fiorenza 1995: 211).

Gal. 3.28, she concludes, is 'best understood as a communal Christian self-definition rather than a statement about the baptized individual' (Schüssler Fiorenza 1995: 213). However, Wayne Meeks says,

The symbolization of a reunified mankind was not just pious talk in early Christianity, but a quite important way of conceptualizing and dramatizing the Christians' awareness of their peculiar relationship to the larger societies around them. At least some of the early Christian groups thought of themselves as a new genus of mankind, or as the restored original mankind (Meeks 1974: 166).

Meeks views much of the Gnostic tradition, and extracanonical texts such as the Gospel of Thomas, as attempts to restore the original androgynous unity (Meeks 1974: 191–97). In Thomas (Saying 22) Jesus says,

When you make the two into one, and when you make the inner like the outer and the outer like the inner, and the upper like the lower, and when you make the male and female into a single one, so that the male will not be male nor the female be female ... then you will enter [the Father's domain] (in Valantasis 1997: 95).

Richard Valantasis suggests that the 'new person' of Thomas 22 is a totally-integrated, third-gender person who simultaneously negates gender, and that 'this new self also demands the recreation of the physical body and its theological signification' (Valantasis 1997: 96). However, this apparently positive appeal to androgyny (and its realization) does not carry through the rest of Thomas; in Saying 114 Jesus says of Mary, 'I will guide her to make her male, so that she too may become a living spirit resembling you males. For every female who makes herself male will enter the domain of heaven' (in Valantasis 1997: 194).[3] In the later epistles of the Pauline school, the strongly realized eschatology flavouring Corinthians and Galatians (and Thomas 22) has been watered down to a lesson about morality – specifically, the moral distinctiveness of the Christian life – rather than a literal recreated unity (Meeks 1974: 204–205). It is this sense which has tended to persist in the Church. Where there

3. Valantasis argues that since this 'living spirit' only *resembles* the males, rather than *being* male, the Saying 'does not seem to manifest a degree of misogyny, but makes the stated goal specifically for women as well' (Valantasis 1997: 195). However, as Marvin Meyer notes, the Gnostic association of the female with the earthly, perishable and passive, and the male with the heavenly, imperishable and active, which renders Saying 114 an attempt at a statement of liberation from the body, is 'shocking to modern sensitivities' (Meyer 1992: 109).

have been attempts to 'transcend' human sex, these have usually ended in negating bodiliness altogether, or in continuing to privilege some types of bodiliness over others.

Those who promote clearly-differentiated gender roles, particularly the submission of women to men, often assert that the apparent eradication of male and female exhorted in Galatians and Thomas is future-eschatological, not for now, as do eschatological feminists who view the subordination of women as undesirable but unchangeable within history (Ruether 1983: 86). A realized, temporal world where there is no male and female – or where biological maleness and femaleness are not the only available options – has seemed too unrealistic or utopian for most theologians to take seriously.

I am not proposing that intersexed individuals are harbingers of the Gal. 3.28-order, liminal or united firstfruits of the coming age. It would be highly problematic to use them in this way. But even if it would be naïve to read Gal. 3.28 as a simple prophecy of sexual androgyny in this present realm, it must be read as questioning something about the way in which females and males relate to one another in God's economy. The Galatians text implies that there is something about participation in Christ, about *perichoresis* between Christ and the church and between humans, which means that even such apparently self-evident concepts as sexed nature are not to be taken as read in the nascent new order. F. Gerald Downing comments,

> To insist that Galatians 3.28 is not "a prescription for the organization of a Christian society" ... is implicitly at least to adopt the Aristotelian social implications and the disjunctions which entail them, rather than adopt the Pauline refusal of them (Downing 2005: 183).

I believe that it is the compound nature of the phrase 'male and female' which is most interesting, in contrast with the dualism of 'Jew *or* Greek' and 'slave *or* free'. This linguistic variation opens up space for dwelling on the possibility of an erasure of the binarism. The assertion that there is no male *and* female in Christ does not necessarily mean that there is no male *or* female; biological reproduction in its present form is therefore still possible. However, what no longer exists in Christ is the all-encompassing cipher 'male-and-female' for humanity. Humanity does not exist in Christ only as male-and-female as they relate to each other. The end of male-and-female is the end of an exclusive, heteronormative system wherein humans are completed as humans only by so-called sexual complementarity. The male-and-female formula in Gal.3.28 obviously echoes the creation narrative at Gen.1.27, but to be made male and female and to be made in God's image are not necessarily identical. As Phyllis Bird holds (below), the Genesis text may be more to do with animal biology than with social status; it may, also, simply be an assertion about binary sex no longer justifiable in light of our present understandings about the science of sex differentiation. It seems to me that the clause 'male and female' in Galatians after two clauses based very evidently in *social* meaning (particularly since the whole point of Galatians 3 is that 'Jew' is a religious and not just an ethnic category, open to gentile converts through Christ) suggests that it is male-and-female as a socially-limiting construct, not male and female as gamete possibilities (among a range of other sex possibilities), which pass away in Christ.

This is particularly interesting in thinking through visions of a society where sex and gender do not work as a binary but rather as a continuum or a multiplicity, and where anatomy (particularly genital anatomy) is not unproblematically used as a cipher for identity. If male-and-female is passing away, then it need not stand for or encompass everyone; human bodies need not be altered to 'fit' it, particularly before those who live in them (like neonates with intersex/DSD conditions) can express an opinion. 'Male and female' in Gal.3.28 is not quite a synonym for what we would now call 'masculine and feminine'; it is not *just* the limiting character of binary gender constructs which is to pass away (though expanded conceptions of what it means to be masculine, feminine or both will certainly be part of the new, just order). Rather, biology is not to be the primary or most defining thing about members of the new community (although reproductive capacity will, at least for some people, continue to be an important aspect of their identity); and biology is not to be considered an *a priori* or incontrovertible 'fact' about a given body. 'Biological sex' is inscribed onto bodies as well as being read off them; 'male' and 'female' are not unproblematic, monolithic configurations, and should not be built up as such.

The 'no more male-and-female in Christ', then, means no more taxonomies of goodness or perfection attached to the success or otherwise of how a given body meets current criteria for maleness or femaleness. The Body of Christ made up of human bodies prefigures and begins to constitute the Body of Christ as it will be; 'perfected' not in terms of homogenization or assimilation but of reciprocity, embrace and grace. The end – the cessation – of male-and-female is the end – the *telos* – for humanity. This is the crux of reading Gal.3.28 in a more than future sense, for a realized eschatology is rooted in the *already*, the possibility for the redemption of this present realm. 1 Cor. 12.24 is potentially subversive of contemporaneous norms of honour and shame, for God has already disrupted expected systems surrounding who is deserving of glorification – but to superimpose unwavering models of honour and dishonour, weakness and strength, risks concretizing patterns of authority which already coincide with the *status quo*. Questions of what comprises 'legitimate' bodiliness – which can stand in its own conceptual right without having to be cured, tidied or redeemed away – cannot be unproblematically figured by the able over against the impaired, the typically-sexed over against the intersexed, the central over against the marginal. Varying human bodies are deemed to fall into these categories somewhat arbitrarily depending on culture and context, and may move categories over time without changing greatly as bodies.

There is a sexual element which is important here, too. Although many people with intersex/DSD conditions identify as masculine men or feminine women, and experience heterosexual attraction, there are also those who characterize their eroticism as neither homosexual nor heterosexual but as something other than either. Discussing the consequences of removing certain parts of the genital anatomy, Angela Moreno says,

> It is very painful for me … to conceptualize that what has been taken is a very specific eroticism, a hermaphroditic eroticism, that must really scare people and … cause a great deal of anxiety … That special part, our … sacred sexuality, has been ripped from us … That very special form of sexuality, arousal, and all of that that was uniquely hermaphroditic was taken. That is the crime (Moreno, speaking in Chase 1996).

Salzman and Lawler note that, within official Roman Catholic teaching, not only are only certain sexual acts (i.e. penetration of a vagina by a penis, followed by male ejaculation inside the vagina) moral ones, but certain 'biologically functioning genitalia' are necessary in order to be able to have such sexual intercourse at all.

Roman Catholic teaching does allow for hetero-genital sacramental union even where couples are infertile (Salzman and Lawler 2008: 122), so there is arguably a space of legitimacy here for sexual acts which could not lead to procreation. But since Catholic teaching also insists on 'communion complementarity', whereby only the male and female genitals' union can create a sacramental union, this excludes not only homosexual couples but also those whose genital anatomy cannot be said to match up to 'normal' male or female genitalia.

Heteronormative theologies which sanction only heterosexual eroticism, then, exclude not just homosexual eroticism but also eroticism which is other, which falls outside signification. Anti-hegemonic theologies must seriously question this, and must query the right of those in positions of privilege to delimit what kinds of eroticism (in practice, normally those which coincide with married procreation) are acceptable and worth celebrating. The existence of intersex/DSD raises problems for those who assert that the only legitimate marriage which can take place is that between a man and a woman. In practice, as we have seen, not all men are male and not all women are female. If marriage must take place between a male and a female, then how are these to be defined? An individual with AIS will probably have female-related external genitalia and live and identify as a woman, but she will also have (or have had at some point) testes, which may or may not produce sperm, and XY chromosomes. For the purposes of marriage, is she male or female? Would those Christians who endorse only male-female marriage really sanction a marriage between a woman with AIS and another woman without it?

Barth, Body and the Significance of Sex

Karl Barth's theology of sexual difference in the *Church Dogmatics* (especially III/1 and III/4) has been of particular importance because of its extensive identification of male-and-female complementarity and response with the supposedly correlative relationship between God and humanity – which have reinforced patterns of binary sex, and assumed that ambiguous sex does not adequately reflect God's pattern for humanity. Barth argues that the human is the only creature essentially differentiated by sex alone, rather than race, species or type as other animals are. This indivisibility, except on the grounds of sex, is part of what mirrors God's image in human beings. Beliefs about humans' sexed status are central to Barth, and he holds that the structure of procession of humans as male and female mirrors the structure of authority from God to Christ to the Church. However, in this, as I argue below, he fails to resist a particular human-centred model of sex and gender – ironically, given his thoroughgoing suspicion of ideology and hegemony (Gorringe 2004: 119; Gorringe 1999). Barth attempts to be true to the Genesis text, yet fails to allow the scriptural witness to stand 'over against' a human model of sex in his insistence that humans are, without exception, either male or female. As such, they must also be 'appropriately' masculine and feminine. Homosexuality, for Barth, disrupts the order in humanity which reflects the order between God and humans, and betrays a rejection of the law of God revealed in Scripture (Barth 1961: 166). Several writers have critiqued Barth's anthropology on the grounds that it is sexist, homophobic, inconsistent, or that it rests on an apparent biological essentialism despite his claims to the contrary; for discussions of some of these tensions see Sonderegger 2000, Fiddes 1990, Mollenkott 2007, Blevins 2005 and Muers 1999. I suggest that Barth's anthropology is unsuccessful not only on these grounds, but also because it does not make sense in light of the existence of intersex/DSD.

Standing Before God as Either/Or: Order and Procession in Human Sex

In *CD* III/1 Barth argues,

> As God is One, and He alone is God, so man as man is one and alone, and two only in the duality of his kind, i.e., in the duality of man and woman. In this way he is a copy and imitation of God ... He repeats in his confrontation of God and himself the confrontation in God ... Man can and will always be man before God and among his fellows only as he is man in relationship to woman and woman in relationship to man. And as he is one or the other he *is* man (Barth 1958: 186).[4]

4. Reading Barth only in translation sometimes obscures the fact that he himself uses two different German words, *Mann* and *Mensch*, which are both rendered 'man' in English, as here in Thomson's translation. *Mann* equates more closely to 'male', and *Mensch* to 'human', but the fact that 'man' in English can be used to mean both 'male' and 'mankind' (that is, all humans) obfuscates Barth's distinction between these terms. Rachel Muers notes that this adds to the ambiguity around what it is that Barth means in his discussion of order and procession in the male-female and divine-human relationships.

Men and women require each other in order to be completely, fully human. Barth insists that God's command comes to man and woman in the relationship *and order* in which God created them (Barth 1961: 153). Order is far from incidental here: it is in the *processional* relationships between the participants that, for Barth, male and female human relationships also most profoundly echo both intra-Trinitarian and divine-human ones. Barth avows that 'man in his divinely created sexuality is a similitude of the covenant, which rests upon the fact that God Himself does not will to be alone but with man and for him' (Barth 1961: 117).

Humans certainly do require interaction with one another in order to allow their humanity to blossom and to echo the perichoretic interactions in God. However, what is less convincing is the assertion that such interaction and mutual need in humans – such being directed to the fellow-human (Barth 1961: 116) – is most basically expressed through the relation of man and woman. Barth says,

> The "male *or* female" is immediately to be completed by the "male *and* female". Rightly understood, the "and" is already contained in the "or" ... For how is it possible to characterize man except in his distinctive relation to woman[?] ... In obedience to God, man will be male or female (Barth 1961: 149).

This is particularly interesting in terms of thinking about intersex/ DSD and of 'transgressive' sexed identities such as transgender, for Barth says,

> Since man has been created by God as male or female, and stands before God in this Either-Or, everything that God wills and requires of him is contained by implication in this situation ... God ... requires that [the human] should be genuinely and fully the one or the other, male or female, that he should acknowledge his sex instead of trying in some way to deny it, ... that he should stick to its limits rather than seek in some way to transcend them (Barth 1961: 149).

She says, 'The temporal sequence of the creation of male and female (itself based on the unargued elision of '*adam* and '*ish*, *der Mensch* and *der Mann*) is transposed into a synchronic "succession": "first and second" becomes "higher and lower". The model of "the woman as answer" itself contains this ambiguity; a question precedes its answer temporally, but, as Barth describes it, the question also determines its answer and thus acquires a priority which is more than temporal' (Muers 1999: 269).

Barth reads male-and-female as defining the whole of humanity on the grounds of Gen. 1.27. Crucially, however, this conclusion is not the only one which either the Genesis text or the scriptural witness in its entirety allows us to reach. Moreover, Barth's insistence that the *Mensch* (the human) is only completed by the male's and the female's presence for each other, risks reducing the Other to being only the completer of the self, the other of the same (as demonstrated in Muers 1999: 268).

Of course, Barth's strong distinction between male and female can be read positively: women are not simply 'deficient men', but have a humanity uniquely their own (Rees 2002: 32). Both men and women are directed to each other and proceed from each other; each should be for the other 'a centre and source' (Barth 1961: 163). They have 'a mutual responsibility' (Barth 1961: 168) to 'answer' each other. This sounds positive and egalitarian – an attempt to give men and women equal responsibility for helping to fulfil humanity whilst not eliding the real differences between them which some individuals find such important loci for their identity. However, what is still problematic in Barth is the inevitability of the 'order' in which this ostensible mutuality must occur. Barth says:

> [Man and woman] are not to be equated, nor their relationship reversed. They stand in a sequence. It is in this that man has his allotted place and woman hers … If order does not prevail in the being and fellowship of man and woman … the only alternative is disorder … Order means succession. It means preceding and following. It means super- and sub-ordination (Barth 1961: 169).

For Barth, it is woman's very vocation to be submissive (Fiddes 1990: 141). Woman must follow the initiative which man must take (Barth 1961: 171). Man and woman are A and B, not A and a second A (Barth 1961: 169–71). Although, Barth argues, this means that they must stand or fall together, that they are free or unfree together, what is central for him is that 'succession, and therefore precedence and following … does not mean any inner inequality between those who stand in this succession and are subject to this order' (Barth 1961: 170).

However, it is not as easy as all that to get around the inherent inequity built into order and procession. Geoffrey Rees argues that conscious differentiation between, and separation of men and women, as in Barth's writings, is actually 'a function of the norm it purports to undergird' (Rees 2002: 22). In other words, sexual difference in binary terms is regarded as normative *only* because of prior heteronormative constraints. It is beliefs about gender, and societal structures based in gender, which affect how sexed bodies are read, not exclusively the other way round (as Laqueur demonstrates). But a significant part of what is actually at stake in getting beyond a concretized binary model of gender is access to power – which includes access to God (Rees 2002: 27, 30). Power is certainly the issue, argues Rees, in a theological anthropology of complementarity such as Barth's. 'Barth explains ... that Jesus himself was all 'A', all Man, that to imagine anything otherwise about Jesus is to dishonour God' (Rees 2002: 38). Therefore, claims Rees,

> The "climax" of sexual encounter between man and woman turns out to be a decidedly male homosocial encounter ... "Master" ... of the woman ... [the man] now finds his will tested (measured) against the will of God ... The result is an intensely sexualized male-homosocial figuration of God-intoxication, as the man "who is tested and must test himself" ... discovers that compared to God's phallus, his own is as *no phallus* (Rees 2002: 35-6).

Even heterosexual intercourse, then, in Rees' reading of Barth, is actually primarily about working out hierarchies and relationships between human males and a God called 'he' – who is given the attributes of human husbands and fathers. This is highly problematic, not least because the use of the male-female relationship as synecdoche of the God-humanity relationship is so appealing that the inequalities outworked in it are sometimes hidden under layers of piety. As Ward comments, 'The attraction of opposite sexes maps too easily onto the logic of those who have and want more and those who lack and are dependant' (Ward 1998: 70).

Of course, even Rees owns that Jesus-as-A is already a complicated picture; it means men must become 'as women' in relation to Jesus (Rees 2002: 37). Moreover, Jesus himself becomes submissive and responsive to God, who might be figured as some kind of super-A. Fiddes comments that, since man's superordination and woman's subordination both echo aspects of Christ for Barth, each deserves equal honour (Fiddes 1990: 143). Moreover, Rees admits that Barth's model of initiation-and-response (God *then* man, man *then* woman) depends less on any actual, particular instance of heterosexual encounter than on the concomitant stability of appropriately 'masculine' identities for men and 'feminine' identities for women. It is not necessary for Barth that *every* individual marry in order that the 'good' of marriage be maintained; human marriage points and witnesses to the relationship between Christ and his 'bride' paradigmatically, but male-female complementarity exists beyond marriage itself (Barth 1961: 124–25). It might therefore be said that Barth's anthropology is not necessarily or ineluctably a reinforcing of heterosexual ideology.

In spite of all this potential disruption, however, to Barth the *project* of male-female marriage must not be destabilized, as when individuals claim 'illegitimate' or 'degenerate' gender roles, for this undermines a specific model of God-humanity imagery by threatening male homosocial norms. Thus, for Barth, argues Rees, 'Women ... don't so much need men to encounter God, as they need to continually make themselves present to men, as conduits of male encounter with God' (Rees 2002: 39). In this model, women are *for* men, finding their own fulfilment, even their own *meaningfulness*, in what they are to men – entering signification by the back door, under men's skirts, just as they will be saved by childbearing (or so the author of 1 Tim. 2.13–15 claims). In their obedient ceding to male initiation, women characterize the humility in relation to men which men should also show in relation to Christ (Barth 1961: 175); they become exemplary, but can only do so after they have already accepted their subordination to men. They gain their status as exemplars for men, as humans co-subject, with men, to Christ, only after they have demonstrated how *unlike* men they are. Men can thereby keep humility at arm's length: it can be held as a 'good' without actually defining who and what men are. In similar vein to Rees, and in an attempt to deconstruct theological objections to homosexual activity, Ward claims, '[Barth] wants sexual difference to be paradigmatic ... But he reads this sexual difference from the male perspective ... His other is not really another at all. It is the other of the same' (Ward 1998: 66–7). Even if, as Sonderegger maintains, the ranking where woman-follows-man is 'purely formal or structural' (Sonderegger 2000: 268), it has become, for Barth, the only option – and thus no option at all.

Barth is not alone in this. Salzman and Lawler argue in their reworking of Roman Catholic teaching on complementarity that 'the Magisterium's complementarity principle is grounded in biological genitalia, the male and female sexual organs, and … this grounding is inadequate as a principle for the construction of a personalist, relationally-centred, sexual ethics' (Salzman and Lawler 2008: 120). They criticize the logic whereby non-heterosexual acts are considered 'intrinsically disordered' because they lack hetero-genital complementarity, even if the personal or relational complementarity between the partners is still present – as has been protested by countless homosexual couples. In fact, the genitalia are not the fundamental markers of a person; rather, they must be understood as 'organs of the whole person, including his or her sexual orientation' (Salzman and Lawler 2008: 129) – so the 'morality' of their use actually depends on the extent to which they communicate the identity and ontology of persons *in their entirety*, sexual orientation and all. It is this which Barth and the Roman Catholic Magisterium have not adequately understood.

Like the Other Animals? Barth's Conflation of Sex and Gender

We now return to Barth's assertion that it is in their distinction as male and female that humans reflect God more perfectly than the other animals, since they are fundamentally distinguished only on this basis. Phyllis Bird criticizes Barth's handling of Gen. 1.26–28 (see Barth 1958: 183) in particular on slightly different grounds. She argues,

> [Barth's] own interpretation of the passage is as problematic as any that he criticizes – and for the same reason. Despite close reference to the biblical text as his primary source, he has failed to discern *its* anthropology – and theology – and has advanced only a novel and arresting variation of the classical trinitarian interpretation, an interpretation characterized by the distinctly modern concept of an "I-Thou" relationship, which is foreign to the ancient writer's thought and intention at all three points of its application (God in the relationship within the Godhead, humanity in the relationship between the sexes, and God and humanity in relationship to each other). At its most fundamental level Barth's exegesis fails to understand the grammar of the sentences he so ingeniously manipulates (Bird 1981: 132).

Humans' sexual differentiation is mentioned here in Genesis 1, says Bird, because the Priestly writer wants to emphasize the way in which humans are *like* the other animals, not unlike them as Barth holds (Bird 1981: 148). The Hebrew terms for male and female in

Gen. 1.26–8 are biological ones, not social ones as in Gen. 2.22–4, she says, and are simply used to clarify that humans, like other animals, can reproduce (Bird 1981: 148, 155). Humans resemble God, but it is as *creatures* that they are male and female (Bird 1981: 149). She concludes,

> There is no message of shared dominion here, no word about the distribution of roles, responsibility, and authority between the sexes, no word of sexual equality. What is described is a task for the species ... and the position of the species in relation to the other orders of creatures (Bird 1981: 151).

Miroslav Volf concurs, 'Men and women share maleness and femaleness not with God but with animals. They image God in their common humanity' (Volf 2004: 161). Barth's exposition of the passage, in drawing from it conclusions about sex roles, the sexes' status relative to each other, and marriage, is thus, holds Bird, illegitimate in terms of the text (Bird 1981: 155). For Bird, the description of male and female in Gen. 1.26–8 is a purely biological one.

This does not necessarily render the text any less problematic from the perspective of intersex/DSD (Bird stresses that the plural term in verse 27 'works against any notion of androgyny' – Bird 1981: 159), since it still seems to suggest the creation by God of a dually-sexed, male-or-female humanity. However, it does mean Barth's particular outworking of the text stands on shaky ground: Gen.1.26–8 may be about the possibility of biological reproduction, but what is ambiguous (or unaddressed) in Barth's writings is precisely the nature of the 'biological' reality to which the appropriate genderedness of men and women is pinned. In this treatment of male and female, Barth 'defines their ethical and social vocation in terms of their biology alone. It is as if he returns to a natural theology his whole theological system is set up to refute' (Ward 2000: 197). As Blevins notes, this renders Barth's ethics unfaithful to his theology (Blevins 2005: 73).

Although it is gender that Barth discusses, and it appears to be gender roles that he believes to echo divine-human relationships, this is projected back into sex, because Barth does not acknowledge that sex and gender do not always supervene. Barth owns that different times and cultures have had different expectations about what constitutes 'man' and 'woman' (Barth 1961: 154) – but he really seems to mean what constitutes masculinity and femininity rather than maleness and femaleness (for male-female complementarity is, first and foremost, about companionship, not reproduction). He takes the latter as read – but we cannot, if we take intersex/DSD seriously. Barth's model of gender seems to rest in an ideal, assumed sex rather than an actual one. This is ironic, since Barth's primary emphasis is on Trinitarian relationship, and human sex/gender is only secondary to it. Ward's recent re-reading of Barth's anthropology through the lens of alterity (Ward 2007) demonstrates that although difference is 'always erotic and therefore sexually charged to a greater or lesser degree' (Ward 2007: 82), it is also the case that – as Barth does not fully realize – 'Sexual difference is not a given, a fundament, a starting point ... It is produced in and through specific acts of encounter ... there is no theology of sexual difference, only the production of sexual difference in a theological relation' (Ward 2007: 82). To reduce a body to its identifiable maleness or femaleness is thus to negate this body's existence as fluid, transitional and interdependent – echoing the ambiguities 'of a God who is three and who is also one' (Ward 2007: 84).

Psychologically Narcissistic and Theologically Idolatrous?[5]
Barth's Elision of Difference

Although humans indeed need to exist in relationship in order to fill out their humanity, this relationship is *not* fulfilling only or specifically as it connects men and women (or males and females). However, a Barthian-type view has come to be repeated in Church statements such as *Issues in Human Sexuality*: 'In heterosexual love ... personal bonding and mutual self-giving happen between two people who, *because they are of different gender*, are not merely physically differentiated but also diverse in their emotional, mental and spiritual lives'(Central Board of Finance of the Church of England 1991: 37 (my emphasis). In fact, whilst gender is important as a repository for identity through which difference and diversity are expressed, it is not the most fundamental thing about being human, nor the only thing in which difference inheres. As Volf and Ward both note, it is ironic that Barth, who proclaims so vehemently that there can be no natural basis for theology, should slip into

---

5. Blevins 2005: 75.

mistaking the apparent indicative of sex for an imperative. Volf says of Barth,

> The characteristics and roles of God, one could argue, correspond more to those of fathers and men than to those of mothers and women. Notice, however, that this is not an argument from *God's* fatherhood and *God's* maleness – from above; it is an argument from below, from characteristics of *human* fathers and *human* males. The argument must go something like this: God, as portrayed in the Scriptures, is more like *what we know* fathers and men to be than *what we know* mothers and women to be ... It is illicit to turn around and argue that since God is thus and thus (more like males as we know them), human beings as fathers or as men should be thus and thus (Volf 2004: 159–60).

Similarly, Gerard Loughlin stresses that creation *must* be seen as echoing the Trinity and not vice versa. We must not allow conceptions of the Trinity to become concretized or narrowed by conceptions of relationships between human fathers and sons, but must remember the figurative status of such metaphor. Rather, says Loughlin,

> We can see that creation is properly a *parody* of the Trinity, a non-identical repetition in the order of created being of the trinitarian relations, which are now seen to be determinative of human bodies, but not of human sexes (Loughlin 2004: 156; my emphasis).

As Gorringe holds, however, Barth has been too close to the pressures of a patriarchal society, and so his argument is compromised (Gorringe 2004: 120; 1999: 207). To resist ideology, as Barth counsels but does not quite succeed in doing in his theological anthropology, is also to resist idolatry; as I argued from the Galatians text, 'male-and-female' is a golden calf, and so is a God back-projected from a 'male-and-female' model of humanity.

So what, cosmically, is actually being superimposed onto human sex in Barth's model? Barth's Jesus, as the fulfilment of the original Adam, is complete not merely through membership of a race which includes both male and female, but specifically in and through his 'wife', Israel (Barth 1958: 203). Barth wants to argue that it is in desire for the other (opposite-sexed) human that human desire for God is reflected. But, according to Ward, 'The economy of desire, linked to eros, is an economy based upon (male) lack and need. It is an economy of privation' (Ward 2000: 190). Barth's whole system of male-and-female cosmic interaction, mirroring God-and-humanity interaction, is based on a desire which possesses and incorporates, which *eliminates* difference. It fetishizes stereotyped 'difference' based on concretized maleness and femaleness, but disallows any move beyond this paradigm, and thus eradicates any kind of otherness which is not entirely predictable. In fact, argues Ward, Barth's man and woman are not a couple at all, for '[woman] does not stand *with* man, or *before* man as other, she stands *for* man' (Ward 2000: 198). Blevins claims, 'Psychologically, the system is narcissistic; theologically it is idolatrous' (Blevins 2005: 75). Barth's attempt to establish sexual difference does not succeed. Similarly, Rachel Muers notes that Barth's attempt to conceive of woman as *being* the answer for man in her silence is highly problematic:

> Barth's interpretation of the silence of the woman in Genesis relies on her being paradoxically both free and unfree. She must be free, because she must signal by her silence her acceptance of her election. She must be unfree, because her silence is decreed from the beginning and by her nature; her creation out of man means she has no choice. Man, in the story as Barth tells it, has a choice: to speak or keep silent; woman is required to be silent in order to symbolize, for man, what his silence might mean (Muers 2003: 113–14).

It is positive that otherness is always already assumed in Barth; it gives at least the beginnings of an opportunity for woman to have her own identity, distinct if not independent from man – but the possibility of difference should not inhere only in sex. Bodies *are* bodies, and *are* sexed, but are *not* condemned by their sexed natures to act in particular ways (except in very specific circumstances such as pregnancy – and, as Georgia Warnke [2001] has argued, this does not make it legitimate to make the entirety of sex-gender identity supervene on reproduction). This goes beyond Barth's reading whereby '[the] self is not known other than in our response to the call of God to become what we are already' (Loughlin 2004: 186) – 'appropriately' male or female as in relation to our 'completing' opposite. Barth would be the first to insist that he perceives intrahuman relationships as mirroring divine-human relationships and not the other way around; yet, because intrahuman relationships are right there in front of us, a handy object-lesson, inevitably they colour the ways in which human-divine relationships (even supposedly in distinction from any kind of natural theology or anthropomorphization) are described. So Barth's theological anthropology is problematic on this level too, and a thorough disruption of 'ranked' gender as metaphor for the relationship to God of Christ and of humanity is entirely warranted.

Ward rightly argues that homosexual relationships in particular can help highlight the fact that it need not always be the case that man acts and woman responds, saying, 'Same-sex relationships displace ... heterosexist symbolics, revealing a love which exceeds biological reproduction' (Ward 2000: 200). Ward also highlights the necessity of analogy in noting the differences in divine and human agency, 'to move beyond the impasses of univocity and equivocity' (Ward 2000: 276). Where there is no difference, there can be no desire (Ward 1998: 53). This is Barth's own motivation when he says that a relationship between God and a humanity made in God's image and likeness 'can never lead to a neutral It ... but rather an inward, essential and lasting order of being as He and She' (Barth 1961: 158). But this is problematic on at least three counts: first, identicality and equality do not exactly supervene; second, the 'order' designed to avoid stasis actually leads to stasis of a different kind; and third, Barth pins difference solely and ineluctably on sex. Loughlin comments, 'Most obviously, the rigid polarity of male and female precludes homosexuality as a possible condition of masculine and feminine existence' (Loughlin 2004: 187). Moreover, it renders intersex/DSD literally nonsensical. Barth 'allows for variability and new possibilities in the meaning of "masculine" and "feminine"' (Loughlin 2004: 187), but will not shift on the compulsory heterosexuality and mutual completion of those sexed male and female, lest this undermine their difference – which might, in turn, undermine the analogous difference between God and humanity.

Gorringe holds that 'We can accept [Barth's] fundamental theological principles without his unacceptable conclusions' (Gorringe 1999: 207), noting for example the reframing of Barth's account of man and woman as perichoresis in the work of Paul Fiddes (Gorringe 1999: 206–207). However, such a failure to resist a given human ideology (complicated by the fact that Barth believes it to be a more-than-human ideology), I believe, compromises not only this part of Barth's argument, but the strength of his injunction to employ suspicion of ideology generally. It thus seems extremely difficult to 'save' Barth for a theology of intersex on his own terms. This is unfortunate, since his ostensible rejection of hegemony is crucial and incisive, and his suspicion of the 'natural' in determining truth chimes more than he might have acknowledged with subsequent feminist and queer deconstructions of biological essentialism.

At least a part of Barth's fear of 'non-difference' between male and female may stem from a fear which Iain Morland (2001b) claims is present in much non-intersexed discourse: that bodies which seem to *cite* 'normal' bodies, without *themselves* being 'normal' or typical, threaten the distinction between bodies perceived as normal and those perceived as pathological. Impaired and intersexed bodies, for example, can usually perform many or most of the functions that non-impaired and non-intersexed bodies can. This shakes the societal structures which rest upon particular manifestations of gender (and other characteristics) as being normative, and their exceptions as being unproblematically 'other'. Picking up only on the anomalies is somewhat arbitrary – so why does it happen? Referencing the story of Cheryl Chase [Bo Laurent], considered a boy at birth but reassigned a girl whilst a toddler,[6] Morland says,

> Chase's penis/clitoris "quoted" maleness and femaleness without actually being either of them. It performed some of the functions of male and female genitals (such as sensitivity and capacity for erection), but it resisted classification as female or male ... It is [considered] unacceptable for intersexuals to have tissue that "quotes" the tissues of females and males. This is because ... such acts of quotation open up a space of questioning (Morland 2001b: 364).

The questioning goes beyond the actual physiological tissue of the body and asks what is at stake when non-males or non-females 'usurp' the privileges of these states. If something (be it tissue or something else) which 'belongs' to males, which is the sole preserve of males, is annexed by non-males (Harper 2007: 78); or if the perimeters of what constitutes access to a given category are blurred; then questions are raised about whether it is the *actuality* of the

6. Cheryl Chase, the pseudonym of Bo Laurent, is the name under which she founded ISNA in 1993. Laurent recently made her original birth and childhood names public and now uses the name Bo Laurent in all areas of her life.

body which has socio-cosmic significance, or merely the passing appearance. Could Barth's archetypal man-who-acts be an XY individual with ovotestes and extreme hypospadias who has been assigned to live as a girl and woman? Or is it gender behaviour rather than chromosomes which matters? If it is the *appearance* of being a man, of living as a man and taking initiative as a man that counts, then why is an XX transsexual man less of a man than an XY male-from-birth? It might be countered that intersexed and (perhaps) transsexual people are 'special cases', who stand outside Barth's cosmic paradigm of sex without thereby entirely deconstructing its reach for the majority of humans. However, the point is that Barth's model leaves no room for exception – because there can be no exception, either, in the initiating activity of God in relation to humanity; because Barth's narrative structure consists of a particular kind of beginning-middle-end, 'mutually constitutive, mutually demanded' (Muers 1999: 267) – so any exception necessarily begins to abrogate the entire project. If it is at its margins that any structure of ideas is most vulnerable (Douglas 1966: 121), then where these structures must take account of bodily configurations and processes themselves deemed to cross boundaries – processes to do with bodily fluids or the detritus of shed skin (Douglas 1966: 121), or configurations deemed liminal or anomalous – it makes sense that this vulnerability will be heightened.

Implications for Human Bodies in the Body of Christ

The Hegemony of the Binary Body

Human bodies are multiple, so it is important to consider how human bodies are conceptually able to relate to God in more than simplistically-sexed ways. Part of considering the Body of Christ *as a body* has usually been an underlying assumption that it is a body as human bodies are bodies. If human bodies are generally unambiguously-sexed bodies, then, the expectation might be that the Body of Christ is also unambiguously sexed. Actually, however, the Body of Christ already behaves in ways *un*like those of most human bodies: Christ's human body is not generated through the usual sexual route but via what might be termed divine inspiration. Lacking a human male biological component in his parthenogenetic conception, Jesus might well have had 'both the chromosomal identification of a woman and the phenotypic anatomy of a man' (Kessel 1983: 135) – a highly unusual state.[7] Remarkably, though not uniquely, Jesus' body walks on water; is raised from the dead; is taken up into heaven.

The fact that the model perpetuated in Western societies, of a male-and-female binary anthropology, continues to occur through identification with a *religious* ideology, gives the model more power and slows the process of its disintegration as a 'given', since there are multiple motivations for maintaining it. The patterns of power and prestige inculcated in it disincentivize those it privileges from leaving it behind. This explains the particular and ongoing focus on appropriate gender roles in certain strands of Christianity, which has privileged behaviour deemed modest, sexually continent and, often, specifically heterosexual. But just as Barth cannot pretend that his model of God and humanity is somehow prior to his own human embodiedness, so 'Theology ... needs to understand ... how what it assumes it knows needs to be critically assessed. It needs to understand also the kinds of bodies its own discourse has been implicated in producing' (Ward 2004: 74). The 'ideal' bodies produced and endorsed by theology are *not* identical with the human and cosmic body of Christ the God, in whose image all humans are supposedly created. However, suggests Holly E. Hearon, it may be appropriate for people keen to resist hegemonies of oppressive sex/gender discourse to question what the use of particular imagery in the theological tradition actually implies:

> Resisting readers ... may be suspicious of the image of the body. This suspicion may arise in part because of our propensity to envision bodies in gendered terms. Just what does this body look like? Must we conform to a particular image of the body in order to be a part of the body? Would it make any difference if this were a transgendered or intersexed body? (Hearon 2006: 611).

7. Any human parthenogenetic conception would result in offspring with XX chromosomes, since the Y chromosome comes from the father. Mollenkott says, 'As for the second Adam, Jesus the Christ, if the gospel statements that he was born of a virgin are taken literally, then like every other parthenogenetic birth, Jesus was genetically female all his life ... This is a problem for literalists. No wonder, therefore, that the Christian scriptures use a great deal of transgender imagery to describe Christ's body, the Church' (Mollenkott 2002). See also Mollenkott 2007: 115–17.

What it is about bodies that we actually want to say in talking about the Church as the Body of Christ?

Jesus Uncut? Christ's Uncertain Body

> Christianity as the religion of God in human flesh ... is almost too trite to say and yet still too disconcerting to think (Jordan 2007: 282).

Through having to have a body which is still a binary body – which *is* certain things and *is not* other things, as human bodies are generally assumed to be certain things and not other things – God has been rendered sexually respectable, and sexually unremarkable. As Mark D. Jordan notes, Jesus has had to *have* some sex or other, and it has been almost universally assumed that this was male, despite the striking absence of what we actually know about his genitals (for example). Indeed, despite this fuzziness, 'Jesus' maleness has been used to justify a number of theological conclusions' (Jordan 2007: 282) – but even staggeringly detailed sculptures of the crucified Christ are unlikely to reveal anything much beneath his loincloth (Jordan 2007: 283). Moreover, Ward notes that the human body of Christ as represented in art and text has varied according to the cultural expediencies of time and situation. For example, he notes that, in many paintings of the fourteenth, fifteenth and sixteenth centuries, Jesus' penis is depicted uncircumcised, despite a contemporaneous focus on Jesus' humanity and vulnerability (which might have been expected to lead to emphasis of his historicity and concomitant Jewishness). Ward attributes this apparent counter-intuition to circumcision's contemporaneously negative associations with Judaism, Islam and slavery. A fifteenth-century Jesus whose penis was cut would have been a Jesus socially and aesthetically inferior to those meant to venerate him (Ward 2004: 79–82). Rather than reflecting the likely historical fact of Jesus' circumcision, then, the paintings 'are accounts of the body of Christ that are grounded upon certain cultural *a priori* about embodiment' (Ward 2004: 82). The story of Jesus' life and body cannot remain uncut – unedited – any more than his Jewish foreskin can. Jordan, too, notes that although it is historically likely that Jesus was crucified naked, he is never shown like this in Catholic art. This says much more about our own foibles and hang-ups than about Christ's actual physical body (Jordan 2007: 284–85). A desire to retain a scriptural image like that of the body for the Church, then, necessitates re-reading and re-examining the image in light of contemporary and shifting conceptions of bodies and embodiment.

Robert E. Goss, for example, is one of many scholars who have traced a certain note of 'queerness' about the body of Jesus, arguing that, in John's Gospel,

> Jesus exhibits the feminine traits of the Sophia Wisdom model of God, but his maleness complicates the feminine aspects of Wisdom ... He takes on a submissive role as a slave or a woman to wash the feet of his male disciples; he is penetrated by the patriarchal Roman system, nailed to the cross. His flesh is penetrated by the phallic system of patriarchal conquest and rule (Goss 2006b: 550).

Goss also argues that 'Christology realizes its ultimate queer potential in a transgendered Christ – full of fluid identities' (Goss 2006c: 637). This kind of imaginative catalyst allows us to explore what happens to Christ's body if its incontrovertibility (as heterosexual, even as male) is liberated – and how that might affect possible reactions to the individual human bodies said to comprise it as the Church. Ward counsels,

> When we are talking about redemption we are talking about bodies and redemption through bodies. And bodies have no stable or autonomous identity. Bodies are not self-grounded and self-defining. A person's physical body, the "one flesh" of the nuptial body, the church's ecclesial body, the eucharistic body and Christ's eschatological body map upon one another (Ward 1998: 63).

Although bodies with intersex/DSD conditions are not unproblematically ciphers of androgygy or more all-inclusive than other bodies, then, there is a sense in which, as 'atypical' bodies, they already map onto the mixed-up, much-inscribed Body of Christ. Jesus' body, too, is a complicated and ambiguous one; for this reason, comments Sally Gross, Jesus became for her an icon of suffering, as her own pain and confusion surrounding bodiliness and issues of gender seemed to be in his body too (Gross, speaking in van Huyssteen 2003). The particular, specific existences of atypically-sexed or gendered bodies can thereby speak to what *all* bodies mean in relation to one another.

Inside-Out: The Ecstatic Eucharistic Body

The notion of bodily interaction and mutual making is particularly significant to considerations of ecclesiology, especially as expressed in sacramental acts such as Eucharist. The 'body of Christ' is whoever participates in remembering it in a given moment, as well as being a distinct body given over in order to allow the Church to become. Celebration of and memorial to the Body of Christ is an institution (a genesis) as well as a commemoration. A religious symbol such as Eucharist, the consumption and dissemination of the body of Christ in order to nourish and perpetuate the Body of Christ, re/presents an event without itself becoming the sole instance of that event; to do the latter would be to negate the uniqueness and specificity of the original event – as well as of every Eucharist-event which follows. Eucharist is not merely a *memorial* of an event, but more literally a re/collection, a *re/membering*. I have seen John Bell of the Iona community break bread during the Eucharistic liturgy and then, with the words, 'Do this to re-member me', fit the broken pieces back together – the implication being that it is in the act of sharing, the act of communion, that Jesus is raised and his followers walk in his way. Loughlin comments, 'In the liturgical celebration of the Lord's Supper, the Church participates in that creative work in which we are shown what the world could be like, what it will be like, and so, in some sense, is already, in the creation of Christ's bodily communion' (Loughlin 2003: 24). Every body which participates in this act affects the other participating bodies, and all these bodies in turn change and constitute the broader Body which is re-made. Carter Heyward's concept of 'godding', of humans actually contributing to the process of the becoming of God through their own loving relationships, also draws on this idea (Heyward 1982, 1996).

No single body can define alone what it is to be a body; no body can be taken as a perfect specimen unless the criteria of perfection are drawn solely and ineluctably from that one body and its substance on one specific occasion. Rather, the definition of what constitutes a body can only come from taking into consideration *all* bodies. However, it is crucial to acknowledge the tension between the self-constituting and the constituted-by-others nature of bodies, as Vannini and Waskul explore in their proposal that a more useful formulation of the body than the dualistic one found throughout much psychology and sociology would be an *ecstatic* one:

> An ecstatic formulation of the body emphasizes the active, interactive, and transactive state of ekstasis – being at once both inside and outside one's self, body, and society and in virtue of doing so annihilating those boundaries (Vannini and Waskul 2006: 189).

This is 'a departure from the spatial limits of one's body by way of expressing fusion with the divine or with other bodies' (Vannini and Waskul 2006: 190). The ecstatic body holds together its old habits and its movement beyond itself into new habits, and, significantly, 'emerges by becoming committed to its future projects' (Vannini and Waskul 2006: 191). Analogously, the perichoretic Eucharistic body emerges (and becomes an abundant body) in and through commitment to itself as an individual body (its uniqueness) and its being-held in all other bodies too.

Barth might oppose the 'newness' inherent in this re-membering and emergence by countering that all human history and activity is *already* taking place within the context of God's history; that no act of Eucharist is new but rather points to a particular moment at which human history changed through the work of Christ. But the history of God as expressed in the history of the Body of Christ is always a fluid history because of the simultaneous 'newness' and 'oldness' of the co-actors of that history. The particular human body, by its actions, changes the particular human body in its history. This also affects the wider Body-community, present and cosmic. It is the *believers* who make manifest God's image by enacting God's healing and saving works; discussing the centrality of the body and sensory experience in Syriac Christianity, Susan A. Harvey remarks,

> Just as Christ defeated Satan in and by his body, so, too, must the victory be rendered in the whole body of Christ: the body of the believer, the body of the church. Thus, what one does with the body, how one lives in the body, what one knows with the body are all matters vital to the process of salvation (Harvey 2002: 9).

If the communion in the celebration of Eucharist is a communion with Christ in his (cosmic) body, as well as an expression of solidarity between the members of the earthly body, then Christ must also be changed, or true communion has not taken place. God is truly present in the body of Christ, and God, in Christ, is changed by the presence of each individual human body which makes up Christ's Body. Through Christ, God and humans are no longer divided from each other; post-Resurrection, God and humans are no longer as different as they once were. Humans are still creatures, but different kinds of creatures, also co-creators with a responsibility for and toward what they create.

The arbitrary divisions between human tropes also begin to be dissolved in Eucharistic interaction, then; difference persists, but difference based on essentialist types will not necessarily be permanent. Loughlin argues that there is always an element of connection between what humans think of as most encompassing us – our own bodies – and what is perceived as most different from us – bodies which are alien. Loughlin says,

> The alien is necessary for its opposite, the self-same, which is thereby never really opposite, never really its own, self-possessed reality ... For the alien is just the other side of our skin; the inside of our outside. While it appears most distant, it is most close, our most inward but unacceptable being. It is thus all too often abjected, disavowed and destroyed. Yet its unutterable proximity holds open the possibility of its embrace, of connecting across the divide, without denying the difference of one side and the other. This is the possibility of the membrane, of the tissue that separates and connects ... It is the difference that unites; the cut that connects (Loughlin 2004: x–xi).

This seems to me to echo Irigaray's claim that when individuals cannot acknowledge the extent to which they already exist in their Others, they always already repress themselves, risk their selves, because this unawareness of when, where and how the Other might appear limits their capacity to embrace change and expansion in themselves (Irigaray 1985: 135). The fear of intersex/DSD and otherwise atypical bodies becomes the fear of all bodies and what they might become or do; the fear of bodies' uncontrollability. Alienated, discomfiting bodies, then, are not necessarily very far removed from the bodies of those who are discomfited. No 'alien' is as alien to us as we can be to ourselves (Loughlin 2004: 125–26). Intersex/DSD bodies are still often felt to be 'alien', to be 'other' from the bodies which speak and act and formulate policy. However, within Loughlin's account, although they might be pushed out of signification by unyielding binaries, they exist in trace even as they are erased.

Bodily Particularity: 'Individually We Are Members One of Another'[8]

The symbolism of the body of Christ as a body is never self-evident, and thus nor is its sexed nature or sundry other attributes that might be ascribed to it. Christ's (historical) body was not every body, never mind everyman.[9] The particularity of his body is echoed by the particularity of each of our bodies as they interconnect with one another. To suppose that participation in the mythic body of Christ should cancel out each body's uniqueness would be a gross irony – for, as Paul writes, 'We, who are many, are one body in Christ, and *individually* we are members one of another' (Rom.12.5). Thus even apparently incompatible entities may be held together, and without judgements as to pathology or echelons of perfection. Eucharist re-members Christ, but this never happens in distinction from those who participate. Even a mysterious event beyond human control, such as transubstantiation, then impacts – and is impacted by – individual human bodies: the bread and wine I consume literally help to build my body, but I in turn help build the body that the bread and wine represent. Human bodies are signifiers of a broader wholeness in God, but also become what is signified. According to the Church of England's Common Worship liturgy, the bread and wine (the body and blood of Christ) *are* the work of human hands, what human hands have made (Central Board of Finance of the Church of England 2000). Human and non-human bodies already are the new creation, even as they help to build it, but human bodies also have the faculty for envisaging a radically different future. Every individual body, then, is a sign of itself, a sign of all bodies (for this body shows something of the category 'bodies'), and also what is always being signified. Dealing with this tension is a key challenge for anyone working in the area of intersex, as Katrina Roen notes (Roen 2008: 48–9).

8. Rom. 12.5.

9. It is through this kind of logic that Tina Beattie refutes the accusation that a male saviour cannot save women; she says that to say this is to ignore the particular male body of the event. According to D'Costa, '[Beattie] shows that if a focus is placed on male gender without considering the *actual particular male* that is being redescribed, and the significations that are generated by that particular body, then to argue that only a man can save men amounts to redemption via anatomical identification – …a narcissistically projected divine' (D'Costa 2000: 59).

It is not simply a case – as for Barth – of an ordered correspondence, an ordered initiation and response, between God and humanity (Webster 2004: 27–8); in the sense that God is reactive and moved by human history, God is really changed by human history, and so is God's body. This means that the understandings of sex, of the implications of sexed bodies, within Christ's Body – within the Church – must be changeable in response to the sexed self-identification and sexed corporeality of the bodies within the Body. If the cosmic, resurrected Body of Christ is a glorified body, a body beyond death, it must encompass, without rushing to 'perfect', bodies and identities which (in terms of not easily fitting human categorization) are intractable.

Hagiography and Narrative

Inscribed with Texts: Bodies as Palimpsests

The biographies of many intersexed individuals serve to illustrate the manner in which the meaning assigned to particular anatomy changes in light of the surrounding context given to it. Consider that of Cheryl Chase [Bo Laurent]. Martha Coventry reports,

> Chase had been born in 1956 and named Charlie. He was a little boy with a little penis. Eighteen months later, doctors found that Charlie had a uterus and ovaries and that each ovary had a small corner of testicular tissue. But because the ovaries were found to be functional, the decision was made to change his sex of rearing. Charlie became Cheryl. *What doctors had considered a "tiny" penis was now seen as a grossly large clitoris.* In order to feminize the toddler, the surgeon incised deeply to obliterate any trace of a clitoris, removing the shaft along with the glans. Chase was left with a smooth, Barbie-doll look and a thin layer of scar tissue with no erotic sensation (Coventry 2000).

The entire history of Chase [Laurent]'s babyhood was also rewritten; she herself says,

> The story of my childhood is a lie. I know now that after the clitorectomy my parents followed the physicians' advice and discarded every scrap of evidence that Charlie had ever existed. They replaced all of the blue baby clothing with pink and discarded photos and birthday cards ... One day Charlie

ceased to exist in my family, and Cheryl was there in his place
(Chase 1998b: 206).

Her family moved away and settled in a new town before she started
school.

Although the 're-born' Charlie's anatomy had to be adjusted to
fit the back-story of Cheryl, in actuality, the resulting smooth, shiny
pubic area would no more have resembled the genitals of a 'normal'
girl than did the excised glans. However, the *meaning* given by
doctors to Charlie's phallus could not stretch to encompass
something called 'Cheryl's phallus', despite the fact that these would
have been physiologically identical entities – and despite the 'gap'
still left between Cheryl's remodelled anatomy and that of other
girls. If the meaning assigned to 'Body of Christ' can stretch to
encompass bodies which queer or subvert what bodies are held to
mean in a heterosexual, male-and-female theological anthropology,
can the meanings of binary *human* sex as invested by mainstream
theology also be stretched to encompass different truths about
humanity?

Using the category of hagiographic texts, Edith Wyschogrod in
Saints and Postmodernism suggests that saints themselves become
'texts' because their bodies become inscribed by meanings given
them by their biographers and those who hear and believe in their
stories. Different 'voices', *heteroglossia*, clamour to be heard, not only
as a result of the chronology but also of the contemporaneous
dissonance between, for instance, the claims of the saint and of
his/her institutional or authoritative context – often shifting in
predominance at different points in the narrative (Wyschogrod
1990: 6). David McCarthy Matzko holds that the cults surrounding
saints 'have shaped their identities far beyond the character of their
own lives on earth' (McCarthy Matzko 1996: 110). The inevitable
distance between 'signifier' (stories, legends and devotions
surrounding the incarnate life of the saint) and 'signified' (the saint's
'actual' body), then, is always in tension with a simultaneous and
inextricable connection between the two; Wyschogrod argues that,
just as the supposedly 'all-seeing' subject is actually limited by
location, so the saint's sainthood cannot be separated from his or
her lived bodily experience. The 'truth' of a hagiographic text still
lies, to an extent, in its perceived historical veracity, although the
meanings read into that historically-located individual's life might

be multiple – just as Eucharist must still be rooted in its historical tradition and its citing of historical events whilst being a new act, a new institution each time.

Wyschogrod's work inspires reflection on where 'truths' about bodies actually lie: where embodied lives are read as exemplary – as in hagiography – does this 'fix' the 'meaning' of a body somewhere outside or beyond itself (thus, arguably, eroding its subjectivity)? In fact, it is conceivable that trying to find a single, synthesized reading (trying to find the 'original' of a word or a body) might detract from the polyphony of truths about bodies which appear where readings jostle for pre-eminence. This raises questions about who has the right to invoke particular readings of a body, or to decide whether some readings attached to intersexed bodies in particular are more legitimate or 'ethical' than others. For Morland, for example, readings of the narratives of intersex must always be multiple, even as they focus on actual lived experience. To those who claim that the reform of the treatment of intersex is a matter of a simple paradigm shift from 'bad' early surgery to 'good' non-intervention, Morland counters that, in fact, *both* surgical intervention *and* its critique are veritable sites of ethical reflection on intersex (Morland 2005a). Any proposed 'reform' of the treatment of intersex should, in fact, be seen 'as a way of *reading* the plurality of narratives about intersex, the ethical outcome of which cannot be determined in advance' (Morland 2005a: 240). Morland critiques ISNA's tabular contrasting of the older 'concealment-centred' paradigm and newer 'patient-centred' paradigm for dealing with intersex/DSD, arguing that for ISNA to insist on 'patient-centred' care *even where* patients actively want their doctors to assume responsibility and act decisively on their behalf is itself deeply problematic (Morland 2008). Activists cannot avoid paternalism, claims Morland, for as long as their patient-centred approach is narrated as inherently ethically superior not only to the 'medical model' but also to what other patients want (Morland 2008). Morland implies that trying to find the 'right' narrative would be as elusive as trying to find the 'original' body, the body behind all the signifiers about what a body is and means.

McCarthy Matzko notes, 'Particular individuals are often set apart as saints only because their lives become access for the church to name its embodiment on this landscape' (McCarthy Matzko 1996: 115). Likewise, it seems to me, particular individuals can literally come to embody a community's understanding of its own bodiliness. The 'good' of this is ambiguous, for whilst the Church (for example) has often paralleled its own felt weakness or lack with real bodies such as those of people who are blind or deaf, in doing so it has normalized the perception of blindness or deafness as weakness or lack. Similarly, whilst there is potential in noting a possible disruption of heterosexual, homosocial norms in unusually gendered or unusually sexed bodies, there is also a risk therein of objectification and misuse. People with intersex/DSD conditions have sometimes been made to bear the weight of unsought connotation: from the mythic associations afforded the androgyne throughout history, through having the 'falseness' of their bodies changed to a 'true sex' via surgery, even through being figured as a 'third' or politically significant liminal figure by activists when all they want is a quiet, unremarkable life (Preves 2003: 39). Preves warns that individuals who politically oppose surgery for genital ambiguity must be wary of making intersex itself an essentialist identity wherein particular experiences and narratives of trauma are also essentialized (Preves 2003: 148). This is one reason why some intersexed people, and groups like Accord Alliance, have moved away from the identity language of 'intersex' and prefer the (debatably) less emotive language of 'DSD'.

Emptying Self of Self: Bodies and the Kenosis *of Signification*

Making a person 'mean' concepts with which they may not wish to be associated risks distorting and misrepresenting them, and might be interpreted as doing violence to their personhood. Interestingly, however, for Wyschogrod, the saints' self-giving in their bodies can be read as a *kenosis* of self-signification (Wyschogrod 1990: 33). Wyschogrod's saints give up their bodies to be used by and for others, but, concomitantly, this means that their bodies also come to be figured by others. Their stories and representations are transmitted by others. Wyschogrod says,

> The saint forgoes self-interest claims, or, in Christian hagiographic language, the soul empties self of self. For theistic hagiography, the "interior space" that is thus hollowed is filled by a transcendent Other. But human others, the recipients of saintly benevolence, may also come to occupy this void (Wyschogrod 1990: 33).

Saints do not ask to be saints *per se*, but they do exhibit comparatively freely-chosen kenotic behaviour, albeit sometimes in response to a divinely-commanded 'call' or vocation. In this way they come to be figured as exemplars or cosmic indicators, but in a manner unsought and possibly undesired. Because 'human others ... come to occupy this void', however, the uncertainty of the saint's history usually risks pious concretization by 'the recipients of saintly benevolence'. Saints give up their own self-determination.

Ecstatic bodies, however, direct themselves as well as being directed. It is thus possible to 'grow' one's identity in a (partially) chosen direction. This is particularly important in light of the objections to the concept of *kenosis* as an appropriate ideal for individuals who have already found themselves marginalized and denied the capacity to self-direct – as raised by Daphne Hampson (Hampson 1990: 155). The last thing people with intersex/DSD conditions need, Hampson might say, is even more ceding of their continence as subject-selves; *kenosis* might be a suitable project for the privileged, but for those who are already conceptually threatened it risks becoming a theologically-sanctioned form of masochism.[10] Ethically 'good' identities, for Morland, should promote the recognition of other identities, including sexed identities (Morland 2005a: 129). The 'character' of any body, then, rests both on its conscious self-projection and on its reaction from, and constitution by, others. Just as the sacrament of Eucharist must commemorate a particular event and institute a unique event too, so too a 'body'

10. Hampson (1990: 155; 1996c: 129–30) writes in response to Ruether 1983: 115–16 (see my comments below, in this chapter). Hampson says that the paradigm of the ideal self being sacrificial and broken for others too easily feeds into a downtrodden 'martyr-complex' already present in some women (Hampson 1996c: 130). Conversely, what is virtuous for the powerless is the courage to claim power (Hampson 1996c: 131). Sarah Coakley has countered that the *kenosis* critiqued by Hampson is not identical with the *kenosis* described by Paul (Coakley 2002: 9), and that the latter can be an important element of holding vulnerability and personal empowerment together, 'precisely by creating the "space" in which non-coercive divine power manifests itself' (Coakley 2002: 5). Coakley reasonably suspects that Hampson is too essentialist in her demarcations of all males as powerful and all females as powerless (Coakley 2002: 22), that Hampson too unproblematically considers power a 'good' (Coakley 2002: 32), and that Foucault's comment that *all* of us wields power in some respect might also disrupt Hampson's claim (Coakley 2002: 34). Some of these discussions are expanded by Hampson, Coakley and others in Hampson 1996a.

made up of other bodies must comprise the truths borne in each body as well as transforming them through their new context in and with one another.

Formidably, then, it may be that those whose bodies are considered *un*remarkable in terms of a sex-gender harmony must be prepared to relinquish the (unsolicited) power and status which currently comes with such a state of affairs. This might be what is meant by giving more honour to weaker members: if one member is felt to be less 'characteristic' of the body than another, if one member lacks what is felt to be a particular good, it might be said that what matters is to somehow give them what they lack. But the implication of Morland's point might be that, in the Body of Christ, rather than making the weaker (or less honoured) members conform to the Body, rather, the Body should conform to them. If it is 'weak' to lack a particular sexed status, then, rather than making those who lack binary sexed status the exception and compensating for them on these grounds, why not make it that *everyone else* cedes the 'honour' attached to sexed status? As F. Gerald Downing comments, the 'weak' elsewhere in Paul's writings are those *bound to convention*, as with the controversies over meat-eating in 1 Cor. 8 and 10 and Romans 14 (Downing 2005: 181). It might be argued that the extent to which binary sex-gender categories are used to demarcate humans in our society is no more than a deep-rooted convention, and one which must not be held in greater regard than the demands of justice. Morland goes so far as to say,

> The sex identities "male" and "female" are indefensible because they do not endorse the recognition of sexual diversity. Quite the opposite: such binary sex identities constitute a commitment to a system that erases intersexuality … Non-intersexed people who seek justice for the intersexed should refuse the identities "male" or "female" (Morland 2005a: 129, 131).

A commitment to 'male' and 'female' as labels entails, argues Morland, a commitment to sexual descriptivism.

Wyschogrod, too, discussing the possibility of sainthood leading to a self-effaced neuter state where body, time, memory and so on have all been handed over to be used by and for others, argues that what is to be given over might include unequivocal gender. Wyschogrod uses the story of the saint Marina/Marinus to explore the manner in which this individual's uncertain, shifting gender identity highlights the questions otherwise often naturalized in narrative, about the 'who' or the 'self' to whom things happen.[11] There are already gender-bending aspects to the story, such as Marinus being left to care alone for the child whom s/he has supposedly sired. Wyschogrod reads the story from a Lacanian standpoint, citing the specular identity that Marina/Marinus has failed to settle on because of a lack of parental figures (a dead mother and cloistered father). The 'signifier' of gender has been buried. The erasure of the girl Marina, through her father disguising her as a boy, also affects the identity formation of the 'masculine' Marinus. Marina/Marinus is neither male nor female because s/he has been made to be both (Wyschogrod 1990: 118). This leads to a collapse of meaning for Marina/Marinus as an individual; her 'desire' is made unspeakable, existing outside cultural meaning and accepted binary structures. However, this also means that Marina/Marinus' body becomes very evidently 'for the other', reinforcing the manner in which it (and its genderedness at given moments) is used for the good of others throughout Marina/Marinus' life (Wyschogrod 1990: 121). Here, then, is a model of not clinging to gender or sex identities which leave no conceptual space for sex 'outsiders' – as Morland urges (above). For Marina/Marinus it was a largely destructive experience as part of a whole narrative of loss and secrecy. But the relinquishing of sexed identities, even those held dear, could be a more constructive, enriching and humanizing part of that ethical action done 'for the other' by the non-intersexed saints – the souls and bodies given as living sacrifices for the Body of Christ which is the human bodies all around.

This could entail a handing-over of identification to those beyond the narrative categories within binary sex signification, and thereby speak of solidarity, of 'standing with' those who cannot be represented adequately within existing systems. Ruether says, 'Jesus as the Christ, the representative of liberated humanity and the

11. The story goes that Marina's widowed father enters a monastery, and later disguises Marina as a boy, Marinus, so she can live there with him. Later, as a young man still living in the monastery, Marinus is accused of having fathered a child, and does not deny it. Marinus is forced to leave the monastery, and the baby's mother later leaves it with Marinus. Marinus looks after the child and, as a reward, is allowed to re-enter the monastery five years later. Marina/Marinus' true sex is not discovered until death (Wyschogrod 1990: 115–16).

liberating Word of God, manifests the *kenosis of patriarchy*, the announcement of the new humanity through a lifestyle that discards hierarchical class privilege and speaks on behalf of the lowly' (Ruether 1983: 115–16). The earthly body of Jesus was understood to have privilege attached to its perceived sex, and thus Jesus lived in a context of the various subversion of embrace of particular aspects of this status. However, the *maleness itself* of his body does not have inherent significance, but simply how that maleness is understood and reacted to. Coakley has questioned whether the *kenosis* described by Paul is really a *kenosis* of masculinism, as Hampson seems to suggest (and which would render kenotic activity problematic for those already disempowered, since it is for Hampson an expression of guilt or compensation) (Coakley 2002: 11–14, 19; Hampson 1990: 155). In fact, then, it is more than a *kenosis* of patriarchy that is needed in the new world; Coakley suggests that a contemplative form of *kenosis* 'may take us beyond ... existing gender stereotypes, up-ending them in its gradual undermining of *all* previous certainties and dogmatisms' (Coakley 2002: 37). The result if not necessarily the process is positive: what is implied is, I believe, a *kenosis* of any signification attached to sex/gender unnecessarily – or where an insistence that a particular model of sex and gender is the only valid one excludes people who do not tick that model's boxes. One's body is neither only one's own nor only part of the world and *not* one's own; rather, 'it is the primary place of their union in differentiation' (Ford 1999: 95). The body always has an availability for meaningfulness (as given by others), but is also always irreducible to being *only* what it is as defined by others. Inside and outside are reversed in the new creation; moreover, inside and outside are no longer discrete categories, for, as in Morland's argument, they collapse into each other.

So although part of what Wyschogrod describes as possible saintly behaviour is the ceding of certainty in sexed and gendered identity, it is not necessarily the case that it is intersexed/DSD people who are called to be saintly or exemplary in this respect. The existence of an intersexed/DSD body should oblige one to reappraise one's views about the meaning of one's *own* body in one's *own* community – particularly when one's body is *not* deemed intersexed or otherwise unusual – before it leads one to presume to investigate any 'inherent' import in what has been designated an 'other' body, even a saintly or exemplary one. Thus it is only from one's own body, in oneself, that one can apply the lessons learned from other bodies. To assume that it is always and inevitably those with atypical patterns of sex, gender or bodiliness whose configurations are problematic is to further exclude them from signification. Clinging to a particular model of human gender because it is thought to be central to human status as being in the image of God is not only unhelpful – as Morland implies – but also idolatrous. For humans to cling solely to what they already believe to be true of God can only limit a fuller understanding of what it is actually possible to know of God. Only accepting as veritable what is already indubitable means some epistemological sites will be deemed irrelevant, or too dark for the light of God to reach. The 'kenotic hymn' of Phil. 2.5–11 counsels that humans are to emulate Jesus, who did not consider equality with God something to be grasped; but to exploit, cling, or grasp at equality with God is exactly what happens when humans decide that a single present or historical reading of gender tells the whole story of God. To claim God as a figurehead for a particular human project – to purport to know exactly what the 'perfected' Body of Christ will look like, and which identities can and cannot exist legitimately within its prototype – is to attempt to stand beyond contradiction.

An authentic giving-over of oneself to be figured by God and the other human will necessarily have uncertain, unpredictable consequences. Ford suggests,

> The self is posited by God in community without that necessarily being a dominating heteronomy. Likewise there is no "shattered cogito" in fragmentation, but there can be a complex gathering of self in diverse relationships (including forms of self-dispossession that require a letting go of control and mastery, often an existential equivalent of shattering) before a God who is trusted as the gatherer of selves in blessing (Ford 1999: 99).

The self-emptying described in the Philippians text involves humans emptying themselves of what they think they know about themselves, and of what they think they know about what it is to be made in the image of God – of which gender constructs have, historically, been part.

What might *kenosis* for non-intersexed/DSD people mean? This will vary from situation to situation, but the gist will be to consciously cede the privilege which comes from having an unquestioned sex. It could be as simple as refusing to declare one's sex on forms or documents when (as almost always) this is not directly relevant or essential information. It could be refusing to ascribe the presence or absence of qualities such as strength, intelligence, empathy, courage, gentleness or compassion to a given individual's (or one's own) maleness or femaleness, acknowledging instead that these are all characteristics available to – and to be cultivated in – humans regardless of sex. Within churches, it could be refusing to participate in disseminating teaching or liturgy grounded in essentialist, complementarist norms of maleness and femaleness on which masculinity and femininity are supposed unproblematically to supervene. Crucially, however, rather than eliding bodily differences (as Mollenkott's 'omnigender' society threatens to do), a multiplicity and immense range of variation should be acknowledged and celebrated.

Giving-Up and Giving-Over: Disrupting the Binaries

For Wyschogrod, saints' bodies are given over into a multiplicity of stories which they cannot control. This has also happened with the ways in which intersexed/DSD bodies have been treated and represented. However, if people whose capacity to self-direct is threatened continue to give themselves over to be figured by others, this may promote a perpetuation of their disempowerment. A giving-up and giving-over should not be done unproblematically by those who already find themselves at the margins of signification. Those painted as the stronger and the weaker members respectively, as those who act and those who are acted upon, give up and give over for one another, but there are ways in which this giving-over might be more evident and more painful for those who have more privilege and status to lose. In this way, bodies continue to construct and inscribe one another.

If Christ's Body is its human members as well as a cosmic entity, it is important that participants in 'filling out' and 'co-creating' Christ in his Body retain their difference, otherness and uniqueness too. Because of its constituents, Christ's Body is always multiple and diverse, grounded in Christ's real physical body and other real physical bodies too. Gavin D'Costa contends that it is highly significant that Christ's physical body is always already reliant upon, as well as co-sustaining, that of his mother Mary. Thus Mary should be viewed as 'co-redeemer'. D'Costa expands,

> The unilateral dependence of the church on Christ is now turned
> around: the church is a filling out and complement to the redeemer
> ... To fill out and complement Christ is to point to a lack, to
> refuse a closure on the incarnation, such that both women and
> men might now be co-redeemers ...The description of who Christ
> is, in his human perfection, is always necessarily a description
> of the women and men ... that are being brought into holiness
> through the Holy Spirit. Hence, *the description of the humanity of
> Christ is never complete* (D'Costa 2000: 196, 198; my emphasis).

By giving up his right to equality with God, Christ allows himself
to be built and fulfilled by his human neighbours. They *make*
Christ's humanity. D'Costa has missed a trick here, however, for
he can still only say that the filling-out of Christ – and thus the
representation of the Trinity – must be *both* male and female (still
based in a binary paradigm, grounded in lack-and-completion)
rather than *beyond* male and female. To suppose that (human) sex
attributes tell the whole truth of God is to settle for a God made in
our image without adequately examining why our self-identification
is as it is in the first place.

Bodies Qua *Bodies: Some (Provisional) Conclusions*

The image of the body as symbolizing wholeness, completion and
co-operation in Christianity is not an unproblematic one, but it is a
valuable reminder of the grounded, carnal locus of our encounter
with God. All bodies are constituted by their wider body – political,
social, religious – and constitute that body. Since each individual
body is synecdoche of the wider Body, any perceived imperfections
must be construed as either symptomatic of the real ongoing
struggles of a Body at war with itself, or as evincing questions
about whether perfection and imperfection, interior and exterior,
imposed identity and self-identity, are categories which can be
maintained as opposites. All these are held within each other and
cannot be excised without smothering the truth of the skirmishes
of community. By analogy, then, individual bodies which seem not
to fit some of the metaphors the Body has held about itself –
particularly, in the current situation, bodies which do not neatly fit
a Barthian economy of invitation and response, male-and-female
binary complementarity, such as bodies which are intersexed/DSD,
transgender or homosexual – raise questions about the fitness of

those metaphors to become imperative rather than merely indicative of a particular self-understanding. The particularity of Christ's body promotes celebration and valuing of every particular body. It might be said that this could have been the logical conclusion of Barth's own underscoring of the centrality of Christ's life, death and resurrection as historically-located events in an historical body – yet Barth's male-and-female imagery (designed for each other; repeating the otherness between God and humanity; completing, by woman, the part that man did not even realize he was missing) only allows him certain norms, an instance where typical is rendered obligatory.

This raises further hard questions about the limitations of body and Body imagery for the Church, in light not just of intersex/DSD but of other real – and not just stereotypical – bodies. Perhaps a metaphor with more fluid boundaries is desirable, or perhaps the attributes of real bodies need to be re-examined for their potential as adding to the image. For example, skin is semi-permeable yet does a remarkable job at keeping organ and sinew contained. It contains where appropriate and lets fluids pass where appropriate. Impermeable skin would lead to death, with sweat unable to escape and cool the body. Similarly, the skin of the Body is pathological when it only separates and divides. Ward suggests that it is crucial that the body of Christ being constructed now is *malleable*, ambiguous, porous, hybrid, even queer (Ward 2004: 85). Artistic images of Christ in glory with still-evident wounds[12] echo the suggestion in Augustine that 'scars' may be present even in the 'perfected' body (see Chapter 5). This idea has been expanded by Hull (2003b) and suggests that the notion of perfection as flawless 'wholeness' is itself flawed, or at least inadequate; Hull notes that Christ's resurrected body possesses a *wounded* power, a paradoxically 'imperfect perfection' (Hull 2003b). If the metaphor of the Church as Christ's Body is to be retained, there are certain other qualities which must be borne with it: a truly Eucharistic body, as Wyschogrod has implied, must be a truly saintly body, a body given over to be figured by others just as Christ has relinquished his body to be figured by those who now consume it at altar rails and in living rooms across the world. Ward exhorts, 'We are called to make meaning in God – this is the

---

12. See, for instance, Rubens' *Christ Risen* (1616) and Grünewald's *The Resurrection of Christ* (the Isenheimer Altarpiece; 1510–15).

particular commission of Christian *poeisis*. That is, Christian theologians have to render visible the operation of the Word, the body of Christ' (Ward 2004: 83). Herman C. Waetjen comments,

> In the new creation all pollution systems, which separated human beings from each other and discriminated against those categorized as unclean and therefore sinful, are invalid. Consequently, if all binary oppositions have been transcended, especially the binary realities of male and female ... the actuality of many individuated selves of human beings, regardless of their sexual or intersexual physiology, regardless of their homo- or heterosexuality, can be united as one body to constitute the New Humanity of Christ Jesus. This is the vision ... which the church of today can begin to actualize and thereby fulfil its destiny as the pioneer of a new moral order (Waetjen 1996: 114).

Human bodies are signs of the regeneration and interaction in God, indicating both what they are and what they are not. The human body more broadly shows the Body which it has already helped to build and the Body which is still under construction, still growing, still regenerating. The questions of meaning raised in and by intersexed/DSD bodies are raised in and by all bodies, with every body as a symbol peculiarly of itself and universally of bodies as a genus. What is vital is that the body of Christ now represents every other body just as every other body represents, re/presents, Christ. The human bodies held in the Body no longer have to be either the same as one another or stereotypically (as along binary sexed and gendered lines) different from one another. The dead-and-resurrected nature of Christ's Body means bodies are *already* partially their transformed selves, yet also, necessarily, exactly their same, scarred selves. Questions of sexed identity and sexual behaviour, of what it is legitimate to *do* to bodies and to *be* in bodies, must be governed by notions beyond those inhering in narrow, constrictive theological conceptions of corporeality. The Body of Christ is intersexed, because its members (or constituents) include intersexed bodies – and because, even for Barth, Jesus comes to be represented as 'nonsexual or supra-sexual, transcending the differentiation', so it might be possible to 'locate the nonsexed, "abstractly human" in the soul or the "inner life", of Jesus and thus of every person' (Muers 1999: 270).

Intersex/DSD is a legitimate conceptual site from which to think theologically. Appropriate kenotic behaviour for those with bodies not deemed unusual or marginal may be to cede their legitimacy, to give up the status that comes from a bodily sex deemed normal or clear. Intersex/DSD is at once marginal and non-marginal, and deserves theological reflection exactly *because* it is both marginal and non-marginal. Where people are marginalized, excluded or swept from signification altogether, this is exactly where ethical praxis demands that theology should speak with and have solidarity with them. *Kenosis* for non-intersexed people necessitates thinking ourselves into the margins – not in order to colonize experience which is not ours, but because intersex/DSD disturbs binary constructs of sex and gender in their entirety. It is in this sense that intersex/DSD cannot remain marginal but must be considered in its status as disruptive and subversive of a whole swathe of socially- and theologically-sanctioned norms which are really hegemonies. It has implications across the whole of theology.

In order to consider further the ways in which the existence of intersex/DSD and its treatment might subvert some naturalized norms of theological anthropology, I now turn to an examination of some existing theologies attached to the first of three specific areas: transgender and sex reassignment surgery.

Chapter 4

REASSIGNING AND REDEFINING: INTERSEX/DSD AND THEOLOGIES FROM TRANSGENDER[1]

> The body is a model which can stand for any bounded system. Its boundaries can represent any boundaries which are threatened or precarious ... All margins are dangerous. If they are pulled this way or that the shape of fundamental experience is altered. Any structure of ideas is vulnerable at its margins (Douglas 1966: 115, 121).

Justice and appropriately kenotic behaviour from clearly-sexed, non-intersexed/DSD people involves thinking ourselves into the margins. In this chapter I consider what happens when mainstream, privileged theologies and their associated hegemonies fail to think themselves into the margins; when, by contrast, they speak from an unreflectively sexed, privileged centre and disregard or devalue sexed and gendered configurations which seem atypical or abnormal. I propose that a more adequate theological response to intersex/DSD might be facilitated by reflection on transgender which does not start from a position of assuming its pathology or inadequacy.

Just as some people with intersex/DSD conditions have described not being 'trusted' as agents or decision-makers by their doctors (Preves 2003: 62), so, too, transgender people must first obtain outside sanction, confirmation or 'approval' for what they consider to be their state – in this case, from the medical profession – in order to gain access to sex reassignment surgery (SRS). In terms commonly used in medical ethics, this might be seen as compromising their autonomy and personhood, their capacity as authors and actors to shape and direct their own lives. There are good reasons for advising a period (usually at least a year) of living publicly in the new gender before surgery takes place. SRS is

---

1. Portions of this chapter appear in '"State of Mind" versus "Concrete Set of Facts": The Contrasting of Transgender and Intersex in Church Documents on Sexuality' (Cornwall 2009a).

serious, invasive surgery, and not easily reversible. However, the fact that transpeople are expected to 'test' their new gender highlights the oddness of the fact that non-transpeople are *not* expected similarly to 'try out' their gender roles before they are 'confirmed'.[2] For most people, the gender in which they are brought up from infancy is assigned solely on the basis of their genitals, and any subsequent deviation from it is deemed exceptional. This is grounded in a largely heteronormative model, one where bodies unproblematically 'tell' truths about individuals.

This kind of essentialist heteronormativity has also coloured theological responses to transgender. Transgender has tended to be viewed with suspicion within the Church, both because of fears that it will lead to homosexual relationships and the undermining of marriage, and because of reservations about the propriety of carrying out sex reassignment surgery in the first place (reservations not usually extended to surgery on children with intersex/DSD conditions, as we will see). In a system where marriage and procreation are so highly valued, it has sometimes been deemed illegitimate to render oneself infertile when this compromises the good of being able to procreate, and to bring this element to sexual intercourse with one's partner. It is interesting that the very word 'testis' is derived from the Latin word for 'witness'; the testes 'testify' to the virility of the individual (Hoad 1986: 488). However, reconsidering and redefining what actually inheres in 'truths' about heterosexual sex and procreation helps to deconstruct this objection to the reassignment of transpeople.

What happened when the Roman Catholic priest Sally Gross transitioned to life as a woman (Chapter 1) is reminiscent of what happens each time a transgender person asserts that the gender in which they have been living until that time now does violence to their person. It is not a case of taking on a 'false' gender, any more than it was 'false' for Gross to transition to a feminine expression of her own identity. However, part of the reason why transgender has often been figured as threatening is because it seems to allow bodies to cross the gulf between male and female physiology, to

2. Likewise, 'an individual who identifies as lesbian, gay or bisexual has no need to engage with the medical or psychiatric profession in order to be able to pursue his or her lifestyle' (Johnson 2007; see also Pauly 1992). This points to an instance of sexuality appearing to be read as more essential or irreducible than gender identity.

undermine the either/or binary on which so much social fabric is built, and to allow an annexation of the privileges and functions of state to which given individuals do not have 'legitimate' access. For Barth, as we saw in the previous chapter, any human who is not a properly masculine male or feminine female is not fulfilling their humanity, and must be figured (negatively) as 'a neutral It' (Barth 1961: 158). But what might appear to be incontrovertible demarcations of sex/gender are bulwarked by discourses *already* sited in a heteronormative mindset where male is *only* male and female is *only* female and each is exclusive of the other. Many Christian attitudes to homosexuality are based on this premise, too, as homosexuality is held to negate something profound about what it is to be a human being in (sexual) distinction from another human being.

However, the existence of intersex/DSD bodies – and the various masculine, feminine, and other gender identities of those who live in them – shows that sexed nature is already more complicated and shifting than binary, prescriptive systems allow. In considering Christian perspectives on and objections to transgender, and particularly transgender surgery, it will be helpful to keep in mind questions of what is actually at stake in insisting on dually-distinct sexed and gendered identities and heterosexuality for men and women, and what might be eroded by a move beyond them.

Some Theological Responses to Transgender

Oliver O'Donovan

Holding as pre-existent 'known fact' that all transgender people are mentally ill or delusional will affect the extent to which they are apportioned legitimacy as authors and actors of their own identities. Sandy Stone notes that, particularly in the early 1960s when transgender surgery was still fairly uncommon, few studies were conducted on 'ordinary' people seeking reassignment, namely those *not* already deemed psychologically disturbed. Data collected on those desiring surgery was not done in specialist gender clinics, but in clinics dealing with a wide range of psychological disorders. It is therefore perhaps unsurprising that most transgender people presented high levels of depressive and bipolar-type symptoms (Stone 1991: 340), since these had probably led to their original referral to the clinics. In the 1960s it had already become broadly believed as a result of only a few clinical studies that transgender people were highly likely to be emotionally and psychologically disturbed, a legacy which still persists. The unproblematic linking of transgender with psychological disturbance and sin is also evident in documents such as *Issues in Human Sexuality* (Central Board of Finance of the Church of England 1991: 7, 26) and *Transsexuality* (Evangelical Alliance 2000).

However, Christians and others might still insist that the apparently superfluous, extravagant nature of the removal of healthy, non-pathological tissue is counter-intuitive, eroding rather than promoting bodily integrity, and threatening the overall well-being of the individual. In *Transsexualism and Christian Marriage*, Oliver O'Donovan argues,

> The body of a living animal is susceptible to moulding only at the cost of its systemic integrity ... Respect for natural forms ... must mean more than the exploitation of plastic possibilities ... The traditional canon of medical practice ... ruled against surgical intervention into a living human body except to protect the functional integrity of that body when it was endangered by disease or injury. The use of craft to manipulate matter had to be ruled by the inherent structural integrity of that matter (O'Donovan 1982: 15).

However, as Meyerowitz comments, ironically the doctors who shared reservations about transgender surgery in the 1950s and 60s were often more than happy to remove healthy tissue from intersexed children 'without apparent qualms' (Meyerowitz 2002: 121). J. David Hester cites an example of a US medical insurance plan which covered surgery done on an intersexed infant but not sex-change treatment for a transperson, as the former was deemed 'medically necessary' and the latter was not (Hester 2004: 216). This case illustrates the way in which the genital tissue of children with intersex/DSD conditions is often already figured as pathological by interventionist urologists and endocrinologists. The genital matter of prospective transsexuals is medically healthy, and would be unproblematic *of itself* in another context, but is simply inappropriate for the context of this particular body.

O'Donovan also implies that, as well as threatening the broad integrity of the person, reassignment surgery for transpeople transgresses the givenness of the particular body as it is, so that to redefine the body sculpturally is to take the cult of autonomy to extremes (Meyerowitz notes that it is not unusual for transsexuals to be painted as 'self-indulgent technophiles' – Meyerowitz 2002: 11). O'Donovan asserts, 'To know oneself as body is to know that there are only certain things that one can do and be, because one's freedom must be responsible to a given form, which is the form of one's own experience in the material world' (O'Donovan 1982: 15). He insists that transgender surgery goes beyond the pale of the limits appropriate for human bodies. However, O'Donovan's argument seems to rest in an assumption that the body itself, the flesh and blood, is the extent of the entity whose functional integrity could be compromised. By contrast, for many transgender people, the pre-operative flesh is *in itself* part of what threatens the unity and integrity of the whole person (psychological and somatic). Yet O'Donovan himself states,

> Self-transcendence, in which the spirit may view the body as an object for thought, has not led, as it ought, to the recognition of the body as self and the acknowledgement of self as obligated to the body's form; it has led to the reduction of the body to undifferentiated matter, on which the spirit proposes to exercise unlimited freedom. In this way we confront the possibility of self-manipulation which is self-falsification; and we discover it to be based on precisely that abolition of complementarity between the body and the soul which was being recommended to us in the interests of a unified conceptual field (O'Donovan 1982: 15-16).

O'Donovan is anxious to avoid a body-soul duality, and there is a positive move toward a suspicion of surgery which is not absolutely necessary to the promotion of the integrity of the person – though O'Donovan is loath to admit that such could *ever* be the case with transsexual surgery. He also seems to view transsexual surgery as inherently cosmetic – and thus superfluous – rather than therapeutic.

Interestingly, however, O'Donovan's views on transgender are not fully transposed into his brief consideration of intersex/DSD. O'Donovan insists that 'the term "hermaphrodite", offensive as it may be, is conceptually truer, suggesting that the condition is one of both-and, arising from a malfunction in the process of differentiation' (O'Donovan 1982: 7). Like the doctors cited by Meyerowitz, O'Donovan seems happy to concede that 'surgery ... is appropriate to resolve the ambiguities of the hermaphrodite ...

The resulting sex ... is the real sex of the hermaphrodite. That is to say, it is the sex to which, in view of the ambiguity, it is sensible to assign him' (O'Donovan 1982: 13). O'Donovan argues that transsexualism and intersex are not two stops along the same road, and that it is less legitimate to accept the transperson's altered sex as their 'real sex' (despite the chromosomal anomaly) as it would be with a surgically-altered intersexed person (O'Donovan 1982: 13). O'Donovan owns,

> There are, of course, rare syndromes in which one might confess doubt as to the patient's original relation to the XX/XY alternative ... But such a doubt cannot obscure the primary fact that human sexuality at the biological level is dimorphic in intent, and that the only way to understand biological ambiguity, even at the chromosomal level, is as a malfunction in the dimorphic programme (O'Donovan 1982: 7).

Intersex/DSD, then, for O'Donovan, can only ever be a failure in a self-evident project of differentiation. But in attempting to resist body-soul dualism he reinscribes it, privileging 'irreducible' bodily sex over complex gender identity. There is an insistence in O'Donovan, as in *Transsexuality* and *Some Issues in Human Sexuality*, that 'sex is God-given' (The Archbishops' Council 2003: 233), but not enough reflection on how sex might actually be defined if it is considered in distinction from heteronormative views of complementarity and marriage and in light of all the instances in which 'males' and 'females' are not males and females at all.

O'Donovan wishes to refute the argument that individuals could ever find themselves 'trapped in the wrong body'; rather, he holds, the body they have, sex and all, is an integral part of who they are. By this logic therapeutic surgery or intervention to remove any kind of congenital disability or deformity would also be wrong (the bodies we have been given *are* ourselves, even if they are not as we might have wished); yet O'Donovan legitimates surgery on 'hermaphroditic' bodies to 'resolve' their 'ambiguities'. There is an error of reasoning here. Hester comments, 'Apparently, not having an identifiable sex is an emergency and something worth correcting, but having the "wrong" sex is not ... This looks to be a serious inconsistency ... when what is at stake in both cases is gender assignment' (Hester 2004: 216).

Another part of O'Donovan's argument against transgender surgery rests on the *artificiality* of the new body parts, and the implications for their cosmic significance during sexual intercourse – assuming that acts of heterosexual intercourse only, and conceivably *penetrative* heterosexual intercourse only, have significance beyond simple physical intimacy and exchange. But theologians' general failure to explore the value of non-penetrative sex is symptomatic of destructively narrow heteronormative attitudes. Genitalizing sex is fetishistic. It devalues non-penetrative, non-genital sexuality. It is highly problematic to accord penetrative heterosexual sex a different cosmic significance from other modes of sex, especially given an awareness that not everyone has the relevant anatomy to engage in it. O'Donovan says that, although it is legitimate to use crutches for walking if the leg is deficient for this purpose,

> The point is simply that such assistance never becomes anything more than a substitute ... Whatever the surgeon may be able to do, and whatever he may yet learn to do, *he cannot make self out of not-self*. He cannot turn an artefact into a human being's body. The transsexual can never say with justice: "These organs are my bodily being, and their sex is my sex" (O'Donovan 1982: 16, my emphasis).

I do not believe the 'homosexual' objection to transsexual sexual activity is an insurmountable one. But in any case, O'Donovan's objection in the above passage seems to be rooted in something prior to this, something about the extent to which prostheses are to be considered veritable parts of the recipients' bodies. Similar arguments might be made about organ transplants from donors; but when the donor is oneself (as when skin from one's own arm or thigh is used to make a vagina or penis) it is more difficult to maintain that the new organs are 'artefacts' or 'not-self'.

Moreover, O'Donovan could not have anticipated the particular advances in medical science in the intervening decades which allow serious discussion of the possibility of growing a penis in a laboratory from a female-to-male transsexual's own DNA and stem cells, as has been done already with skin and ears (Prosser 1998: 91–92; Liao and Boyle 2004: 461). If such an organ is cultivated from an individual's own cells, it becomes even harder than with a donor organ to argue that the new organ is not authentically 'them'. There is a certain inconsistency in appealing to the good – and therefore sanctity – of nature when nature has produced something desirable, but intervening to alter it when it has produced something objectionable, as O'Donovan seems to do; Catherine Harper notes that, in terms of variant sex/gender, 'nature is not all that manifests, but all that is deemed to be "naturally" manifesting' (Harper 2007: 180). There is technological intervention involved in stem-cell organ growth, but this is also true of every skin graft, hip replacement and pacemaker operation. Perhaps these new medical technologies muddy the waters rather than clarifying them; in any case, they open the gates for wholeness to go beyond happenstance.

Fraser Watts

As we have seen, the perceived 'good' of the body in which one finds oneself is not always self-evident. This accounts for the range even within the limited number of theological treatments of transgender, several of which have responded specifically to O'Donovan's work. Fraser Watts says,

> It is clear that not all aspects of our nature are a given that must simply be accepted. Most Christians would raise no objection to operations that corrected minor physical deformities … It is also clear that Christians do not accept their personalities as a given that they should simply accept (Watts 2002: 75).

Watts simultaneously raises the desire for sex transition to the level of a physical condition and legitimates a 'correction' of physical conditions viewed as problematic. Watts himself draws links between transgender and intersex/DSD, arguing that the very existence of 'hermaphrodites' demonstrates that it is over-simplistic to say everyone is 'clearly either male or female' (Watts 2002: 66). Watts holds that, just as people with intersex/DSD conditions are 'anomalous' in one respect, so might transpeople be in another respect (Watts 2002: 66). He rejects Kessler and McKenna's position that all gender is socially constructed (Kessler and McKenna 1978: vii), saying that most people *are* made either male or female as Gen. 1.12 and Mk 10.6 state; however, he holds that *even if* the distinction is a gift of God in creation and something to celebrate, this does not mean there are no exceptions to it (Watts 2002: 79). He argues that 'drawing a less sharp boundary between male and female would allow people to operate much more easily in an in-between area', so that 'transsexualism as we know it would be rendered unnecessary' (Watts 2002: 70).

In contrast with the 2000 Evangelical Alliance policy report which he cites (discussed below), Watts believes there is no good reason why transpeople should not become clergy – although, he says, they would probably require time away from the ministry to readjust to their new state (Watts 2002: 81). He cites the case of Peter Stone, the first serving Church of England priest to undergo SRS, whose parish in Swindon was keen for her to return as priest after transitioning gender. The *Daily Telegraph* quoted the Right Rev. Barry Rogerson, Bishop of Bristol, as saying at the time that there were 'no ethical or ecclesiastical legal reasons why the Rev. Carol Stone should not continue in ministry in the Church of England' (O'Neill 2000). In an interview in June 2000 before her final surgery, Stone said,

> In January, I wrote to the Bishop, telling him my life story, my agonies … It was a letter that has been in my heart for the 22 years of my ministry. I've never known anything else but the call to serve God in Holy Orders and I've never known any deeper desire than to be a woman (in Jardine 2000).

After the bishop had explained Stone's situation to the congregation at St Philip's church in Swindon, a member of the congregation said, 'We loved him as Peter, and as Carol we will give him our full support' (Jardine 2000). Stone returned to resume ministry at St Philip's in November 2000, and said, 'It is time to live a normal life … I want to get back to the bread and butter work of the Church. I have a wonderful congregation … and they are full of love, encouragement and humour. I am very grateful' (in Combe 2000). Criticisms came, however, particularly from the Evangelical Alliance. Stone's situation demonstrates that it is by no means impossible for a transperson to continue in the priesthood, though it would have been far more difficult in a denomination which did not recognize women as priests. However, the fact that controversy followed the 2005 revelation that Sarah Jones, an Anglican curate in Herefordshire, had undergone gender transition ten years earlier, suggests that much education and debate are needed before transgender priests will become as relatively accepted as female-born priests are. Watts argues that it would depend on the needs and reaction of the particular parish whether it would be appropriate for a transgender priest to continue there (Watts 2002: 81); this, however, does not mean that bishops should pander to the prejudices of a vocal minority. In actual fact, although the Bishop of Hereford had known of Jones' transition before he ordained her, they both decided not to make this information public to her new parish in Ross-on-Wye, since, says Jones,

> There's a difference between privacy and secrecy. It wasn't that we were holding a secret, but it's that we all have information which is ... properly private. And ... if I'd have turned up at that church and the first thing people knew about me was my ... medical gender history, we felt a lot of them would say, "Why are you dumping this baggage on us? ... We come to church to worship God" (Jones 2005).

Rodney Holder

Holder's work, though brief, significantly informs the chapter on transsexualism in *Some Issues in Human Sexuality*. Holder is keen to distinguish transsexualism from 'other conditions of ambivalent sexuality' (Holder 1998a: 90), in which he includes 'hermaphroditism' (referring to a range of conditions). Unfortunately, Holder is sweeping in his assertion that 'hermaphroditism ... is a congenital disorder in which both male and female gonads are present and the external genitalia are not clearly male or female' (Holder 1998a: 90). In fact, only a very few individuals, those called in the past 'true hermaphrodites', have both ovarian and testicular tissue; most intersexed/DSD people do not have both male and female gonads. Nor is it always true that the external genitalia are ambiguous, which is why conditions such as AIS and 5-ARD sometimes go undetected until puberty. Holder asserts that surgical reassignment for intersex/ DSD is 'uncontroversial', and that 'immediate post-natal surgical sex assignment seems to work in that individuals rarely suffer gender identity disturbance' (Holder 1998a: 90). This suggests only cursory engagement with intersexed/DSD people and their testimonies, although these had already begun to appear by 1998.

Holder also cites traits such as 'excessive femininity in boys or masculinity in girls' (Holder 1998a: 89) to characterize gender dysphoria. This evidences pre-existing assumptions about the binary nature of gender, further bolstered by Holder's observation that 'it has proved impossible to construct a functional penis in the female-to-male case – a fact which might well impinge on an ethical judgement as to the validity of marriage following the operation in this case' (Holder 1998a: 90). This is telling, for Holder's definitions of 'function' and 'success' are based in capacity for participation in penetrative penis-in-vagina sex alone (Holder 1998b: 131). What is at stake here is not whether *same-sex* relationships are marriages (as for O'Donovan) but whether *unconsummated* relationships are marriages. It is still, a decade after Holder, difficult to create a vagina which can self-lubricate, or be erotically sensitive – but this broader functionality seems unproblematic to Holder as long as it can be penetrated. This feeds back into Holder's readings of Gen. 1.26–28 and 2.18–25 as necessarily inferring heterosexual marriage (and procreation) as ideal and the only truly legitimate arena of sexual gratification for the Christian (Holder 1998a: 95–96; 1998b: 132). Holder comments that although the purposes of marriage are not limited to procreation, neither is procreation the only purpose frustrated when one partner is transsexual. He says, 'Transsexualism clearly presents a problem … also for the relational purpose, because the latter normatively comes to fulfilment in consummation' (Holder 1998b: 130).

In this mindset, even when procreation is impossible, the only kind of sexual intercourse legitimated – the only kind deemed truly fulfilling – is the same kind that would be legitimate if procreation *were* possible. Consummation equals penetration. This is despite the fact that, as Holder himself notes, the Book of Common Prayer specifically allows for the marriage of people past child-bearing age, on the grounds that sex is unitive as well as procreative and helps avoid fornication (Holder 1998b: 130–31). The restriction on sexual activity to that which could, all things being equal, lead to the conception and birth of a child, *even where* the specifics of the participants' individual or collective biology would not allow it, thus seems profoundly counter-intuitive. Acts of sex where one or more partners is transgender will almost always be acts of sex where procreation is not biologically possible, either because the individual has had their capacity for producing gametes removed or suppressed, or because they may be having sex with someone producing the same gametes. But the non-procreative nature of these sex acts is only as significant and as insignificant as non-procreative acts where the partners are intersex, male and female, or any combination. If contraception, sterilization, oral sex, sex for post-menopausal women, and sex for couples fully aware that one or both of them is infertile are legitimate, then sex for transpeople cannot be rejected on the grounds of non-procreation alone.

Issues in Human Sexuality

The 1991 Church of England statement, *Issues in Human Sexuality*, is extremely heteronormative throughout, presenting the monogamous, heterosexual married couple as the unproblematized ideal (Central Board of Finance of the Church of England 1991: 9). In this light, it may be considered unsurprising that anyone who elects to 'compromise' their capacity to marry and to bear children should be thought of as perverse. As might have been predicted, transgender itself is addressed in *Issues* entirely in one short paragraph which also deals with the 'problems' of sex addiction and those who find genital sex difficult or impossible (such conflation being revealing in itself, with its implication that transgender bears reflection only as a discomfiting curiosity). The statement reinforces throughout its early assertion that 'sin can disturb the delicate balance of the man-woman partnership' (Central Board of Finance of the Church of England 1991: 7). As such, transgender can only be understood as arising from and being symptomatic of this sin:

> Human sexuality is a very fragile system, easily distorted and broken. There have always been a certain number of both men and women ... whose sexuality feels to them at odds with their bodies, so that they become convinced of their need for sex change, or enter the world of the transvestite. Damage to sexuality, sometimes irreversible, can be done very early in life. The personality is given a twist which puts normal sex out of reach (Church of England 1991: 26–27).

The whole, brief discussion of transgender is sandwiched between the languages of damage and perversion.

The statement's overbearing heteronormativity is extraordinarily limiting: since *Issues* cannot conceive of homosexuality as a fully legitimate identity, it cannot think it into the minds of those whose experiences it purports to present either. Undoubtedly, the 'normal sex' which is put out of reach here is the kind of sex which happens between a male man and a female woman, ideally within a marriage. This is reinforced by the rather obsessive emphasis on procreation, even unwittingly (one hopes) echoed in language like that found in the claim that even the homosexual, through becoming Christlike, can participate in 'the final consummation of all things' (Central Board of Finance of the Church of England 1991: 41).

But why is this attitude which considers heterosexual, penetrative sexual intercourse the norm, and any variation from it deviant or inadequate, quite so strong? This becomes evident later in the document: the *a priori* given to which other factors must be subsumed is gender complementarity:

> It is important for the mature development both of individual men and women and of society that each person should come to understand and to value ... complementarity ... The fact that heterosexual unions in the context of marriage and the family are of such importance for the fostering of true man-woman complementarity seems to us to confirm their essential place in God's given order (Central Board of Finance of the Church of England 1991: 37–38).

This obsession with complementarity means that human identity is caricatured, 'immature' development (which presumably means any non-standard understanding of sexuality and gender) stigmatized, and difference pinned solely on sex rather than on any of the other elements contributing to the tension of sameness and difference within which human interaction takes place:

> In heterosexual love ... personal bonding and mutual self-giving happen between two people who, *because they are of different gender*, are not merely physically differentiated but also diverse in their emotional, mental and spiritual lives (Central Board of Finance of the Church of England 1991: 37) (my emphasis).

In fact, as in Barth's anthropology, this is a grossly inadequate representation of otherness.

Intersex is not acknowledged in *Issues* at all, and so cannot be contrasted with transgender, adequately or otherwise. However, it is important to note the worldview and attitude to transgender – and to sexuality more broadly – assumed in *Issues* since these underlie the fuller 2003 document *Some Issues in Human Sexuality*. What we can take from this brief look at *Issues* is its profoundly heteronormative bent, and its deep investment in gender complementarity as providing the correct basis for human sexual relationships. This is particularly important because it hints at the kinds of background work most valued by the compilers of *Issues* and *Some Issues*.

The Evangelical Alliance

Transsexuality, a 2000 report by the Evangelical Alliance Policy Commission, is particularly invested in presenting intersex/DSD as natural (that is, based in genuine biological ambiguity) and transgender as chosen (because the biology is understood as unproblematically pointing to a certain narrow conclusion). This seems to be done in order to bolster a heteronormative agenda and present non-heterosexual sexualities as illegitimate. Its handling of intersex/DSD is also telling, and the document is worth examining in some detail.

Transsexuality lists both 'hermaphrodite' and 'intersex' in its glossary. Although it is positive that distinctions between hermaphroditism and intersex have been drawn, since the two are still so often conflated, it is a shame that this was not done more accurately. I cite these definitions at length in order to show up the muddled and misleading thinking contained within them:

> *Intersex*: Refers to a number of rare medical conditions where people are born with ambiguous sexual characteristics, and nearly always due to physiological causes. Commonly, this may be shown by the presence of intermediate forms of external genitalia. *Congenital adrenal hyperplasia*, in which a girl is born with a masculinised clitoris, and chromosomal abnormalities such as *Turner's syndrome*, are among the medical conditions known as "intersex". When an intersex condition is present there is usually a clear physiological causal condition ... Despite frequent arguments to the contrary, transsexuality should not be regarded as a genuine recognised "intersex" condition. Most biological investigations of transsexuals have found no abnormalities in chromosomal pattern, in the gonads (which include the internal and external sexual organs), or in sex hormone levels that could account for the condition (Evangelical Alliance 2000: 3-4).

> *Hermaphrodite*: One of a number of rare clear physiological causal medical congenital conditions where the sex of newly born babies is ambiguous due to the presence of gonads and genitalia of both sexes, such people being termed "hermaphrodites". An individual with *testicular feminisation syndrome*, for example, appears normal at birth, but actually has testes as well as a clitoris. The condition is usually treated in early childhood by surgery and hormone therapy (Evangelical Alliance 2000: 3).

Like Holder, the authors of this document have made the mistake of believing that 'hermaphrodites' have both gonads and genitalia associated with males and females. 'Testicular feminization syndrome' (an archaic term for the condition now known as AIS) is an example of intersex, but not of hermaphroditism as the document suggests. Finally, referring to an individual with CAH as having a 'masculinised clitoris' (as opposed to one which is simply larger and more prominently hooded than average) is extremely controversial and betrays a dualistic, essentialist picture of sex, which stigmatizes difference.

That the entry on intersex makes clear its 'physiological causes' is obviously deemed so important that it is repeated only two sentences later. It soon becomes clear why: this is the primary way in which intersex is contrasted with transsexuality, for which 'most biological investigations' have found no explanation. The entry for transsexualism stresses repeatedly that transsexual people are 'biologically normal'; that there is 'no doubt' about their 'actual biological sex' (Evangelical Alliance 2000: 5). Indeed, *Some Issues* takes this up straight away, repeating and reiterating that, 'in the case of transsexuals, there is no doubt about their biological sex' (Archbishops' Council 2003: 223). The implication is clear: since transgender is not biological, it can only be a psychological condition, and since 'healthy' psyches are heterosexual psyches, transgender must be a problem, a result of living in a sinful world. It can therefore only be pathological. '[Transsexualism] is largely concerned with a state of mind ... rather than any concrete set of facts' (Evangelical Alliance 2000: 38). This total dismissal of psychological states as having any kind of actuality is bizarre, and apotheosizes biological 'truths' to a dizzying extent.

The sense in the Evangelical Alliance's document that conditions which are 'merely' psychological can be eradicated through therapy – even if some transgender people may reject this (Evangelical Alliance 2000: 23) – is a dangerous one. It implies they can be explained away and 'disappeared', rather than dealt with head-on as real and permanent aspects of identity. That one's 'state of mind' cannot, in this account, be considered part of a 'concrete set of facts' about one's integrated body-self is profoundly dualistic, heightening the problematic distinction drawn between 'real' and 'false' evidence about sex-gender identity. This is unfortunate, particularly since the writers seem motivated by a genuine desire to ensure that people with gender dysphoria can access therapy for any underlying issues such as poor self-esteem, parental rejection and peer pressure, rather than being fobbed off by doctors who may see reassignment surgery an easy fix (Evangelical Alliance 2000: 26). But although counselling and extensive discussion are, of course, crucial precursors to gender reassignment, the *a priori* assumption in this document (and in *Issues*) that gender dysphoria always means that the mind must be changed and not the body will colour the manner in which transgender people are considered. Just because transgender people cannot help being that way, states *Some Issues*, 'this does not necessarily mean … that a transsexual person cannot come to accept his or her biological sex' (Archbishops' Council 2003: 227). Biology is still the immutable *a priori* which must be 'accepted'; not 'accepting' biology signals the beginnings of 'a gnostic dualism in which the body is seen as separate from the self' (Archbishops' Council 2003: 249). But holding as pre-existent 'known fact' that all transgender people are mentally ill or delusional profoundly undermines their legitimacy as authors and actors of their own identities, and fails to disturb the genital-centric model of human sex which often seems to win through in the Church statements despite their acknowledgement of other models.

The unquestioned privileging of genital-appearance-at-birth over other matrices of sex-gender identity can be clearly seen elsewhere in the 2000 Evangelical Alliance report:

> We need to start by distinguishing between sex-*ambiguity* as a physiological fact at birth (the phenomenon of the "intersex" or "hermaphrodite" state constituting examples of such ambiguity), and transsexual phenomena. Something which is ambiguous between two distinct things, and where ambiguity is regarded as bad, will need to be resolved if possible into one or other of these distinct possibilities (Evangelical Alliance 2000: 58).

But what the report does not acknowledge is that intersex does *not* only exist as an example of something which stands between two distinct things; actually, it problematizes the model of their being two distinct things in the first place. Intersex shows that human sex is *not* a simple binary; and, since any exception to a dualistic model necessarily undermines the model in its entirety, this makes essentialist assumptions about what constitutes 'concrete facts' even more precarious.

The Evangelical Alliance report, however, will not acknowledge this, insisting instead,

> Sex is fundamental to being human; each person is, inevitably, male or female. Sometimes the process of sexual typology is not straightforward, as the "intersex" case has shown. But that merely confirms sexual typology to be a matter of interpretation of a reality distinct from the judgement made (Evangelical Alliance 2000: 63).

This, however, is a circular argument. It presupposes that the attempts to make the bodies of people with intersex/DSD conditions fit into a 'typology' at all are correct, and fails to ask whether the so-called 'reality distinct from the judgement' has itself neglected to take account of the 'exceptions', which may well turn out to be, after all, not so exceptional. There is no sense that the binary model of masculine maleness and feminine femaleness might be a provisional or inadequately narrow one. Indeed, and almost unbelievably, the report admits that even if it could one day be demonstrated that transsexualism were a kind of late-onset intersex, 'the case for the essential givenness of sex, as argued in this report, would remain largely unchanged' (Evangelical Alliance 2000: 67). There seems to be an implication that any discovery of a 'physical causation' of transgender might necessitate 'potential corrective physical or genetic treatment' (Evangelical Alliance 2000: 23). Ironically, given the repeated assertion that transsexualism is to be contrasted with the genuine biological state of intersex, it is very clear here that any new evidence about a biological basis for transsexualism is to be subsumed to the existing biblical witness – as it is interpreted – about the nature of human sex and gender (Evangelical Alliance 2000: 48). As Adrian Thatcher comments in response to the use of Scripture in *Some Issues*,

> Genesis 1 and 2 are required to bear an impossible weight of interpretation ... To say Genesis provides a "framework for understanding what it means for us to be male and female before God" is already to offer interpretation well beyond what the text itself is able to authorize. There need be no objection to such interpretations, of course, provided that they are understood as the outcome of the engagement of some readers with the text. But the bishops want far more than this. They are able to derive

"what it means" to be male and female, and just from this text!
(Thatcher 2005: 21–22).[3]

The writers of the Evangelical Alliance report are doing something
very similar, pinning their responses to transgender on biblical
texts which do not claim to be telling 'scientific' truths about
human sex. Theology must absolutely defend its capacity to critique
modern science and culture, but doing so on the basis of a shoddy
bibliolatry gets no-one anywhere. Mollenkott is right that the
'gender mountain' is particularly vast in religious circles, and
that unfortunately it is not usually the case that people of faith
immediately 'repent of their oppressive attitudes and open their
hearts to a transformation' when they learn about the reality of
intersex and transgender (Mollenkott 2007: 89).

The Evangelical Alliance's 2006 document, *Gender Recognition*, is
an attempt briefly to update the lengthier 2000 report, and to explain
specifically how the Gender Recognition Act 2004 might impact
legally on churches. The 2006 document specifically stresses the
difference between transsexualism and intersex, accepting the latter
as a legitimate (biological) medical condition, whereas the former
is seen as an issue solely of psychology. In answer to the question
'Is transsexuality a medical condition?', the document states,

> Transsexuality is considered by objective medical opinion to be
> a psychological medical condition. However, if the term "medical
> condition" is used to imply that transsexuality has an underlying
> biological cause, then the answer is "no" (Evangelical Alliance
> 2006: 3).

The assumption that 'psychological' conditions could not also have
biological connections is already dangerous; besides which, some
(debated) biological bases for transsexualism have in fact been
proposed (as the booklet itself acknowledges – Evangelical Alliance
2006: 21–22). Although the document is positive in its acceptance of
the 'reality' of intersex conditions, its desire to distance them from
transsexualism again leads to some demarcations between the
two being drawn where they do not necessarily exist. For
instance: 'Intersex conditions result from a chromosomal disorder.
Transgendered people by definition do not have a chromosomal

---

3. For another critique of the use of Genesis 2 in Anglican texts on sexuality,
in terms of a naïve conflation of biblical and present-day understandings of
marriage and gender relations, see Shaw 2007: 226–27.

disorder and therefore show no evidence of physical sexual ambiguity' (Evangelical Alliance 2006: 5). Not all intersex conditions do, in fact, arise through chromosomal disorders; it is not only inaccurate for the report to claim they do, but also bizarre, given that the same document later cites a survey of medical literature which acknowledges that at least a portion of intersex conditions have 'no discernable medical cause' (Evangelical Alliance 2006: 21). As with the 2000 document, the Evangelical Alliance seems keen to differentiate intersex and transsexualism, on the logic that something with a biological cause cannot be pathologized in the same way as something which has 'only' a psychological cause or which is a conscious choice. But intersex/DSD and transgender differ not predominantly because one is biological/unequivocal and the other is non-biological/uncertain. Intersex/DSD, too, has been called a medical, historical and cultural construction, not an 'evidently' biological one. It is therefore odd for Church documents to draw on intersex in order to demonstrate how 'unreal' transgender is.

The Evangelical Alliance report also endows transsexualism with a sinister moral bent: because it assumes sex must always 'match' gender, the Evangelical Alliance's unyielding insistence that gender must also always map onto chromosomes (2006: 4) leaves it using the language of 'deceit' (2006: 25), 'secrecy and deception' (2006: 9), and 'dangerous legal fiction' which privileges 'illusion over reality' (2006: 5), particularly with regard to new birth certificates. Since, for the Evangelical Alliance, sex and gender *must* correspond, the fact that actual sex-change is not possible already rules out the possibility that gender identity could be authentically other than what typically 'fits' one's chromosomes – though the report seems to have no difficulty in accepting that this does not apply in the case of intersex/DSD. It counsels 'the resolution of any gender confusion through acceptance of one's God-given sex and gender identity' (2006: 4), without entertaining the possibility that one's God-given sex and God-given gender may not cohere. The recommended support to enable resolution includes advice that 'the transgendered person should be encouraged not to hold onto links with former associates ... The outcome is invariably counter-productive' (Evangelical Alliance 2006: 17). The whole report hinges on the repeated assertions that God made all humans either male or female; that gender should map unproblematically onto sex; that any sexual relationship outside heterosexual marriage between two people of opposite birth sexes is wrong; and that this is reality and any attempt to say otherwise is fantasy. Its essentialist bent might partially be explained by an investment in much of the contemporary evangelical tradition in maintaining strong gender divisions when it comes to authority and leadership in the Church community and the biological family in particular.

Some Issues in Human Sexuality

Some Issues in Human Sexuality, the Archbishops' Council of the Church of England's 2003 guide to the sexuality debate, itself focuses in some detail on transgender, mentioning intersex ('true hermaphroditism' or ovotestes) only briefly. *Some Issues* touches on some interesting concepts surrounding transgender, but will only run so far with them. This may be because its strong emphasis on male and female being the human types created by God allows the transsexualism chapter to appeal to 'God-givenness' – individuals should not seek to change or escape from their sex-gender configuration as given by God (which, it is assumed, will be a non-transgender configuration). For example, it cites an unpublished paper by Peter Forster, which suggests that transgender should *not* be viewed monolithically as a solely psychological disorder necessitating solely psychological treatment, but does not pursue these ideas. Forster says that, through living in a fallen world, bodies and minds are sometimes out of alignment, and may exhibit 'fault lines' such as the belief that one should be a different sex. It should not be assumed that the physical 'evidence' about sex automatically overrides the self-perception of gender (Archbishops' Council 2003: 238). It might, then, be appropriate to adjust transsexuals' bodies, as long as it is accepted that this is still risky and provisional, within the uncertain nature of a dynamic and evolving world (Archbishops' Council 2003: 238, 239). Further reflection on Forster's approach would have been valuable. 'God-givenness' seems suspiciously heteronormative, since 'healthy' manifestations of gender are presented only as those which supervene on (unproblematized) biological sex, and promote gender-based complementarity. More engagement with scholarly work assuming a model of human sex and gender which is, at least in part, socially constructed, would have allowed for both a non-pathological understanding of transgender on the part of the bishops, and a recognition that contemporary understandings of biology are neither divinely-ordained nor set in stone.

With reference to the suggestion in *Some Issues* that transgender is based in a Gnostic-style dualism which undervalues the somatic body, Christina Beardsley, a transgender woman who is an Anglican healthcare chaplain, argues that

> The transition journey, in which the subject's body is subtly or dramatically changed by hormones and surgery, is not the Gnostic rejection of the body, or a dismissal of its importance, but a quest for a fuller embodiment of the person. Indeed, after starting on hormones people frequently say, "It was as if my body had been longing for these and was at last being satisfied" (Beardsley 2005: 343).

On this reading, to refuse SRS might be as dualistic as to allow it. Beardsley also makes other important critiques of the handling of transsexualism in *Some Issues*, where sex-change is read as negation of the 'true' body. Beardsley argues that *Some Issues* falls short in relying too much on Scripture and tradition which has not taken into account pastoral care changes which should have occurred in light of medical and psychological work done on transsexualism, including not acknowledging any work suggesting a biological basis for transsexualism; in making unsubstantiated assertions as, for instance, claiming that to bless same-sex couples would undermine heterosexual marriage without adequately explaining why; in not using transsexual individuals' own experiences; in employing a 'circularity' of method, whereby the Gen. 1.26-27 reference to 'male' and 'female' 'is assumed to denote self-evident concepts that support the authors' preconceived ideas about marriage and gender' (Beardsley 2005: 343); in arguing that it is appropriate to refer to transsexuals with the pronouns of their birth-assigned gender rather than the gender they have adopted; in a failure to discuss, or at least acknowledge, the existence of third-sex and third-gender categories in other cultures; and in a failure to engage with the specific problem of social exclusion faced by many transsexuals.

Nobody can know for sure that the child born with testes and an acceptably-sized penis and who is assigned 'boy' accordingly will continue to identify as a boy and man as he grows up. As Warnke, Laqueur, Dreger, Gilbert and others have shown, sex has not always been assigned in exactly the same way as it is now. It is therefore conceivable that it will not be assigned this way forevermore, and that the particular 'biological' distinction which the Church documents tend to draw between intersex and transgender will no longer stand, because different biological or non-biological characteristics will have come into vogue as more significant signposts of sex. So the authors of *Some Issues* are naïve in their insistence that 'physiological and psychological factors are not susceptible to change in the same way as social factors' (Archbishops' Council 2003: 226).

Transgender Christians

Several authors have written about how transgender identity affects and is affected by religious faith. Mollenkott and Sheridan, among others, assume the non-pathology of transgender and aim to help congregations engage sympathetically with the gender-variant individuals in their midst, as well helping trans Christians find resources and healthy identity in the tradition. Mollenkott variously calls herself a transgender lesbian, masculine woman and 'two-spirited woman'. This rather loose definition of transgender echoes Mollenkott's belief that 'most liberated people' are transgender to an extent, given that they would likely want to reject what Western culture considers traditionally masculine or feminine (Mollenkott 2002). Her practice of calling a wide range of people 'transgenderists' is controversial given that many people with intersex conditions/ DSDs, and many homosexual people, would refute any classification as transgender. Her appeal to intersexed people as speaking of a more pure or primal state of humanity may be deemed to stereotype or annex them in undesirable ways.

Mollenkott believes that there are several reasons why Christians may be particularly hostile toward transgender and cross-dressing. These include a lack of awareness about gender oppression among religious people; the conflation of gender privilege with divine blessing (Mollenkott 2007: 90); over-rigid readings of the Genesis 1 creation account (Mollenkott 2007: 97); a lingering belief that femaleness is polluting or second-best (Mollenkott 2007: 105), so that it makes no moral sense for a healthy individual to want to transition from the 'cleaner', more blessed state of manhood; and a failure to recognize that the Pauline injunction in 1 Cor. 11, where long hair is specified for women and short hair for men, is a time- and culture-specific imperative to ensure the early Christians could be distinguished from Greek and Roman priests (Mollenkott 2007: 107), not a once-and-for-all prescription about appropriate hairstyles.

Sheridan, a more traditionally transgender woman, wants to educate people about the differences between sex, gender and sexual orientation since, she says, many Christians do not understand the distinctions between these and tend to lump together everyone they consider deviant. She uses elements of liberation theological hermeneutics to promote transgender people's capacity to struggle for justice and acceptance, showing that 'good news of liberation, salvation, and redemption to the poor, the outcast, the suffering, and the oppressed' (Sheridan 2001: 57) is profoundly *for* those who are transgender. Even if the Christian Church has rejected and marginalized transpeople, she suggests, it is still part of their own spiritual heritage, not to be dismissed or easily let go (Sheridan 2001: 56).

In his book *Trans-Gendered: Theology, Ministry, and Communities of Faith*, Justin Tanis, a pastor in the Metropolitan Community Church and Program Manager of the [US] National Center for Transgender Equality, attempts to present a biblical basis for accepting people with variant gender in church congregations. He figures gender as a *calling* rather than something inevitably mapped onto a particular biology, and suggests that the experience of living with variant gender is one of following an invitation by God to take part in a new, abundant, holistic way of living, transforming one's body, mind, and spirit (Tanis 2003). Tanis is also the co-author of *Opening the Door to the Inclusion of Transgender People*, which advises LGBT organizations on how to become fully inclusive of transgender interests (Mottet and Tanis 2008). The latter also gives specific advice for communities of faith on how to be more transgender-inclusive. Suggestions include acknowledging the reality of transgender in theological consideration of justice, hospitality and the diversity of creation; and ensuring that the religious education of children and young people also covers reflection on gender identity and expression (Mottet and Tanis 2008: 62).

Malcolm Himschoot, a United Church of Christ minister, was the subject of a feature-length 2005 documentary film, *Call Me Malcolm* (Parlagreco 2005), which followed him as he travelled around the United States meeting other transgender people. Himschoot, who transitioned to living as a man during his time as a seminary student, says,

Some people hear, just by who I am, ... the sermon about stepping into who God has called you to be, and undergoing transformation even if it's hard ... I wasn't really ready to do anything while I was going by the name Miriam. I was a sort of a lonely person, and I don't think that's a way to head into ministry. So I don't think I, as Miriam, could have been a minister, or much of anything ... I was hitting a dead end that way (Himschoot speaking in Parlagreco 2005).

The voices of Himschoot, Tanis, Sheridan, Kolakowski (below) and others cannot be done justice to here, but are crucial in providing a transgender perspective which other churchpeople will recognize as belonging to their own discourse. They thereby provide something which Christina Beardsley identifies as being missing from *Some Issues in Human Sexuality*, namely stories from the direct experience of those who are both Christian and transgender.

Transgender and Scripture

The responses to transgender by the Church of England and the Evangelical Alliance in particular often seem to rest in particular (limited) scriptural texts, and do not necessarily adequately question heteronormative readings of these. In fact, there is so little biblical material which could be interpreted as speaking specifically about transgender issues that it is dangerous to try to build a Christian theological-ethical response purely on the basis of it. Responses to transgender are often actually grounded in verses about cross-dressing and eunicism, and I now consider them briefly.

Victoria Kolakowski argues that the lack of biblical condemnation of eunuchs – even those who have 'made themselves eunuchs' as in Mt. 19.12 – and the premise that 'compassion is superior to the Law' (Kolakowski 1997a: 22) open the way for a non-condemnatory Christian ethical response to transsexualism too. The Ethiopian eunuch in Acts 8, for instance, is baptized into the community with no special mention made of, or significance attached to, his genitals (Kolakowski 1997a: 24). If it assumed that at least some eunuchs have undergone surgery which has altered their genitals, this implies that, even on purely scriptural grounds, it is not possible to reject genital surgery out of hand as a legitimate path for some individuals. Indeed, Kolakowski explicitly wants to claim eunuchs as the biblical 'ancestors' of today's transpeople (Kolakowski 1997b: 43). However, says Deryn Guest,

> While tracing a transsexual or transgender ancestry to ancient times might understandably be popular and have strategic advantages, the very different constructions of gender and sexuality in different places and times seriously undermine such ventures. Certainly, the application of [Deuteronomy 22.5] to (post)modern transsexual transition would not have been envisaged by any ancient author (Guest 2006: 134).

Guest is right to urge caution in trying to build a castle on a pebble; indeed, it is extremely problematic to apply verses out of context to a substantially different situation. Simply picking out a verse like Deut. 22.5 (discussed below) and applying it to transsexualism is neither exegetically nor hermeneutically sound. The same might be said about the tactic employed by male-to-female transsexual, Malinda, in the documentary series *Sex Change Hospital*, who uses Jesus' words in Mt. 5.30 and Mk 9.43 to claim that since her male genitalia do, indeed, 'offend' her, they should, indeed, be cut off (in McKim 2007). I am aware of the similar limitations of trying to 'find' intersex/DSD in the biblical texts. I acknowledge Guest's caution, but still consider it expedient to reflect on biblical attitudes to eunicism – *not* because it is necessarily synonymous with transgender, but because it provides one instance whereby a condition 'missing' from the scriptural narratives might be read analogously into it.

Transvestism

In terms of appeal to biblical ratification for the impropriety of transsexualism, Deut. 22.5 is the verse of choice: 'A woman shall not wear a man's apparel, nor shall a man put on a woman's garment; for whoever does such things is abhorrent to the Lord your God.' However, this total conflation of transvestism (changing clothes) and transsexualism (changing the body), is problematic, even if the verse is accepted as normative teaching for today. Deut. 22.5 uses dress as shorthand for appropriate, non-transgressive (gendered) behaviour. There is no suggestion that, by wearing a woman's garment, a man *becomes* a woman; the issue is that he could be *mistaken* for a woman, which matters very much in a context where women and men operate in clearly-defined and segregated spheres. The act of cross-dressing itself cannot be said to transgress any universal law, but is contingent on the practices of a given community. The verse thus seems in much the same vein as Deut. 22.11 ('You shall not wear clothes made of wool and linen woven together'): it is to do with not 'mixing' (or mixing-up) things which should remain distinct. Those who have rationalized to themselves that the latter verse need no longer be followed might, by the same logic, be able to question the former, for cross-dressing's disruption of the 'natural' order is far less thunderous if the 'natural' order (in this case, what can and cannot legitimately be mixed-up or mixed together) is itself already acknowledged as being culturally constructed.

This is very significant in terms of intersex/DSD, for it is a reminder that what we consider unusual or atypical bodiliness is always affected by what we already consider normal or unremarkable. The ways we respond to intersex/DSD in a given culture, climate or environment are coloured by our pre-existing assumptions and wants. Since theologians and other Christians can help to speak, make and influence the cultural narratives being endorsed and disseminated in society at large, this means theologians can also stand for particular goods such as justice, love and compassion which must always be promoted. Morland's work is a compelling reminder that responses to intersex/DSD are fundamentally to do with narrative, and (in particular) whose narratives are given most weight and why. Reflecting on the ways (good and bad) in which transgender has been 'narrated' by and alongside the theological tradition is therefore an important precursor to being self-reflective and self-critical of the ways in which we engage with intersex/DSD.

Some transgender people and other commentators have welcomed verses such as Deut. 22.5, and the appearance of eunuchs who play central roles in some biblical narratives (West 2006: 280), for at least appearing to acknowledge the existence of cross-dressers and transgender or unusually-gendered individuals in the Hebrew Bible. However, many transsexuals stress the distinction between actual gender dysphoria and mere cross-dressing. Jan Morris, for instance, says, 'The transvestite gains his gratification specifically from wearing the clothes of the opposite sex, and would sacrifice his pleasures by *joining* that sex ... Trans-sexualism is something different in kind. It is not a sexual mode or preference. It is not an act of sex at all' (Morris J. 2002: 5-6). This link with a specifically sexual practice or fetish may be another reason why the whole area of transvestism is regarded with unease by a Christian church where vanilla, non-kinky sex is the ideal.

Marcella Althaus-Reid discusses the manner in which transvestism is potentially subversive of a hegemonic sexual theology. She claims that, in Latin America, cross-dressing is symbolic of the rejection of a particular cosmic, sexual and economic order disseminated by the *conquistadors*. Transvestism, in this account, might in fact be a political act. By spurning accepted narratives of appropriate sex and gender roles, the (economically or spiritually) poor may also spurn the narratives which have helped to keep them poor: a continual drip-feeding of suggestions that they are helpless, sinful and so on. Argentinian carnival parades feature saints in drag, hermaphroditic Magdalenes; Althaus-Reid says, 'Political identities are sexual identities. Gender and sexual confusion are chaotic in intention: it is not, however, the chaos of the flesh, but the chaos of sexual premises in our trusted ideologies which we should be scared of' (Althaus-Reid 2000: 199). Cross-dressing, then, might stand for a far broader rejection of repressive ideologies.

Eunicism

Kolakowski notes that Deut. 23.1 and Lev. 22.24–25, which prohibit admitting to the assembly of the Lord anyone whose testes have been crushed or penis torn off, and offering for sacrifice animals whose testes have been bruised, crushed or torn off, have been used to oppose SRS (Kolakowski 1997a: 18). As Kolakowski says of the Leviticus passage, however, 'It is clear that this must be an extrapolation from and not a literal interpretation of the verse' (1997a: 18). Both passages are clear that the problem is that the body has become 'blemished' by the removal or crushing of the testes, and that it cannot participate in procreation or ritual circumcision – *not* simply because of a shift in sex. David Tabb Stewart concurs that it is at least unclear 'whether stigma develops from the "feminization" of a man's body or whether from a kind of handicapism – or at least ableism' (Stewart 2006: 93). Mollenkott suggests, after Leslie Feinberg, that the Deuteronomist's forbidding of penectomy is a cultural imperative stemming 'from repudiation of cross-gendering among priests of the various goddesses' (Mollenkott 2007: 135).

J. David Hester notes that ritual castration within early Christianity was not uncommon, and, far from being viewed as reprehensible self-mutilation (as often occurs with transsexualism), was considered admirably ascetic. By standing outside the context of male-female procreative complementarity, Hester argues, eunuchs draw attention to the oddness of the binary sex paradigm and concomitant heterosexist assumptions (Hester 2005: 38). Significantly, he says,

> Jesus heals the blind, the paralyzed, the possessed, the fevered, the leprous, the haemorrhaging, even the dead, in every case restoring them to full societal membership. In the case of the eunuch, however, there is no implication whatsoever of "illness" or social "deformity" in need of restoration. Instead, the eunuch is held up as the model to follow (Hester 2005: 38).

Eunicism might be used as a metaphor for other forms of chosen or unchosen transgression of clearly-sexed, heterosexual norms. Thomas Bohache and others have suggested that 'eunuch' could be glossed so that, in Mt. 19.12, Jesus is 'referring to a broad category of people who, from their birth, have not "fitted" the predominant expectations of gender and sexuality' (Bohache 2006: 510). The verses about eunicism might be applied to transgender in other ways too: just as eunuchs have often been 'desexed' in contemporary parlance to make them less threatening (where 'eunuch' has come to be a synonym for 'neuter'), so theologies which insist on celibacy or asexuality for transpeople might be ignoring the possible subversive quality of the sexualities of these individuals.

Hester argues that although, particularly in light of biblical references such as Mt 19.12, eunuchs have often been figured as asexual and unthreatening, in fact the later 'celibate' reading of eunicism results from masculinist assumptions where penetration is everything and sexual activity without penetration is not deemed legitimate sexual activity at all (Hester 2005: 17). In fact, says Hester, because eunuchs in the early centuries of the common era were not considered a threat by their male masters, they were allowed far more freedom to interact with women. However, 'Eunuchs were not celibate. Indeed, they were not even viewed as chaste. In fact, eunuchs were universally characterized by the frequency, ease and adeptness with which they performed sexual acts with both men and women' (Hester 2005: 18). Thus eunuchs threatened phallocentric patriarchy not only by being reminders to non-castrated men of the phallic power so vulnerable to excision (Hester 2005: 19), but by living out the fact that sex itself was not all about top and bottom, penetration and power. It is said that eunuchs were notoriously good at oral and anal sex (Hester 2005: 22), and were popular sexual partners for women because they posed no risk of impregnation (Hester 2005: 24). This removed sexual pleasure from its purely economic context where top and bottom mapped incontrovertibly onto social status, where women incubated child-commodities. Thus, says Hester, eunicism came to be condemned as much for its embodiment of a loss of male prestige (Hester 2005: 28) as anything; it is in *this* sense that it is 'unnatural' (Hester 2005: 29). This makes it even more significant that the Jesus of Mt. 19.11-12 seems actually to view eunicism as a gift.

As I note above, *Issues in Human Sexuality* is heteronormative in the extreme, and follows the Revised English Bible's translation of these verses: 'For while some are *incapable of marriage* because they were born so ... others *have renounced marriage* for the sake of the Kingdom of Heaven' (my emphasis) (in Central Board of Finance of the Church of England 1991: 25). Although the sidestepping of marriage is a possible reading from the text, the REB's dynamic-equivalent translation ties it too unequivocally to this one exposition, eroding the broader nature of eunuchs as sexual, potent individuals. Possible readings of the passage are, in fact, various: Jesus may be acknowledging the Graeco-Roman belief that 'the most virile man was the man who had kept most of his vital spirit – that is, who lost little or no seed' (Brown 1988: 19)[4] – thereby subverting Jewish norms which equated fecundity and virility with status. Jesus could be counselling that eunuchs are better fit to renounce sexual temptation (despite the fact that eunuchs were known to be popular lovers) and not be tied down by a wife and children, thus having more time to dedicate to the work of the kingdom – as Paul also implies, 'in view of the impending crisis', in 1 Corinthians 7. Jesus might be speaking subversively (Hester 2005: 29), acknowledging that male-female marriage could be unjust and repressive to all concerned, but particularly the disenfranchised women, children

4. Brown continues, 'Far from crumbling into a presexual formlessness, as was the case with those castrated when young, the full-grown man who made himself a eunuch, by carefully tying his testicles, became an *asporos*, a man who wasted no vital fire on others' (Brown 1988: 19).

and slaves of the household – thereby profoundly shaking his (male) disciples' beliefs about their own rights and privileges as married men, and prompting them 'to choose to operate under a new definition of being male' (Talbott 2006: 40).[5]

It seems to me that the implication of the eunuch passages is that, just as eunuchs are 'beyond' the societal strictures which mean that men and women cannot be alone together but eunuchs and women can be, the crux of there being no male and female in Christ is that, *in Christ*, non-eunuch men and woman can also be alone together, for the meaning of their *social* bodies (and, therefore, their very physiology) has changed. These multiple interpretations may prompt theological endorsement of 'transgressive', 'indecent' or queer lifestyle and sex-gender configurations.

Although the situation of the biblical eunuch and the present-day transsexual is by no means identical, the phenomenon of transgender also provides fertile ground from which to question more general assumptions about bodies and embodiment, particularly in terms of autonomy and self-determination, as well as the fixity of the mapping of gender upon sex or vice versa.

What Does Transgender Threaten?

I will now reflect more broadly on the goods and norms which transgender (and particularly sex reassignment surgery) might be said to threaten, and will ask whether these goods are really beneficial or irrefutable, given that if they can be demonstrated to be arbitrary or unjust it may no longer be justifiable to pull them out of the arsenal against intersex/DSD.

Lever Fabergé's 2003 television advertisement for the Lynx deodorant range depicted groups of men in a range of physically close (and clammy) circumstances: hugging after a football victory,

---

5. This view echoes that of Countryman, who says, 'The eunuch … was one of the few "individuals" in the ancient world – a man with no intrinsic relation to a family. Jesus was acknowledging, then, that his prohibition of divorce effectively dissolved the family and made eunuchs of all men, for it deprived them of the authority requisite to maintain their patriarchal position and keep their households in subjection to themselves as the unique representatives of their families. What may appear to be a pronouncement about details of sexual ethics … actually spelled the end of the entire hierarchical institution called family' (Countryman 1989: 176).

reclining in a sauna, dancing wildly together in a crowded nightclub. The tagline cautioned, 'Men's sweat only attracts other men'. The kinds of male-bonding settings portrayed by the commercial are also, it could be argued, exactly those which also help to reinforce the 'homosocial' structures underlying the less sweaty norms of society: the man-on-man action which can never quite be called homoerotic but which provides the social glue for the business and social dealings which men still, largely, in many contexts, control.

This conceptual scenario echoes a Lacanian model whereby 'phallic exchange' must be mediated by a symbolic repository of meaning and power: a woman, a child, capital. To circumvent this through male-on-male sexual (phallic) activity, to depart from heterosexual (and homosocial) norms of commodity-exchange, would be, argues Geoffrey Rees, to '[undermine] the possibility of male receptivity of phallic dominance – transacted through women – from God to men' (Rees 2002: 36). Rees contends,

> When Barth and his multiple followers characterize same-sex sexual desire as a species of narcissism, what they are actually describing is the narcissism of their own male homosocial desire in its tendency to demonize sexual relations, in its need to obsessively define manhood and male homosocial bonds as a function of sexual relations between men and women (Rees 2002: 42).

Men's sweat only attracts other men; the 'sweat' which bonds them is complex social ritual which defines themselves (by identification) and their others (by distinction). It is this, not homosexuality, which is homogenizing and narcissistic. In the homosocial account, men who do not behave as men *should* behave open a space for others to transgress *their* rightful spheres too. Rees says, 'When discrimination between men and women deteriorates, the current structure of the male homosocial continuum becomes unstable, so that men become liable to suffering some of the indignities – and pleasures – associated with women' (Rees 2002: 26).

This, it might be argued, is part of the real reason for theologies which insist on clear distinctions between the spheres appropriate for men and women – not simply because (it is believed) this will allow fullness of being for each gender, but because a deconstruction of sex-gender norms would lead, too, to a deconstruction of who has power over whom and in what this is actually based. To diminish some of the artificially-imposed 'gaps' between men and women might also lead to a questioning of what it is about males which 'necessitates' their being fulfilled and completed only in a position of leadership over and above females. Rees concludes that it is, therefore, misguided to view (heterosexual) marriage as a necessary or inevitable occasion for God's self-revelation (Rees 2002: 45). Arguably, male-female marriage as an institution has been about social (and often male-controlled) pre-eminence just as much as it has been about providing a repository for sexual morality. But God is not limited by such human-created social structures. God, in fact, exists and self-reveals beyond the range of socially normalized, socially legitimized male-and-female relationships. Importantly, then, it is also unnecessary, in terms of revelation, for each and every *body* to fit a heteronormative system: the intersexed/DSD, transgender or otherwise unusual body need no longer carry the weight of *making* God via the status and power-exchange sometimes reinforced in acts of heterosexual commerce.

One major Christian objection to transsexual surgery has been that, if homosexual acts are wrong, then acts between a post-operative transsexual and someone of their original sex are also wrong, since SRS cannot *really* change something as basic as one's sexed nature. Some Christians therefore oppose SRS, or people living permanently in a transgender identity role, because this will lead to homosexual relationships. However, this argument against transsexualism from homosexuality is extremely shaky. It is sometimes claimed (as Rees notes) that homosexual relationships are inevitably narcissistic, because same-sex partners delight in another who is essentially *like* them rather than one who is unlike them. But, holds Ward, a relationship between a man and woman can be just as narcissistic as that between two men or two women, since sex and gender are by no means the only or ineluctable markers of affinity or inconsonance. Ward concludes,

> There is no desire without difference. But exactly what is "other" in a relationship between two "women" or two "men" becomes indefinable ... There can be self-designated "heterosexual relationships" whose structure of desire is homosexual, and so-called homosexual relationships whose structure of desire is heterosexual. True desire, that is, God-ordained desire can only be heterosexual (Ward 1998: 70–71).

As we saw in Chapter 3, it is Barth's 'complementarity' that is narcissistic (Ward 1998: 67; Blevins 2005: 75), since it relies on ostensible difference which turns out to be sameness. *True* difference, prompting Godly desire, is not inherently more present in man-woman than man-man or woman-woman relationships.

Rees and Ward show that homosexual acts are read as deplorable *not just* because they are believed to jeopardize some kind of cosmic order (often the conscious rationale for opposing them). They are also deemed to refute structures of dominion, based on power, submission and subjection – a far more hidden and insidious agenda, deeply naturalized and become almost unconscious. If it is accepted that there is more going on in masculine-feminine gender relationships than meets the eye, however, and that hierarchical structures are usually about controlling access to power, then they will be deeply shaken by models of God where God relinquishes status, ceding power and supremacy, in solidarity with those at the margins. Top-down structures of power, and their associated social norms based on repressive hegemonies, are thus theologically indefensible. For both Ward and Rees, the proverbially 'hetero'-sexual, that which is *by definition* grounded in an acknowledgement of otherness, can actually be oppressively homogenous. Where male power and prestige are viewed as a legitimate mirroring of divine ascendancy, male-to-female transsexualism (and voluntary eunicism) becomes decidedly blasphemous.

Changing Sex: The 'Real' and the Phantom

The oft-cited and oft-proclaimed transsexual yearning to make body match psyche, to reclaim the efficacy of the 'outer' layer in telegraphing and (literally) embodying what one believes oneself to be, is arresting in terms of the notion that integrity of self supervenes upon integrity or wholeness of body. The argument runs that, if transgender persons cannot accept their outer appearance as 'really them', then it *must* be changed in order to promote their psychosomatic unity. This is condemned by O'Donovan (above) as falling back into a kind of dualism where the existing body is seen merely as dough for the 'self' to mould as it sees fit, rather than inextricably *being* the self that simply is. Theologies from disability demonstrate that the Christian tradition, too, has invested in images of completeness representing the whole (or able) person (see Chapter 5) – but the extent to which this 'self' must necessarily include the physical body is unclear.

The notion that body and identity must match, as propounded by many transpeople and by surgeons who perform corrections on children with intersex/DSD conditions, contrasts with the erstwhile position of ISNA and some activists: the latter suggest that gender and genitals need not, in fact, correspond for emotional wellbeing to be promoted (http://www.isna.org/faq/gender_assignment). This is an area in which the testimonies of transsexuals and the vision, as of Kessler and McKenna (1978: vii) and Mollenkott (2007) of a world of sex-gender haziness conflict. The positive experiences of some boys with micro- or absent penises who have grown up without medical intervention suggest that it is not always necessary to 'have' the right body parts in order to 'have' sexual identity: Diamond and Sigmundson (1997a) report that many boys with absent penises reassigned as girls in infancy later transitioned back, living successfully as men.

Although this might be seen as suggesting that transsexual surgery is unnecessary (for transgender people, too, should be able to inhabit their new identities without having the 'bits' to 'prove' it), it also, conversely, bolsters the 'authenticity' of the phantom-type body-parts which many transpeople already experience. Prosser uses Oliver Sacks' work on proprioception (Sacks 1985: 42) and phantom limbs (Sacks 1985: 63-66) to explore transpeople's feeling that body parts which are absent are actually present and belong to them, just as people who have lost a limb often experience an apparent awareness that it is still there – the *belief* of ownership having more strength than visual evidence that the body part is lacking. Prosser suggests that transpersons' desired sex could be described as their 'phantom sex'; in this model, all that surgery does is to concretize what the individual *already* knows and experiences to be present: 'Sex reassignment surgery may then be grasped as healing and changing the transsexual subject in that it serves as the antidote to both of these body image distortions' (Prosser 1998: 85). This pivots on *redefining* certain characteristics of body and identity. Kessler insists, 'One argument for reducing the number of intersex surgeries hinges on changing the meaning of variant genitals, such that a large clitoris does not necessarily mean "offence", a small penis does not necessarily mean "not a real man", and an absent vagina does not necessarily mean "not a real woman"' (Kessler 1998: 9).

For Kessler, it is necessary to change our ideas of what variability signifies, so that not all variation is figured as pathological by default, rather than eradicating the variation itself.[6] Just as an individual with an intersex/DSD condition does not need to have a penis to be a real man (if he feels he is a man, if his body and identity largely tells him he is a man), so a transman who was born female does not need a penis to be a real man if he feels he is a man, if his body and identity largely tells him he is a man. If we can accept that the latter individual, who might have ovaries and a vaginal opening and a high voice register, is *really* already a man (without being really *male*), then the question of whether or not that individual then goes on to have constructive surgery to attach a penile appendage or to lengthen the existing clitoris becomes rather moot.

Myra J. Hird says,

> To effect the incorporation of an intersexual surgically assigned as "female" involves a determination as to the constitution of femaleness. Any definition of "woman" that retains any corporeality must be able to define that corporeality, and this is exactly where the problem begins in definition based on "sex" ... An intersexual [woman] will have any combination of partially or totally surgically created vagina, labia and breasts ... If being female does not entail the possession of particular anatomical parts, then the artificial creation of these body parts is inconsequential. But our current assumptions about the constitution of "sex" struggles with such a reality (Hird 2000: 353).

To accept that to be a (cultural) man need have very little to do with physiology is not only vital if one acknowledges any element of social constructionism in gender, but is also all but self-evident given the enormous range of bodily appearances of those considered men. Warnke, noting that identifying and classifying bodily sex from a particular, limited set of properties is as arbitrary as assigning race in the same way, argues,

> The merit of recognizing sex as an interpretation is that we can consider its point or validity in the same way that we consider the point or validity of any interpretation: according to its internal

6. Kessler also wishes for a move from pinning male 'adequacy' entirely on penis size, as has tended to happen in intersex/DSD surgery, to more focus on interpersonal and communication skills (Kessler 1998: 38).

coherence, its compatibility with other interpretations we take seriously, and its ability to illuminate a subject-matter for us (Warnke 2001: 133).

There seem to be two apparently contradictory positions here, then: one, that surgery to provide appropriate body-parts is not, in fact, necessary to bolster gender identity; and two, that surgery to provide appropriate body-parts is both therapeutic and legitimate. However, these can in fact be held in a reasonable tension: the body *can* express and authentically be the identity of an individual even if its gender and genitals do not supervene in a typical way, but, simultaneously, valuing and respecting the integrity of this body does not necessarily mean outlawing any surgical work, including genital surgical work, done on it.

The question of the reality of sex has influenced another significant aspect of Christianity's suspicion of transgender: a reluctance to own that it is within the legitimate remit of humans to 'change' something as fundamental (or as 'real') as sexed identity. This is not exactly the same as the issue about compromising the overall integrity of the body; it is more about holding that sex and gender in particular are fundamental goods and givens which contribute to the person as God intended them to be. Sex reassignment surgery in particular has been figured as 'playing God'; of course, *any* medical or surgical intervention can be (and often has been) labelled in the same manner, but some types of procedures become more accepted and 'naturalized' than others. If it is accepted that SRS can be therapeutic then it is only as controversial as other therapeutic surgeries.

But whereas something like surgery to remove cataracts might be seen as actually *enhancing* the wholeness of the person by restoring or enabling sight, SRS is rarely considered in this way by its opponents. Transsexual surgery has usually been figured as invasive, not therapeutic. Jay Prosser comments that many people consider SRS 'unnatural' simply because it is not curative of an 'evident' ill: ostensibly, there was nothing 'wrong' with the body in question to begin with, so there is nothing to fix. As with cosmetic surgery such as rhinoplasty and breast enlargement, SRS is sometimes viewed as unnecessary and superficial – a matter of putting oneself through the dangers of anaesthesia and surgical invasion for the sake of vanity, and leaching medical resources which could be better used elsewhere for more 'serious' problems.

However, what others might see as mutilation, transsexuals often perceive as *restoration*, making the body more as it should have been in relation to the psyche (Prosser 1998: 81-2). Jenny Kirk, who underwent SRS in 2006, says, 'After the operation I felt that a huge weight had been lifted off my mind. It was like being reborn. I remember being in hospital thinking, "Gosh, this is what people who aren't transsexuals must feel like"' (Kirk 2007: 57). Transgender priest Malcolm Himschoot says, 'I didn't ruin or disfigure anything or destroy anything. And I know that it might look that way, and I'm very sorry for that. But I came to the point where I had to live into the future or I was not *going* to live' (Himschoot, speaking in Parlagreco 2005). Rather than having bodies which manage authentically to communicate their 'core selves', many transpeople believe their bodies' expression of their identities is erroneous (Rubin 2003: 150). Interestingly, Henry Rubin's findings from his study of female-to-male transsexuals suggest that the actual surgery they had undergone, particularly that to create a penis, was much less significant in terms of selfhood than was receiving supplements of testosterone, which was 'valued because it alters the most important features used in the sex attribution process' (Rubin 2003: 153): secondary characteristics such as voice pitch, facial hair and broad build. Several of Rubin's subjects claimed that taking testosterone had not altered their (self-perceived) identities, but merely their bodies and certain aspects of their behaviour (Rubin 2003: 153). Interestingly, says Rubin,

> Testosterone has little effect on who they [FTMs] are inside. From their point of view, they are becoming the men they always already were. They do not claim that testosterone transforms them from women into men ... A few men report that transition changed them, but they deny that testosterone has anything to do with these changes (Rubin 2003: 153–54).

The changes in identity for Rubin's interviewees, then, have come about as a by-product of the whole transition process, not simply and ineluctably because of testosterone itself. It is, of course, also possible that part of the shift in perception from within the individual resides in coming to recognize in oneself characteristics which one already (culturally) associates with 'being a man' – and this is complicated by the subject's particular background and cultural context.

Transsexuals' agnosia about body parts related to their pre-operative sex have prompted another reservation surrounding SRS from the Church: if people believe that they have been born into the wrong body, does this not *in itself* suggest they have a deep-seated psychological disturbance, and might not SRS therefore compromise the already-fragile mental health of transgender patients through what might be considered a 'collaboration with psychosis' (Billings and Urban 1982: 274)? This fear was expressed by some doctors in the 1950s and 60s in the early days of SRS; Billings and Urban (1982: 269-70) give a variety of citations from medical literature of the 1960s portraying people seeking SRS as psychotic, paranoid schizophrenic or neurotic. However, overwhelmingly positive post-surgery follow-up reports did not appear to corroborate such suspicions (Meyerowitz 2002: 124). Of course, it is possible that 'post-operative patients could ill afford to be critical of such a profound alteration as genital amputation' (Billings and Urban 1982: 273); but, although counselling and extensive discussion are crucial precursors to SRS, the *a priori* assumption that gender dysphoria itself *always* means that it is the mind which must be altered and not the body will colour the manner in which transgender people are responded to by healthcare professionals. Besides, as Milton Diamond and Hazel Glenn Beh argue, transpeople have just as much right to make decisions about their bodies which later disappoint them – in sum, just as much 'right to be wrong' about their own bodies – as anyone else does (Diamond and Beh 2006).

Male All Along? The Historicity of Individuals

Questions stemming from the issue of the historicity of individuals, and the extent to which the persistence of an integrated personhood might be said to be compromised by surgical intervention on the genitals, have affected Christian responses to transgender and may colour responses to intersex too.

For example, concerns about the permanence and legitimacy of existing marriages where one partner is transgender or has undergone SRS have prompted Christians to ask questions about the legal and ecclesiastical recognition of transpeople's new states. The Corbett v. Corbett (April Ashley) case in 1970 led to Lord Justice Ormrod's ruling that transgender individuals in the UK could not legally change the sex that appeared on their birth or death certificates, or marry (Nataf 1996: 15). Since April 2005, in light of the Gender Recognition Act 2004, it has been possible in the UK for transpeople to apply for a Gender Recognition Certificate. This allows the acquisition of a new birth certificate with the new legal name and sex (http://www.grp.gov.uk/). If the individual was married at the time of SRS, the document given will be an interim gender recognition certificate valid until the marriage has been dissolved, at which point a full certificate will be given. Proceedings to dissolve the marriage must start within six months of the interim certificate being given, which, interestingly, means that the individual *cannot* get a full gender recognition certificate without dissolving the pre-existing marriage. This goes against the view of Kolakowski that there might be sound theological reasons for not dissolving the marital covenant, and that 'outsiders should not attempt to separate what God has joined' (Kolakowski 1997a: 28). Kolakowski recognizes a continuity of identity in transpeople which is thereby carried over into their relationships. The record of the person's birth sex will not be totally excised from the register, but will not be publicly accessible; any published lists of births from the year in question will contain the new name and sex. Transpeople may marry in their new sex, but Church of England and Church in Wales clergy are not obliged to marry people whom they believe to have changed sex. If transpersons do not disclose their SRS to their proposed spouse, but the spouse discovers after the marriage that SRS took place, the spouse may seek to have the marriage annulled. Holder suggests that ideally, those with transgender feelings before marriage would realize that that debarred them from the vocation of marriage; however, since this does not always occur, Holder believes that, if they subsequently have surgery, they should be celibate in their new sex out of respect for the former spouse and any children (Holder 1998b: 133).

The issue of whether transsexuals' birth certificates should be legally changed after transition raises broader questions about the historicity of individuals. A person born and registered female who undergoes SRS aged 30 and acquires a birth certificate reading 'M' is essentially seeking verification that they were 'male all along'. This is, indeed, what many transsexuals do claim, saying that their external morphology has merely been adjusted to reflect the truth of what they always were (Rubin 2003: 143, 149-51). However, regardless of whether or not the individual's self-identification is considered valid, changing the birth certificate seems to 'disappear' the history of having been *perceived* as a particular sex for at least part of that time. This might be viewed as negative or anti-incarnational. One opposition to male-to-female transition from some feminists is that men are hijacking women's circles without having lived through the struggles of having women's biographies; Janice Raymond, in *The Transsexual Empire*, argued that male-to-female transsexuals were 'raping' women, invading their space, just as much as men who invaded women literally with their penises or fists.[7] Rosemary Auchmuty says,

> Transsexuals ... don't have a woman's past. They weren't brought up as women and because so much of the women's movement was premised on personal experience and sharing that experience and theorizing out of that, feminists argued for [the] exclusion of transsexuals ... It's very difficult for people to lose the habits of their gender upbringing. Male-to-female transsexuals in women's groups dominate, in my experience. In this society women have little enough space and time for their voices to be heard (Auchmuty in Nataf 1996: 37–38).

Myra J. Hird, however, criticizes the biological essentialism inherent in some feminisms – like that betrayed in Auchmuty's remark – in her exploration of the manner in which both intersex and transgender radically challenge the sex-versus-gender binary (Hird 2000).

Although some transpeople freely admit to their histories in a different sex, the apparent unwillingness of others to acknowledge their own gendered and sexed past might be viewed as a rejection of one's body as it appeared for a significant proportion of one's life when one was related to in that body, and – concomitantly – as a rejection of the good of that incarnation and portion of one's history. However, where an experience of being embodied was profoundly alien and psychologically painful, the legal sex-change on the birth certificate can be a catalyst for healing. By ratifying the new status and hugely reducing the chances that people will face prejudice when applying for jobs or in other situations where it is

7. Stephen Whittle claims, 'The repercussions of Raymond's book are still being felt ... with many Rape Crisis Centres refusing to help transsexual women, and transsexual women being excluded from women's courses, women's centres and other women's spaces' (Whittle 2000: 51).

necessary to show a birth certificate, the gender recognition certificate symbolizes an investment in this new and what the transsexual believes to be more authentic incarnation. In fact, the Gender Recognition Act 2004 explicitly states,

> Where a full gender recognition certificate is issued to a person, the person's gender becomes for all purposes the acquired gender ... [This] does not affect things done, or events occurring, before the certificate is issued; but it does operate for the interpretation of enactments passed, and instruments and other documents made, before the certificate is issued (as well as those passed or made afterwards) (Gender Recognition Act 2004, Section 9, subsections 1–2, online at http://www.opsi.gov.uk/acts/acts2004/40007−a.htm#9).

In other words, the granting of a certificate does *not* eliminate the history of the individual which took place beforehand; it may simply mean that access to information about the individual in their original sex is far more strictly limited. Transpeople who prefer not to discuss their pre-operative pasts are not necessarily denying they ever happened – they might simply be protecting themselves from prejudice from those unaware of their transition, or focusing on the present rather than being negatively affected by bitterness about a time when they felt constantly divided from their own bodies.

Interestingly, as Alison Jasper notes (Jasper 2005: 44), the Gender Recognition Act also states that the gender recognition certificate will be given only on condition that the awarding panel is satisfied the transitioning individual intends to continue to live in the new gender for the rest of their life. This endowing of permanence of gender as a 'good' even after an acknowledgement, in the very granting of the certificate, that it can be changed, may be designed to make subsequent legal statuses and arrangements (such as marriage) less complicated than they might otherwise be. Arguably, however, being known as an historical individual by one's community need not entail permanent gender; indeed, part of one's historicity might include having been known and embraced by one's community throughout one's changes of gender (as with Carol Stone, above). Katherine Johnson notes Billings and Urban's argument that 'the medical image of a stable life-long transsexual identification does not adequately represent some individuals' experiences and motivations' (Johnson 2007: 450). ISNA counsels openness to the fact that one's intersexed child might choose to change gender, and, moreover, that *any* child, intersexed or not, might change gender, since any gender assignment is only ever preliminary (http://www.isna.org/faq/gender_assignment).

There are sound theological precedents for accepting and supporting this kind of change. God remains faithful even as circumstances shift, and, claims the Psalmist, has known each day before it comes to be (Ps. 139.16). This might be interpreted as an assurance that no change in circumstance can go beyond the reach of God to exist in compassion with, to be alongside, those whose identities undergo large shifts.

Transgender as Essentialism

Some, including Preves in *Intersex and Identity*, have argued that, far from being a subversive disrupting of binarized gender norms as is sometimes claimed, elective transsexual surgery in fact affirms, rather than challenges, the polarity (Preves 2003: 45-46), rendering SRS part of what makes society so inhospitable to non-binary bodies such as those of people with intersex/DSD conditions. Generally, transpeople speak in terms of 'transition' from one (sexed) state to the 'opposite' state. Arguing from liminality as a positive ideal, Preves suggests that SRS supports the hegemony which insists that physical gender signifiers *must* 'match' the lived gender in order for psychological well-being to persist (which, in turn, feeds back into the mindset that intersexed anatomies must be fixed or adjusted). Transpeople, runs the argument, are bolstering the very fixity in which they themselves have been unable to fit. However, Joanne Meyerowitz, in her history of transsexual surgery in the USA, argues that whilst, in the 1950s and 60s, many transgender people unabashedly did wish to be assuredly either male or female, so did the vast majority of other individuals (Meyerowitz 2002: 12). In its context, the desire to be unambiguously sexed, and for sex and gender to match, was even less remarkable than in present-day British and North American society. Aspiring transsexuals were as likely as others to wish to avoid homosexuality, and even many lesbian and gay people believed that to abscond from accepted gender binaries was undesirable (Meyerowitz 2002: 178). Even so, could it be argued that SRS is ethically inappropriate within a theological mindset which seeks to deconstruct binary notions of sex and gender, and to anticipate the kind of post-Galatians 3.28

world where sex-gender norms, overtly oppressive or not, are no longer to be bolstered?

Although many transpeople feel unambiguously members of their new sex and gender and do not wish to be recognized as anything other than an unremarkable man or woman, there are others who wish to embrace what might be called the 'queer' aspect of sex-change. Some transsexual bodies, like some intersexed bodies, appear unusual or ambiguous after surgery. This is particularly true of female-to-male transsexuals who have had surgery and/or hormone therapy to enlarge the penis, but also choose not to have the vagina sewn up. It is thus possible for them either to penetrate or to be penetrated, and to participate in a range of sexual roles and behaviours. This refusal to close off possibilities might be viewed as simply another aspect of psychological disturbance; an unwillingness to fully go along with an altered sex because that is not what one 'really' is, and one knows it deep down even if one attempts to repress it – for, in a mindset where everyone must be unambiguously sexed, voluntary indeterminacy is pathological. However, there is also promise here for relationships neither demarcated nor delimited by the bulwarks of gender. If it is not possible to tell for certain the gender or sex of the person with whom one is in relationship, this will profoundly affect the nature of that relationship. Pragmatic matters of who can and cannot become pregnant will certainly be deserving of consideration; but the point is exactly that this conversation *will* be necessitated, rather than omitted through assumption. To engage in relationships where one is unsure of the partner's sex will prompt a whole series of questions about the roles and responsibilities in those relationships.

Transgender as Performativity

As we have seen, some Christians and others argue that transgender is not a 'real' condition but a psychological disturbance, and should therefore not be 'confirmed' through SRS. It has been claimed from other quarters, however, that transgender may be 'unreal', that is, fabricated, in a different way. Billings and Urban go so far as to claim,

> Transsexualism is a socially constructed reality which only exists in and through medical practice. The problem of transsexual

patients does not lie "in their minds" ... The legitimation,
rationalization, and commodification of sex-change operations
have produced an identity category – transsexual – for a diverse
group of sexual deviants and victims of severe gender role distress
(Billings and Urban 1982: 266).

Billings and Urban suggest that, rather than healing the body or
the mind, doctors who carry out sex reassignment surgery 'perform
a moral function', being 'accorded moral authority to sponsor
passage from one sexed state to another' (Billings and Urban 1982:
266). In this way, transsexualism can be said to be an artificial
construction of the healthcare profession (a status which has also
been proposed for intersex/DSD). Doctors have been part of what
has shifted transgender from social deviantism to a legitimate
'medical' issue, partly in response to patients and – it has been
claimed – partly because the 'new' phenomenon of transsexualism
in the mid-twentieth century opened up new surgical and psychiatric
arenas for research and, thereby, professional prestige (Billings and
Urban 1982: 269).

Billings and Urban hold that, like other 'negotiated illnesses',
transgender holds moral and social as well as medical meanings
(Billings and Urban 1982: 276), but that its figuring as medical entity
'pushes patients toward an alluring world of artificial vaginas and
penises rather than toward self-understanding and sexual politics'
(Billings and Urban 1982: 276). They claim, 'At the level of ideology,
sex-change surgery ... reflects and extends late-capitalist logics of
reification and commodification ... The fulfilment of human desires
is less a matter of public discussion than a technical accomplishment
of social administration' (Billings and Urban 1982: 277). Making
transgender a medical phenomenon legitimates medical (surgical)
intervention, which actually 'disappears' it, since 'patients whose
subjective histories are subsumed under the unifying rhetoric of
transsexualism win operations but no language adequate to express
[their] disparate and diverse desires' (Billings and Urban 1982: 276).
The 'pseudo-tolerant gender-identity clinics ... are implicitly political
and, indirectly, intolerant' (Billings and Urban 1982: 277). Thus
medical intervention to cancel out gender dysphoria or different
experiences of being a sexed/gendered body does not expand
societal notions of what it is to be a sexed/gendered body in the
first place.

Whilst it might be true that SRS sometimes reinforces a binary view of sex and gender, and that some transpeople may 'fail' adequately to 'queer' sex-gender norms, the crucial point is that there is no reason why transgender people should have to do this *on behalf of* everyone else. Transpeople still have to survive in a largely binary society. The privileges which some feel they gain from passing in a given gender are exactly the same as those which non-transpeople would also gain. To suppose that *only* transgender is 'constructed', then, argues Prosser, both denies the constructed nature of all gender identity and undermines the transperson's agency, eroding 'the subject's capacity not only to initiate and effect his/her own somatic transition but to inform and redefine the medical narrative of transsexuality' (Prosser 1998: 8).

Prosser remarks that many readers of Judith Butler's *Gender Trouble* seized upon it as yoking together transgender and homosexuality, as if the trans life were the only one which could authentically disrupt and queer gender. Prosser asks, 'My concern is the implication of this harnessing of transgender as queer for transsexuality: what are the points at which the transsexual as transgendered subject is not queer?' (Prosser 1998: 27). Prosser argues that the over-emphasis given to Butler's reading of gender as performative, a relatively minor element in *Gender Trouble* but often sedimented into a necessarily queer performativity, has frequently led to an assumption that transsexuality is always and exclusively subversive (Prosser 1998: 31). In fact, retorts Prosser, transgender is *not* always queer or subversive, but is no less legitimate as a result: 'There are transsexuals who seek very pointedly to be nonperformative, to be constantive, quite simply, to *be*' (Prosser 1998: 32). Since *Gender Trouble* seems to imply that 'sex' is *always* a result of performed gender, usually 'typically' straight gender, Prosser says it 'cannot account for a transsexual desire for sexed embodiment as *telos*' (Prosser 1998: 33). For Prosser, the feeling of being 'trapped' in the 'wrong' body is common and central to almost all trans autobiography,[8] and yet it is exactly this for which Butler cannot allow space in *Gender Trouble*, for it would

8. Jan Morris' entire history and biography is set in light of this assertion: 'I was three or perhaps four years old when I realized that I had been born into the wrong body, and should really be a girl... It is the earliest memory of my life' (Morris J. 2002: 1).

open the door to the possibility of 'interior' heterosexual sex too, whereas Butler is so careful to demonstrate its constructed character.[9]

Sandy Stone notes that the accusation that transsexuals make stereotypical converts (ultra-feminine women and ultra-masculine men) who reinforce heteronormal hegemonies may not so much reflect a 'truth' about transsexuals themselves, but is, rather, an overhang from the early practice of gender clinics only to accept for SRS those individuals *already* 'gendered' appropriately (Stone S. 1991: 347; Johnson 2007). Thus it was in the interests of a prospective male-to-female to exaggerate his interest in clothes and make-up in order to come across as 'more feminine'. Billings and Urban's own observations from a gender clinic in the 1970s led them to conclude,

---

9. By the late 1990s, Butler more explicitly acknowledges some of the more unchosen elements of the performance of gender. She says, 'Even ... family relations recapitulate, individualize, and specify preexisting cultural relations; they are rarely, if ever, radically original. The act that one does, the act that one performs, is, in a sense, an act that has been going on before one arrived on the scene' (Butler 1997: 409). This is not to say that bodies are merely inscribed; rather, 'The gendered body acts its part in a culturally restricted corporeal space and enacts interpretations within the confines of already existing directives' (Butler 1997: 410). The actor is still an actor and not a puppet, even if the action takes place within certain bounds. Butler concludes that it will come to be in the very *insignificance* of gendered acts that it will be possible to critique politically gender 'realities': 'The redescription needs to expose the reifications that tacitly serve as substantial gender cores or identities, and to elucidate both the act and the strategy of disavowal which at once constitute and conceal gender as we live it. The prescription is invariably more difficult, if only because we need to think a world in which acts, gestures, the visual body, the clothed body, the various physical attributes usually associated with gender, *express nothing* ... The prescription ... consists in an imperative to acknowledge the existing complexity of gender which our vocabulary invariably disguises and to bring that complexity into a dramatic cultural interplay without punitive consequences' (Butler 1997: 414). This assertion builds on Butler's argument in *Bodies That Matter* (1993), an attempt to re-examine the category of 'sex' after criticisms that *Gender Trouble* was too quick to throw out materiality altogether. Butler claims in *Bodies That Matter* that to seize on the performative nature of gender does not necessarily entail negating the way in which, for example, some bodies can become pregnant and others cannot. However, she says, it is still essential to ask questions about why some bodies are figured as legitimate subjects and others are not (Butler 1993: 3), and to accept that materiality is an ongoing process that gives the *effect* of boundary or fixity, rather than an actual static site or surface (Butler 1993: 9).

> More than anything else, physical appearance enables patients
> to control screening interviews; successful cross-dressing often
> truncates the screening process. When patients appear at a clinic
> convincingly cross-dressed, verbal slips or doubtful accounts
> are set right by covering accounts – or are simply glossed over
> because physical appearance confirms the gender claimed. On
> the other hand, discrepant appearances are taken as alarming
> signs (Billings and Urban 1982: 275).

Billings and Urban add that interviewing doctors in the 1970s
sometimes 'prompted' or 'coached' patients to offer expected,
'ritualized expressions such as "I always played with dolls as a
child"' (Billings and Urban 1982: 275) in order to be able to tick the
right boxes. Stone and others report that it became common for
transpeople not to tell doctors the whole story of their sexual tastes
in case this earmarked them as 'unsuitable' for surgery. Prospective
male-to-females would not admit to obtaining sexual pleasure from
their penises, probably because of a hangover among the medical
establishment of Freud's view that phallic (clitoral) pleasure in
women was infantile and adult women should orgasm vaginally.
Stone says,

> The prohibition continued postoperatively in interestingly
> transmuted form, and remained so absolute that no postoperative
> transsexual would admit to experiencing sexual pleasure through
> masturbation either. Full membership in the assigned gender
> was conferred by orgasm, real or faked, accomplished through
> heterosexual penetration (Stone S. 1991: 348).

Butler adds that, even now, 'It is for the most part the gender
essentialist position that must be voiced for transsexual surgery to
take place, and ... someone who comes in with a sense of gender as
changeable will have a more difficult time convincing psychiatrists
and doctors to perform the surgery' (Butler 2001: 632).

So it is not somehow *trans itself* which must 'necessarily subvert
or affirm dominant forms of masculinity' (Rubin 2003: 145); rather,
says Rubin, 'Transsexual men have the potential to generate either
alternative or hegemonic forms of masculinity ... [and] to resignify
what it means to behave like a man. Transsexualism is neither
essentially normative nor essentially counter-hegemonic' (Rubin
2003: 145). To seize upon transpeople as naïvely and single-handedly
reinforcing oppressive gendered constructs is to fail to recognize
that transgender both informs and is informed by wider societal

beliefs about gender. It must thus be acknowledged that transgender self-description and self-determination is both as valid and as muddied as that of individuals whose 'born' sex and gender seem unremarkably to coinhere. As Butler warns, whilst self-description is to be honoured for it is in self-description that an individual gives the language through which he or she wishes to be understood, self-description 'takes place in a language that is already going on, that is already saturated with norms, that predisposes us as we seek to speak of ourselves' (Butler 2001: 630). It would thus be unfortunate to negate the desire of those who cannot persist in their 'natural' bodies to undergo surgery or other intervention to live more comfortably. It is not always enough to live 'as a man' when one still has female genitalia or when one has not yet undergone the secondary physical changes associated with testosterone injections such as increased body temperature and broadened shoulders (Rubin 2003: 155). The desire to undergo surgery may, in some cases, be largely connected with a fear of violent recrimination from those whom one has 'fooled' into believing that one's lived gender reflects one's sex: Brandon Teena, whose story became well-known through its dramatized film version, *Boys Don't Cry* (Peirce 1999), was raped and murdered at the age of 21 when acquaintances of his girlfriend Lana Tisdel discovered that he was morphologically female.

Transpeople are therefore no more 'inherently' subversive of binary sex and gender than anyone else. However, Prosser claims that there are some important ways in which transgender bodies differ from non-trans ones. Rejecting Butler's view in *Gender Trouble* that it is not possible to describe the process by which a body comes to be marked by sex, Prosser claims that transgender narratives tell this very tale. Transgender bodies must be consciously imbued with sexed meanings, new meanings; female-to-males must come to call tissue taken from their arms or groins 'my penis'. This is 'a refiguring of the sexed body that takes place along corporeal, psychic, and symbolic axes' (Prosser 1998: 67); a gendered *becoming*, heavily invested in fleshliness. Prosser draws an interesting metaphor from the Eucharist, commenting that, like transsexualism, transubstantiation both literalizes and deliteralizes, making the real elements metaphorical whilst the Godhead is concretized (Prosser 1998: 50). The 'surface' of the body is not simply a covering, but the very locus of sexed identity.

As far as medicine is concerned, with rare exceptions, the body of the (physiologically) non-intersexed/DSD person (which might include transpersons) already unambiguously describes its own sex and must not be compromised. Conversely, however, the body of the intersexed infant cannot be trusted, because it is 'misleading' or might become so if left unchecked. 'Of course Bianca would have to look like a little girl', said Patrick Malone, consultant urologist at Southampton General Hospital where surgery was carried out to 'hide' the clitoris of the baby with CAH in question, 'because she *was* a little girl' (in Godwin 2004). Arguably, Bianca's visibly large clitoris would not have stopped her being a little girl; she would simply have been a little girl with a large clitoris. But this body could not be allowed to tell its own story unedited; Kessler comments that even the 'facts' of intersexed bodies are edited, so that 'The adolescent is typically told that certain internal organs did not form because of an endocrinological defect, not because those organs could never have developed in someone with his or her sex chromosomes' (Kessler 1998: 30).

Some Conclusions

To declare transgender illegitimate is often to fail to examine the prior heteronormative constraints which render gender 'transgressions' remarkable. The same is often true of intersex/DSD: theologies which claim an immovable model of male and female, masculine and feminine (which also happens to outlaw homosexuality), and which allow no conceptual space for exceptions, risk 'protecting' and fetishizing a truth which does not exist in the first place. As Rees argues, this is largely to do with access to power. Although the existence of individuals with intersex/DSD conditions is less well-known than that of transpeople, the former also expose the discomfort felt when those with socially (and scripturally) sanctioned authority find that the binary paradigm on which their own legitimacy is based is an arbitrary one. Issues around redefining and reassigning bodies show themselves to be about redefining socially-sanctioned 'truths' too. The existence of intersex/DSD and transgender highlights the fact that 'biological' theologies of complementarity such as Barth's turn out to be based more in appearances and assumptions – which raises questions about what 'makes' social sex to begin with and what is really being 'defended' in some quarters from erosion by homosexuality and women in leadership. Both transgender and intersex/DSD question why it is that non-trans, non-intersexed sex and gender are so 'obvious'. Biblical injunctions to overturn human social standards which divide – as in Gal. 3.28 – should prompt a reconsideration of sex-gender norms too. The biblical verses about eunicism sometimes used in relation to trans might also be used in the consideration of intersex/ DSD, but – as we have seen – this necessitates a deliberate consciousness that this is to read into the text something which its original authors were not explicitly addressing.

Questions about the legitimacy of the performance of SRS are particularly interesting when considering theological responses to them, for intersex/DSD is often coming from the opposite extreme: whilst many transpeople battle for surgery to alter their bodies, for the parents of intersexed children the battle is often for them *not* to have surgery. However, issues of autonomy and self-determination apply to both intersexed and transgender people. Theologically, whether or not SRS is considered legitimate seems to come down to whether or not it is deemed necessary, therapeutic surgery, although this has not always been extended to intersex/ DSD surgery. Whereas the social 'good' of having a gender identity and genitals which match is considered fundamental in the treatment of intersex/DSD – and is sanctioned as such by O'Donovan – the same is not true of transgender. Conversely, however, whilst the intersexed person is expected to fully synthesize their altered anatomy into their sense of self, it is almost expected that the transsexual will be unable to, because they will 'know' that their new anatomy is not really 'theirs'. The theological application of O'Donovan's assertion about the authenticity of body parts is thus brought to inconsistent conclusions.

Transgender is less to do with sexuality than with being in harmony with one's body. However, this does not mean transpeople should be asexualized. Both these things are also true for individuals with intersex/DSD conditions. The Church has a duty to stand with those whose bodies are sources of discomfort or disturbance to them, and to support them in their own decisions in regulating their bodies, whether this involves surgical intervention or not. Crucially, however, this must include support for those individuals and their families who have decisions to make regarding surgery. It is vital that Christian communities welcome and embrace bodies as they are, particularly when they have been rejected elsewhere. This should be motivated not by a desire to colonize these bodies but to accept them; for, as Althaus-Reid argues, an embodied theology must embody the unknown, the stranger at the gate. It is in encountering strangers that 'a different body theology occurs: a theology made with the different shapes that come from the encounter' (Althaus-Reid 2004a: 104). Individuals who undergo transition, whether or not this includes SRS, should be welcomed as full members of their worshipping communities and helped to settle into their identity-expressions.

The declaration that there is 'no doubt' about the biological sex of transgender people – as evident in *Transsexuality* and *Some Issues*, as well as in plenty of non-theological texts which assume transgender to be inevitably connected with deviance or mental illness – is troubling for a still deeper and more profound reason. Such an assertion assumes that human sex is generally something which *can* be known without any doubt – that it is somehow *beyond* doubt, except in the case of 'abnormal' people. This is extremely problematic once we have recognized the provisional and arbitrary nature of all human sex assignment. Breaking down the notion that sex, gender and sexuality always supervene in one of two ways is a crucial step toward recognizing the non-pathology of gender variance, intersex/DSD and non-heterosexual orientation.

In the next chapter I consider the ways in which theologies of disability and the impaired or 'imperfect' body, as well as beliefs about what happens to bodily imperfections at the resurrection, complement theologies from transgender when used to reflect on intersex/DSD.

Chapter 5

REMEMBERING AND RE-MEMBERING: INTERSEX/DSD AND
THEOLOGIES FROM DISABILITY[1]

'People with impairments ... constitute a particular threat to the
orderly functioning of society because they occupy an ambiguous
position – not wholly ill, not wholly healthy – and because the
boundary between "us" and "them" is not only in flux but is
constantly being transgressed by people we know ("us"), who,
outrageously, suddenly turn into "them" ... The creation of a
group of people called "the disabled" is hermeneutics, not
ontology' (Scully 1998: 21).

As we saw in Chapter 4, theological treatments of transgender have
been affected by the status of the transsexual body as existing on
conceptual boundaries, a position it shares with intersexed/DSD
bodies despite the differences in how and why each body has been
altered. In this chapter I demonstrate that impaired bodies transcend
conceptual boundaries in a slightly different way – straddling the
usually mutually-exclusive categories of health and pathology and
thus challenging the theological or moral significances sometimes
attached to each state – and explore whether the bodies of people
with intersex/DSD conditions might also be said to exist on such
a cusp.

Whilst some impairments inherently prevent certain physical
activities possible for non-impaired bodies, more and other
disabilities arise from the ways in which the concrete social
environment is structured. Similarly, whilst many intersexed bodies
cannot do some things which many non-intersexed bodies can do –
for example, women with AIS cannot menstruate or become pregnant
as most other women can – there are also things about intersex/
DSD only rendered problematic by societal assumptions. In this
chapter I argue that, just as disability need not necessarily be deemed

1 Portions of this chapter appear in 'Theologies of Resistance: Intersex,
Disability and Queering the 'Real World''' (Cornwall 2009b).

pathological, either socially or theologically – in spite of the real inherent differences in ability arising from some impairments – likewise, intersex/DSD also need not necessarily be deemed pathological. I explore issues of the real versus constructed nature of disability, and how this impinges on the autonomy and subjecthood of those deemed disabled. I consider some of the ways in which disability has been figured within theology, focusing particularly on questions about the eschatological body, and how notions of the resurrection body in Augustine might help to build a non-pathological picture of intersexed and otherwise 'imperfect' bodies.

I work from the premise that intersex/DSD conditions are analogous to physical disabilities, not intellectual ones. People with developmental intellectual disabilities face exclusion from society in many ways, and raise their own extensive and significant set of questions which have been discussed in detail elsewhere (as by the contributors to the *Journal of Religion, Disability and Health*'s special edition on Hauerwas' theology of disability – Swinton 2004 – and in Young 1990). Although it is artificial to separate physical and intellectual disabilities in this way – since many physical impairments result from various kinds and extents of brain damage, and since the brain is, after all, absolutely a part of the body – I do so in order to consider more precisely the nature of physical functional impairment without entering in detail into the enormous issues of personhood and autonomy for people with intellectual disabilities to which I cannot do justice here. However, a recent article by Morgan Holmes specifically compares parental attitudes to intersexed children and those born with severe neurological impairments (Holmes 2008).

Intersex/DSD and Disability: Areas of Resonance

To what extent might considering disability and intersex/DSD analogously begin to open the way for a fuller theological understanding of intersex/DSD? Some people with intersex/DSD conditions do not wish to be considered politically in the same breath as transsexual or homosexual individuals, because such alliances are felt to erode the particularity of the issues faced by intersexed/DSD people. However, it is conceivable that the 'difference' of intersexed/DSD bodies might resonate with the 'difference' of impaired bodies less problematically than with bodies deemed sexually other.

One example is the case of D/deafness. Like intersex/DSD, deafness is not universally accepted as a tragic or disabling condition – although it is often figured in this way by non-deaf medical professionals. For some Deaf parents, having Deaf children is a cause for happiness, since they will be able to participate fully in the parents' particular culture. One couple, Paula Garfield and Tomato Lichy, celebrated when they discovered that their baby daughter, Molly, was deaf, despite the strident view from medics that deafness was pathological and problematic (R. Atkinson 2006). Garfield and Lichy, who were both made to wear hearing aids as young children, decided not to force Molly to wear them until she was old enough to make her own decision. Far from deafness impeding her development, as medical professionals have argued, Garfield claimed when Molly was 14 months old that her vocabulary was equivalent with that of hearing children of the same age. Crucially, said her parents, hearing aids or cochlear implants in babyhood might in themselves limit or damage Molly – just as surgical intervention for intersex can create undesirable side-effects which are more traumatic than the condition itself. Lichy said, 'It's an important time for Molly to learn about her body in its natural state … How to use her hands and her vision. To give her hundreds of decibels straight into her ear with an amplifying device, when she can't control the volume herself or say if it's painful, is just wrong … How can she learn to play, to focus, to concentrate with noises like that blasting into her ear? We refuse to do it to our baby' (in R. Atkinson 2006).

The claims made by doctors that not having hearing aids is unfair to Molly, and will isolate and disadvantage her, are akin to those made by surgeons putting pressure on the parents of intersexed/DSD infants to have them surgically corrected. Indeed, Lebacqz (1997: 215) notes links between the 'politics of difference' as propounded by ISNA at the time and the model of difference put forward by Deaf people who reject cochlear implants. Arguably, however, rather than trying to ensure reassigned intersexed children will never have to know about their original sex, intersexed children, too, should be able to get to know their body in its original state before later making the decision about whether to have surgery. Garfield states, 'These doctors, and many other people generally, know so little about the deaf community, culture and language, yet they assume they know what is right for us. They have a perception that deafness is a physical failing that needs to be corrected. For us, it's just a different and equally valid way of being' (in Atkinson 2006). Just as hearing people find it difficult to understand how an absence of hearing does not equate to a lack, so unambiguously-sexed people generally perceive unambiguous sex as advantageous and (thus) necessary. Esther Morris says, 'I was labelled with "sexual dysfunction" because I couldn't have intercourse ... But I had discovered my own sexuality so I was very confused ... My doctors recommended vaginal reconstruction so I could have a normal sex life with my husband when I got married. I never had a chance to want a vagina; I simply had to have one' (Morris 2003). For Morris, as for the parents of Molly, her physiology was simply 'a different and equally valid way of being'.

Emi Koyama of Intersex Initiative argues that approaching intersex/DSD issues from the perspective of the radical disability rights movement sidesteps some of the problems associated with alliances made with LGBT or queer groups (Koyama 2006). She notes that, as with many physical disabilities, the absence of a vagina can be figured as less problematic in itself than living in a society which insists, arbitrarily, that having a vagina is necessary. She also draws links between the relationship of intersexed/DSD children to the medical professionals who deal with them, and that of people with disabilities to their own caregivers, claiming that children with impairments are encouraged from early on to conform to a particular 'impaired role', characterized by the sense that a disabled person 'must act as the passive mirror of other people's affection and good will, so that non-disabled people can affirm their own goodness. The forced lifelong immersion in this role makes it extremely difficult to question or to challenge potentially self-serving or manipulative motives behind others' presumably altruistic actions' (Koyama 2006). Nancy Eiesland, in her theological reflection on disability, suspects that church communities have also consciously or unconsciously encouraged complicity with the impaired role and thereby with the marginality of people with disabilities (Eiesland 1994: 20). Christopher Newell notes that the tendency to medicalize and mark out impairment has meant that it has been found 'difficult to allow for more tentative and paradoxical conclusions as to who is disabled and who disables them' (Newell 2007: 325). This is particularly interesting in terms of considering the extent to which the rest of society suffers by the stigmatization of impaired and intersexed bodies, and of utilizing theological and critical tools to query established binary models of pathology and 'health'.

Koyama traces parallels between medical responses to intersex/ DSD and to other conditions. She concludes, 'Medical categories can be useful if [they exist] solely to identify people's needs for medical services and technologies and to provide them' (Koyama 2006). Koyama believes that the majority of people with intersex/ DSD are not, in fact, motivated to join queer-identified activism groups – contrary to a vocal minority. Mainstream media coverage of intersex/DSD, Koyama notes, usually homes in on individuals with particular gender identity struggles, or ongoing medical complications, rather than those leading ordinary, unremarkable lives (for, as she hints, this does not make good television).[2] She claims,

> For the majority of intersex individuals who do not particularly feel the need to explain their gender status because they are not trans or genderqueer, or to re-live the horrors of childhood trauma by telling their stories in front of an audience … because they are not activists, there is nothing that motivates them to speak about their intersex experiences (Koyama 2006).

Drawing on the experiences and political engagements of people with disabilities, rather than those with 'sexual' issues centred on the queer-identifying community, then, might allow non-queer-identifying intersexed/DSD people to demand what *they* need. Morgan Holmes also makes a case for viewing intersex through the lens of disability, saying,

> There is a need to wrest intersex management away from the medical domain. And there is good reason to address intersex principally through a critical disability studies apparatus that

2. A notable exception is Channel 4's 2004 documentary *Secret Intersex*, which included the story of half-sisters Ilizane and Xenia (aged 16 and six at the time), who were being brought up in a climate of complete openness about their AIS, and whose parents encouraged them to view themselves as 'inters' rather than girls or boys. This non-hysterical approach was carried on by the programme makers – although the *Sunday Telegraph*, which ran a piece on the family before the programme was shown (Craig 2004), chose the more sensational strapline 'Half Boys, Half Girls: Inside the World of the Hermaphrodite Siblings'.

may hold in abeyance the commonsense attitudes that not only
fail to provide well-being, but which are moving in the face of
that failure, to eradicate intersex altogether through the use of
invasive prenatal technologies, including selective termination
(Holmes 2008: 170).

Commentators on disability, including some theologians, have
argued that certain conditions figured as pathologies might be more
usefully figured as variations. For example, deafness or blindness
can be reckoned different and specific life conditions, without
necessarily having to be considered totally negative. It is possible
to appreciate that there are certain activities made impossible or
much more difficult for people who are deaf or blind without thereby
pathologizing the entire conditions. The theological tradition has
often focused on what is problematic about particular impairments
rather than on what might be advantageous or simply unremarkable
about them – which has not encouraged speaking and acting from
within these particular 'problematic' bodies. However, influenced
by feminist and other methodologies, there has been a move toward
valuing marginal and polyphonic voices in theology. But although
impairments have begun to be figured as legitimate sites for
reflection, there has been far less impetus to move beyond similar
pathological figurings of sexual variation such as intersex/DSD and
transgender. An examination of the different ways in which it is
possible to represent disability in and from the Christian theological
tradition, however, opens the way to finding other ways to read
physical sex variation beyond the male-female binary too.

'Perfect-ability': The Problem of Perfection in Ability and in Sex

People with disabilities, it has been noted, are not, in many respects,
particularly unlike 'normal' people. As a result, they serve as
reminders of what the able body could easily become. The able are
forced to face the possibility that they themselves could (and
probably will, in old age if not before) become the disabled; that
they are, in fact, only 'temporarily able'. In fact, the 'ableness' of
able bodies, just as much as the 'disabledness' of disabled ones, is
contingent on particular norms (Rappmann 2003).The unshakeability
of binary sex, too, is far more precarious than it seems. If the able
are only temporarily able, the unambiguously 'sexed' are also only
temporarily (and arbitrarily) sexed: the current criteria for defining

maleness or femaleness will not necessarily remain so forever. Benchmarks for the size and appearance of the genitals, and the sexed import ascribed to particular physical characteristics, have changed across time and culture and may change again. Gender norms, too, undergo shifts: Ken Stone picks up on Butler's argument that they 'are continually haunted by their own inefficacy' (Stone K. 2005: 126; Butler 1993: 237), because 'the embodiment or materialization of gender norms ... frequently fails to live up to the ideals on which it is based' (Stone K. 2005: 127). Even 'normal', unremarkable men and women constantly do things which might be said to conflict with their gender identity. Any insistence on binary gender and bodies to match – as with early genital surgery for intersex/DSD – always already acknowledges that the binaries are at risk and must be reinforced.

The philosophical 'perfections' assigned to God are, it might be held, nothing but human wish-fulfilment writ large, stemming from a desire to worship a maximized version of ourselves. John M. Hull argues that the Bible more often than not portrays God as 'super-abled', with sensory and other powers beyond those of humans – like us, but more so. The notion of omnipotence is particularly problematic to the idea that human perfection must replicate God's perfection, since humans are clearly not all-powerful, and impaired humans may in some respects be even less powerful than others. It might therefore be held that God's image is more wholly reflected in humans who are more 'perfect' – which might come to mean more powerful or able – than other humans. The problem with such a model is that it is a circular one: while it ostensibly starts with God as a model for humans, actually, it inevitably starts with humans as a model for God. It is contingent on humans having a right idea of what constitutes perfection in the first place. It is dangerous for the same reasons as Barth's theological anthropology: in this account, God's 'perfection' inevitably reflects, and is a projection of, the ideals of a perfect *human* bodily existence, since it is in human selves and bodies that the doctrine is constructed and understood.

Exacerbated Disability and Stigmatization: 'You Shall Not Revile the Deaf or Put a Stumbling-Block Before the Blind'[3]

Both people with impairments and intersexed people are often portrayed and categorized as having limited choices about their bodies and lives, and may have their authority as actors and decision-makers usurped by others. This has happened for many reasons; Stanley Hauerwas argues that one is the medicalization of disability. He says,

> The medical model is particularly destructive for the handicapped in that it puts them in a disastrous psychological and sociological situation: They must define themselves as permanently dependent if they are to receive the advantages of the sick role ... This robs handicapped persons of their most effective means of doing something about their situation, namely, politics ... They have been robbed unjustly of power that is rightfully theirs (Hauerwas 2004b: 171).

Hauerwas follows Gliedman and Roth's claim that societal assumptions about the limiting nature of disability mean that we *already* expect people with disabilities to be abnormal or unable to participate in mainstream life. In order to justify this we seize as identifiers predominantly on those characteristics which confirm impaired persons' difference and atypicality. However, because we have convinced ourselves that the difference lies solely in biological or medical grounds, we absolve ourselves of any contribution to their exclusion (Hauerwas 2004b: 170).

We see this echoed in attitudes to atypical sex/gender configurations too. It is analogous to doctors seizing on the few things that some intersexed people cannot do rather than on all the ways in which their bodies are like those of anyone else. This is not to elide the difference of bodies with intersex/DSD conditions, nor to dismiss Bo Laurent's salient reminder that such bodies may have particular health concerns; but to focus *only* on the difference of intersex/DSD contributes to making them seem teratological. Moreover, doctors, by giving so much weight to the differences that can be altered or 'eradicated', may conceal all the ways in which people are damaged or marginalized *by the medical intervention itself* – what might be termed iatrogenetic harm. Preves argues, 'The persistent focus on the abnormality of intersexed bodies further reifies the "normalcy" of bodies that are not intersexed' (Preves

3 Lev. 19.14.

2003: 126). Rather, intersexed individuals can build a positive identity by 'recasting' their difference and recognizing that 'the genesis of the problem [is] external rather than internal' (Preves 2003: 87). Georgia Warnke says, 'The idea that we just are essentially male or female is ... less an idea about nature than it is an interpretation of natural properties, one that begins with the activities and presumptions of gender and works backward, as it were, toward the body' (Warnke 2001: 130). It is a prior assumption that the difference of intersexed people is dangerous, monstrous or pathological which leads to reading their bodies in exactly this way. This is another aspect of erotic domination, where a good desire for order or cohesion in society degenerates into a project of subsuming and eradicating the different and other. This means texts on impairment from throughout the ambivalent Christian tradition must be continually re-examined in light of new discourses and hermeneutics, against the elusive but imperative gauge of love and justice.

Disability activists often argue that physical 'abnormalities' are only disadvantageous if society is structured so that, for instance, buildings are accessible solely by the physically 'normal'. Similarly, it can be argued, the major reason why intersexed bodies are perceived as dangerous in their difference (and why they must therefore be altered) is because of imposed norms – which become moral imperatives – of how decent, clearly-sexed bodies should look and behave. Bodily states which are not actually life-threatening come to be made out as emergencies because they offend aesthetically (Kessler 1998: 37), and jeopardize the dual hegemonies which say that power, potency and ability – sexual or otherwise – are the goods to which every body must aspire, and that heterosexuality and procreation are self-evidently normal and desirable. People with impairments who refuse either to submit to a role as victim, or to erase their difference and particularity by denying their impairment altogether in order to seem as normal as possible, help to question what constitutes normality and acceptability in the first place. If an impaired body, or a body which does not fit into the sex binary, speaks up for itself and claims its share of audience and consequence, this subverts ableist and heteronormative assumptions.

Part of this, for theologians, involves resisting particular notions of legitimacy and signification. Disability theologians have successfully done this by reframing assumptions about weakness, strength, power and perfection; theologians who reflect on intersex/DSD must do likewise. Power arises from everywhere, holds Foucault; there is always the possibility that it can be transformed and redeemed. Power can generate as well as repress. This means that the political and social liberation of impaired individuals, with which theologians have attempted to think and speak, is itself under continual scrutiny because of the uncertainties and controversies arising in it. Feminist philosopher of disability Susan Wendell asks, 'How can people fight collectively an oppression based on a category without using that category, without organizing around it? But then, if they do use it, do they not build a collective interest in maintaining it?' (Wendell 1996: 76). Within intersex/DSD activism, too, there has been debate over whether intersexed/DSD people should emphasize their difference by ascribing to alternative gender categories such as 'third' or sex categories such as 'inter', or should rather embrace a more mainstream gender binary but without thereby condoning surgical intervention as necessary to authenticate belonging to one of these categories.

Similarly, Preves has commented that the use of 'medical jargon', even by intersexed people when discussing their own intersex/DSD conditions, 'reflects the widespread acceptance of a medical paradigm, which makes it difficult for lay persons to question medical opinion and authority' (Preves 2001: 532). In this instance, the use of the terminology disseminated by the medical establishment is read as tacit evidence of the extent to which the medicalization paradigm exists across discourses. By contrast, self-identification and self-naming have been held to be important aspects of asserting a positive and emancipated personhood (it has been pressure from intersexed people themselves which has led to the terminology of 'hermaphroditism' and 'pseudo-hermaphroditism' largely having been dropped), which is why some self-identified intersexed people reject what they consider to be the imposition of medical language and discourse in 'DSD'. However – as we see in the intersex versus DSD debate – these, too, can become sites of essentialism and stigmatization. As theologians who engage with these issues, it is important that we do not settle for fixed and monolithic answers; all kinds of power have the potential to desiccate into distortions of the good.

Disability in Scripture

Blemish, Curse, Confusion or Blessing?

The scriptural canon does not directly address intersex/DSD. However, a brief reflection on its apparent attitudes toward impaired bodies helps shed light on biblical assumptions about health and goodness in embodiment *per se*.

The scriptural tradition throws up various metaphors of sickness as curse (Exod. 15.26), and, conversely, restored health as reward for obedience (Hos. 6.1). Wellness generally often indicates righteousness (as for the friends of Job). This is not really surprising given – as Fontaine notes – the biblical context of 'a medically naïve society, one based on agricultural production, [where] those who cannot participate fully are naturally seen as existing in a more precarious, and less desirable state' (Fontaine 1994: 110). Although this attitude sometimes prompts injunctions to take particular care of people with disabilities, Fontaine argues that the underlying sense is still that they are at risk – and that, if God intervenes to give special treatment to the lame or blind, 'this emphasizes the remarkable compassion of the one doing the good deed, not the deserving nature or dignity of the recipient' (Fontaine 1994: 110). Appreciating the likely social context in which these texts arose does not mean accepting their cosmology as positive or normative for today, but negative hangovers from scripture do persist (Lewis 2007: 61–65). Partially as a result of this, Eiesland posits, Christianity has tended to see people with disabilities as either overly blessed or overly damned (Eiesland 1994: 70), with no middle way acknowledging the profound normality of lives lived in impaired or otherwise limited bodies (Eiesland 1994: 75).

Marcella Althaus-Reid asserts,

> Impurity, in the scriptures, is a very corporeal category. That is the reason why it needs to be associated with body disfunctions, such as leprosy, blindness and, of course, menstruation.[4] Impurity is without doubt what exceeds the normativity of the body as religiously constructed and it is important to recognize that

4. Although it has been argued that menstrual 'taboos' might in fact mark menstruation out as holy, or allow women a mechanism by which to refuse men's sexual demands for a time (Greenberg 1985: 133; Raphael 1996: 167); that it was women themselves who extended *niddah*, the time during which intercourse at and after menstruation must be avoided, from seven days to twelve days (Greenberg 1985: 122); and that the Orthodox Jewish *mikvah* or

"impurity" is not a given but rather is a legal category imposed
upon a person (Althaus-Reid 2006c: 521).

Althaus-Reid's point seems to be that what is and is not deemed
pure or impure – which includes some instances of impairment – is
always already based on prior but constructed readings of purity.
Another interpretation, famously given by Douglas in *Purity and
Danger*, is that what the Levitical law demands is completeness
(Douglas 1966: 51), which can be compromised by ritual defilement
such as the emission of bodily fluids (Douglas 1966: 51–52), having
a physical blemish, or by being socially 'incomplete' through failing
to live up to what is expected of one, for example, fearlessness
from warriors in battle (Douglas 1966: 52). Impairment might
certainly be figured as fitting into the last two of these three
categories, undermining what is perceived to be a pure, whole and
undefiled state. It might also be considered to be a confusion of
different classes of things, the healthy and the pathological, whereas
Douglas identifies that 'holiness requires that individuals shall
conform to the class to which they belong' (Douglas 1966: 53), and
that holiness requires a keeping-distinct of different categories of
creation. In this reading, confusion, contradiction and hybridity
compromise holiness (Douglas 1966: 53, 56).

Impairment may be figured as boundary-transcending, because
the impaired person is neither wholly healthy nor wholly unhealthy,
and cannot go through a period of ritual cleansing to remove what
it is that is making them other than wholly healthy – thus blurring
the boundary between definite sickness and definite health. The
'purity' of staying within legitimate borders in our own context is
less commonly figured in moral terms. We are more likely to appeal
to unusual or distasteful phenomena as 'unnatural' than as 'impure',
though there is certainly some overlap between these terms and
the senses in which they are used. As we saw in Chapter 4, although
what is 'natural' is often also sanctioned 'normal' and thereby held
as a good to be reinforced, the very notion of reinforcing or
protecting nature demonstrates that it is always already at least in
part a cultural construct. The fact that some post-surgery reports

ritual bath after *niddah* is not inherently unfeminist or simplistically to do
with cleanness/uncleanness (Greenberg 1985: 123, 125), Melissa Raphael holds,
'There seems little doubt that the biblical traditions have and continue to
find menstrual blood repellent to the holy. It is quite outside or profane to
the mechanisms of atonement and salvation which are lubricated by male
sacrificial blood' (Raphael 1996: 171).

describe circumcised penises as 'more natural-looking' than their pre-circumcision versions (Kessler 1998: 39) demonstrates that this extends into readings of genitals too. More pertinent than focusing on 'nature', though, would be to consider whether particular bodily states are states which are *life-enhancing* or *life-negating*, and to what extent any negation of life or flourishing comes about in societal response to the impairment rather than because of the impairment itself. As we have seen, with rare exceptions, intersex/DSD conditions are not physically life-negating in childhood; far more life-negating are the narrow societal models of acceptability for bodies, and the genital surgeries done in response, eroding what Gorringe terms 'life chances' (Gorringe 2004: 149).

Part of the recent movement surrounding disability rights has lain in seeking to problematize the prevalence of a drive for physical perfection based not on the views of the individuals affected but of a society whose desire for perfection stems, in part, from its fear of difference. God does not see with literal eyes nor hear with literal ears (although humans sometimes talk as though God does so – as, for example, in Isa. 37.17), so those humans who do see and do hear do not, by virtue of these abilities, more closely represent the image of God than do blind or deaf people. Even so, Christian traditions which have too unproblematically apotheosized 'unblemished' bodies, after death if not in this life, influenced by the notion 'that physical disability is a travesty of the divine image' (Eiesland 1994: 72) have thus fed into broader mores surrounding the eradication or concealment of the abnormal, thereby filtering what 'normality' is in the first place. The image of God as aseitic, complete in Godself, all-powerful and able to act independently of human activity, has informed the notion that human dependence is something undesirable and less-than-perfect, and that humans who are more than usually dependent on others – that is, those with certain impairments – are thereby even more imperfect (Hull 2001: 72–73). Physical and philosophical perfections are obviously different from one another, but the drive for corporeal perfection has now annexed even medically 'normal' bodies when they are deemed to be cosmetically imperfect – hence the rise of surgery to reduce the labia minora or to 'rejuvenate' (i.e., tighten) the vagina, as seen in glossy magazines alongside 'gruesome down-there pics' (Rolison 2008: 102–103). Kessler points out that such surgery further reduces the range of what is considered acceptable and might thereby increase the likelihood of genital surgery for infants (Kessler 1998: 117) – making notions of normality and perfection into moral and ethical issues even if they were not to begin with.

Although impairment is not unequivocally linked with uncleanness, it is possible to trace links between impairment and moral impurity – as Eiesland has done – throughout the Bible. In the daunting Lev. 26.14-16, a jealous God threatens 'consumption and fever that waste the eyes and cause life to pine away'. As well as making sickness and impairment a direct consequence of God's anger, such passages, if read uncritically, can add to the figuring of people with disabilities as 'other'. Impairment is made something to be feared – leading to its demonization – rather than a common occurrence in numerous ordinary lives, including those which have formerly been able. Eiesland says that exchanges such as that in Luke 5 where Jesus asks whether it is easier to forgive sins or to tell a person with paralysis to stand up and walk, and then heals the man unable to walk, 'have frequently been cited as proof that disability is a sign of moral imperfection or divine retribution for sin' (Eiesland 1994: 71). This is, she notes, extremely problematic – but there is a possible subversion of the attitude by Jesus in John 9: 'His disciples asked him, "Rabbi, who sinned, this man or his parents, that he was born blind?" Jesus answered, "Neither this man nor his parents sinned; he was born blind so that God's works might be revealed in him"' (Jn 9.2-3). Although this does not entirely erase a possible reading of God as capricious or inconsistent, using some individuals as object-lessons for the rest, it does question the concretized association between impairment and personal or ancestor sin which existed in the minds of the disciples and has reappeared at certain points since. Moreover, whilst there is a sense that God *allowed* the man to be born blind, there is no necessity to read the text as stating incontrovertibly that God deliberately *made* the man blind; impairment can thus be figured as simply part of a free universe (as Gorringe suggests), rather than a mark of judgement for sin.

Deborah Creamer's use of what she terms the 'Limitness' model in her theology of disability emphasizes the fact that no one individual or group can encompass the entire range of human experience. This is central to formulating non-stigmatizing theological understandings of impairment, intersex/DSD, and otherwise unusual bodies. None of us can access everything about what it is to be human *per se* or in relationship with God. Not just those with specific impairments or conditions, but *each* of us, is limited in different ways (Creamer 2003: 65). Although it is (as Eiesland notes) treading on dangerous and somewhat assimilationist ground to hold that each of us is *impaired* (Eiesland 1994: 85), it is certainly true that each of us is *limited* by our own position and perspective. Any attempt to propound a universalized, idealized redeemed version of the body as able, as sexed and so on, should therefore be subjected to a scrutiny which is critical at the very least. It might be 'natural' (that is, desirable as a product of a particular cultural perspective) for a non-impaired person to assume that everyone else would be better off non-impaired, or for an unambiguously-sexed person to assume that everyone would be better off without an intersex condition/DSD. However, this risks privileging and rationalizing the world as it is now, a world set up for life as unambiguously sexed, gendered, and able, to be easier all round. It is a little like saying that it is more difficult to be black than to be white and that we will therefore all be white in the resurrection – rather than accepting that it is white privilege and racial prejudice which will pass away. Allowing the voices of the conceptually poor and marginal to be heard and to influence the ongoing story of salvation history is central to doing a just theology.

'Real Worlds' and the Ideology of Dominance

Hannah Lewis, in her recent liberation theology from Deafness, comments that much theologizing done on D/deafness in the past occurred either to provoke pity (and thus charity) for D/deaf people, or to address 'the perceived pastoral "problems" of deaf people' (Lewis 2007: 2). Although this is slowly changing, she suggests that the marginalization of D/deaf people and their concerns cannot be undone without changing 'the dominant theological discourse itself' (Lewis 2007: 3). In order to create space for D/deaf voices to be heard in theology and the Church, she suggests, they must be privileged over those of even interested and involved hearing people, in order to 'balance out the hearing-centred discourse that has dominated Deaf life' (Lewis 2007: 6). This may be 'partial' and 'subjective', but it is necessary. Challenging a hearing hegemony might also mean rejecting other norms: many Deaf texts, notes Lewis, are not written down but signed or performed, and even where written may not exist in an academically-acceptable form (Lewis

2007: 6), but are still legitimate sources for reflection. Lewis holds that practices such as expecting deaf children to survive mainstream school by lipreading are always setting them up to fail, since they will never follow what is going on by this means as effortlessly as hearing children do (Lewis 2007: 29). Both the medical model of deafness, and responses by bodies such as the Church of England, have assumed hearing to be the norm, essential to full human experience. Many chaplains and missioners to deaf people are themselves hearing; and early church services in Britain ostensibly 'for' deaf people, aimed to integrate them into the hearing church and encouraged the use of spoken English rather than British Sign Language (Lewis 2007: 160). This did not value the specificity of deaf experience and relationship to God. In short, says Lewis,

> The power of the medical model has always been its appeal to apparent "common sense". It seems self-evident that someone who lacks one of the "five senses" should be limited in what they can do and need help from those with everything in full working order, that it is "normal" to communicate via hearing and speaking and that this is the natural order of things ... It may be normal for a hearing person to pick up the phone and speak into it and listen to the answer. It is equally normal for me to type my message into the "minicom" and read the answer off the screen in front of me; it is the only way I have ever used the phone for a conversation (Lewis 2007: 29–30).

It might be countered that the very necessity of technological intervention such as the minicom phone for deaf quality of life is 'evidence' that deafness is not a normal, natural state of being; however, this assumes that the more 'mainstream' technology, the ubiquitous speech telephone, is somehow natural in the way a minicom phone is not.

John M. Hull, who has lived life both as sighted and as blind, gives a fascinating reading of scriptural episodes from the approach of blindness (Hull 2001, 2003).[5] Hull does not skim over passages

5. See also 'Sight To The Inly Blind', Hull's overview of disability metaphors in hymns (Hull 2002). A particularly notorious offender is Charles Wesley in 'O For a Thousand Tongues to Sing', who counsels, 'Hear Him, ye deaf; His praise, ye dumb, / Your loosened tongues employ; / Ye blind, behold your Saviour come; / And leap, ye lame, for joy'. Interestingly, a later verse including the assurance that Christ will 'wash the Æthiop white' is excised from modern hymn books; the racist undertone, even if unintentional, is no longer acceptable, but the metaphors of disability persist.

he deems oppressive of blind people, but emphasizes that they were written from a sighted perspective which is not necessarily the only, right or 'real' one. The blind world, he insists, is very different from the sighted one but no less authentic and legitimate, since both are constructions from particular, non-universal bodily positions. He says, however, 'It is unusual to find a sighted person who knows that he or she lives within a world which is a projection of the sighted body ... Although sighted people know that they know through sight, they seldom realize the epistemic implications of vision' (Hull 2003a: 26).

Until sighted people realize that what they know they know from one particular standpoint, however, blind people will never be truly valued and accepted. The normalized hegemony of sightedness (Hull 2003a: 30) goes hand-in-hand with dichotomous discourses of sex, race and so on – for, he says, 'uniformity goes with centrality, with authority, and with power' (Hull 2003a: 30). The hegemony of sightedness, of ableness in general, is an ideology of dominance which Christianity must resist. To come to understand that to be perfect as God is perfect need not mean to be perfect as other humans consider themselves perfect is a vital step both for those excluded from legitimacy and those purporting to speak on behalf of God:

> It is [the] concept that there is one "divine image" to be a travesty of ... which constructs the concept of disability as abnormal, a perversion of or deviation from the norm. People with disabilities cannot be created in the image of a "perfect" God and are therefore somehow less "human" than non-disabled humanity ... there is no way they could be created in the image of "our" God (Lewis 2007: 68–69).

The links with understandings of the intersexed body, as contrasted with the 'clear' and 'normal' male and female bodies of theological anthropology, are striking.

So it is not just questions of ability and impairment that are at stake; Hull insists, 'Once the hegemony of the single world in the relation between able and disabled people is broken, a challenge is mounted against all other human worlds that claim to be absolute' (Hull 2003a: 26). In other words, the differences of the worlds experienced because of differing bodily states should not necessarily be synthesized or assimilated; there will continue to be tensions there. However, acknowledging the plurality of human worlds provides a way in to figuring disability as something other than deficiency or lack (Hull 2003a: 21–22).

In similar vein, Fontaine suggests that reading the voices of the marginal in Scripture as central rather than peripheral will reframe the texts and bring a new and sometimes surprising sense, resisting readings which only make sense to and for the non-disabled. For example, she says, since many people with disabilities have an important sense that they are more than the bodies which cause them so much pain, the injunction to 'cast off an offending member to achieve a greater good' is not a particularly problematic one; rather, she says, 'these are the kind of compromises that make up our daily struggle' (Fontaine 1994: 113). In this sense, people with disabilities are in a stronger position for understanding this particular text than those without.

Hull's and Lewis' appeals to theology as subversive or resistant to ideologies of dominance can apply to theologies from intersex/ DSD too. For the normally-sexed male-and-female to truly take account of differently sexed bodies, it will be necessary to move to an understanding that the dichotomously-sexed world is not the 'only' or 'real' world. Clichéd metaphors based on disability as spiritual lack, fear and pride as paralysis, deafness as obliviousness to the call of God and so on, hurt not only those they misrepresent, but everyone whose horizons are kept narrow. A disruption of existing assumptions is crucial not only to include intersexed/DSD people and those with disabilities but also to expand and diversify imagery to everyone's advantage (Hull 2003a: 22). Impaired and unusually-sexed bodies are part of the Body of Christ and if they suffer further marginalization and conceptual erasure, the rest of the Body suffers too by perpetuating a false image of its own make-up. If we can query the theological and ethical good of 'normalizing' deaf people by insisting they learn to speak, we can also query normalizing genital surgeries.

Perichoresis, *Particularity and Pain*

Hull's work in particular demonstrates that scriptural attitudes to disability are ambiguous and capable of being read very differently if the 'impaired perspective' is held to be the vantage-point, rather than something external or peripheral to how the text should be understood. This does away with the idea that only able people are the 'insiders', the inevitable authors and agents of the Christian tradition. What, then, of variant gender and sex? Biblical texts were written from a particular sexed perspective, but neither the sexual norms of that age nor those of this age are the only 'truth' about the world. Likewise, biblical texts which sanction particular models of sex, gender and family should be recognized as contingent on the contexts in which they were written, and not unproblematically to be transposed into our own society. Biblical texts surrounding disability and sex, then, are and remain problematic, and it may be necessary to formulate theologies in spite of them, drawing on other traditions and resources.

Disability has by no means always been figured as a curse or punishment in the Christian tradition. The converse argument also persists: disability is sometimes deemed a sign not that one is more sinful or less faithful than others, but that one is actually morally exemplary, gaining courage and fortitude from God in order dutifully to bear one's burden and not decry the injustice of one's situation – thus demonstrating how everyone else should respond to their smaller struggles. However, to portray people with disabilities as exemplars of quiet endurance and patience who do not question their lot, or to hold the 'thorn in the flesh' picture of disability as an unproblematic one, risks refusing to address what it is about the way human societies are ordered – and, conceivably, the way God encourages faithfulness and perseverance – that conspires to make the lives of certain individuals more of a burden than they need be. A central aspect of Eiesland's argument is that the whole notion of 'virtuous suffering' can encourage defeatist resignation to one's state. She says, 'Similar to the practice of emphasizing self-sacrifice to women, the theology of virtuous suffering has encouraged persons with disabilities to acquiesce to social barriers as a sign of obedience to God and to internalise second-class status inside and outside the church' (Eiesland 1994: 73). A stressing of moral goods such as patience and fortitude for people with disabilities has risked making impairment itself a moral issue, a proving-ground for goodness and piety, rather than simply another aspect of life experience. As we have seen, intersex/DSD has also been figured using oddly moral language, and this is also problematic, since it contributes to the sense that intersex/DSD is itself something other than an unremarkable variation of human existence.

Discourses surrounding disability have sometimes figured impaired bodies as existing somehow on behalf of the rest of society, as a projection of particular social perceptions. For example, there is a notion that not only might impairment provoke patience or fortitude in the individual, but that people with disabilities somehow exist to help others become better people – which is extremely problematic. Frances Young, who has written extensively about living with her severely brain-damaged and microcephalic son, Arthur, reflects on a comment made to her by a doctor that her son was not solely her own responsibility, but was that of society as a whole, for, said the doctor, 'society needs handicap' (Young 1990: 109). Young expands,

> Handicapped people remind us that life is not all go-getting and individual achievement. There are more fundamental human values. Handicap demands mutual support, a sense of communal sharing. Handicap fosters compassion and helpfulness, care and concern. It challenges our selfishness and our ambition and sectional loyalties. Society needs handicap (Young 1990: 109).

This comment is extremely interesting, and does appear to an extent to recognize (and reinscribe) the message that human life and intercourse is supposed to be built on values of mercy, interdependence and *perichoresis*. In terms of theodicy, however, it is not an adequate response. The existence of the suffering sometimes attached to disability may indeed (like a war, or a road accident) bring the best out of people, promoting selflessness and mutual concern – but this does not mean that these things could not come about any other way, or that wars and road accidents, like excessive pain, should not be figured as undesirable things. Disability is not the necessary or inevitable catalyst; society does not need handicap. This does not necessarily mean wishing away every unusual or different body, but it does mean a continual questioning of attitudes which border on figuring people with disabilities as object-lessons, or as sites of reception for everyone else's activity. Young argues,

> Handicap is not straightforwardly a punishment for sin. But it is a kind of judgement, a *krisis*, because it has that effect. Society ... is judged by the way it treats handicapped people ...

[Handicap] shows up people and their relationships and their values for what they are (Young 1990: 143).

This reading of the 'judgement' of disability (Young notes that the meaning of the Greek krisij encompasses discrimination, separating out or deciding between, as well as condemnatory judgement – Young 1990: 148) as being for the whole of society positively moves away from the notion that disability is punishment for personal or ancestor sin (as we saw Jesus do), but still somehow figures people with disabilities as being exemplary, as being *for* others. Lewis incisively criticizes the Church of England for figuring Deaf people as having 'special gifts' and 'simple, childlike faith' which is 'untrammelled by the complexities of knowledge and understanding' (Committee for Ministry Among Deaf People 1997: 61), noting that 'Deaf people blessed with such "gifts" are expected to spend their lives inspiring and encouraging others rather than getting on with whatever they want to do' (Lewis 2007: 76). Seizing on people with disabilities as inherently disruptive of able, individualist, go-getting hegemonies is as problematic as expecting intersexed and transgender people to single-handedly deconstruct all the injustices and assumptions of patriarchal and heteronormative sex-gender hierarchies. To acknowledge – as Young does – that interactions with people with disabilities may well change oneself is not necessarily problematic; but any mindset which figures people with disabilities as predominantly there to inspire sentimental wonder or to be treated with kindness by others will erode their own capacity to be actors, and render them passive, essentially to be ministered to. This actually removes them from a reciprocal relationship with the rest of society.

Accepting the normality of impaired bodies, however, does not mean burying the fact that people with disabilities do sometimes experience pain and indignity as a direct consequence of their impairment. This physical pain should not be downplayed. As well as the physiological discomfort of the acute or chronic pain attached to some impairments, people who were once able-bodied and have late-onset impairments have spoken of an element of regret for what they could once do and cannot do any more which is limited simply to physical ability. There might also be lasting particularities (including special health concerns) attached to life as an intersexed person which leave them with a legacy of difference in certain respects. Hauerwas, reflecting on the power of individuals in difficult situations to 'transform events into decisions' by naming the particular difficulty as integral to one's identity, counsels, 'I am not suggesting that every form of pain or suffering can or should be seen as some good or challenge. Extreme suffering can as easily destroy as enhance ... Some forms of suffering can only be acknowledged, not transformed' (Hauerwas 2004a: 94). What is crucial is that the negative elements of some bodily conditions or configurations, like excessive pain, are not made the only thing there is to say about them. Impaired bodies, and the bodies of people with intersex/DSD conditions, are not exactly the same as other bodies (though they may be less unlike them than we realize); they have their specific challenges, but this does not in itself negate the goodness of these bodies' stories, and does not mean that any eschatological projection should unproblematically erase them.

'Sown in Weakness, Raised in Power'? The Hope of Healing

It is not possible or desirable to consider the body as simply a 'shell' or casing for the 'real' self, a disembodied soul or spirit. Bizarre as the notion of bodily resurrection might be, it necessitates a non-dualistic understanding of human personhood, and means that bodily specificities, even where they seem problematic, cannot be deemed secondary or peripheral to the experience of being human. So what might this imply for theologies from intersex/DSD in particular?

If the new and coming Kingdom is one whose incoming has not as yet been completed – and if human bodies are sown perishable but will be raised imperishable, and are sown in weakness but will be raised in power (as Paul holds in 1 Cor. 15) – it might seem fair to assume that this means those 'sown' with impairments will be raised non-impaired, or that those 'sown' with intersex/DSD conditions will be raised non-intersexed. But if this is the case, we need to ask hard questions about whether people with physical impairments or people with intersex/DSD conditions will even be recognizable in their resurrected states. What does the idea of a bodily resurrection mean for the persistence of identity and the value of lives lived in impaired, and intersexed, bodies here and now? What does it mean if we figure healing as a prefiguring or incoming of an eschaton where bodies will no longer be painful or troublesome as they sometimes are in the present world?

For some commentators, healing in itself is a problematic concept because 'the relentless characterization of the disabled as objectified beneficiaries of divine healing robs them of their true status as courageous, coping, creative persons – persons who are valued just as they are' (Fontaine 1994: 112). However, as Fontaine also comments, the Christian notion of healing as linked with faith can also help to provide hope when the kind of healing available from medical science has been pronounced useless, or when an individual has been told they will never walk again – especially as some studies have suggested that the hope of those with a religious faith leads to higher rates of recovery or management of health problems than for those without a religious faith (Fontaine 1994: 113). Healing, then, is ambiguous, and attitudes toward it from people with disabilities are sometimes ambivalent. However, the hope that healing is possible is read by some theologians of disability as a positive symbol of the attainability of social as well as psychosomatic change. Fontaine says, 'The Bible, in suggesting that our attitudes and expectations shape our experience and ability to receive healing, gives us back the power to imagine ourselves differently and to craft a reality that more accurately represents our talents as survivors' (Fontaine 1994: 114). God does not, apparently, heal all those who are sick, suffering or disabled, either in the Gospel accounts of Jesus' ministry or after present-day intercession. Healing is far broader than a simple removal of whatever is challenging, particularly if it is only challenging by the narrow standards of an unimaginative society. Abraham Berinyuu says, 'Healing is an act, event, system, or structure that encourages or facilitates God's empowering, renewing, reconciling, and liberating processes in order to reverse the negation of God's intended good for God's creation' (Berinyuu 2004: 210). Healing is thus not the sole task of God. Eschatology affects lived attitudes here and now: a belief that bodies will be 'fixed' after death sometimes makes it too easy to dismiss the struggles faced currently, but an attitude that human beings might be co-redeemers with Christ encourages doing everything possible to eradicate enforced discommodity and promote inclusion. Hester notes that one strategy for overcoming the marginalization of people with intersex/DSD conditions might be one which recognizes that '"healing" is not "healing from", but living comfortably and healthily with oneself as intersex' (Hester 2006: 48). This disruption of the link between healing and curing, and of doctors as the healers, also prompts a reconsideration of medical norms based on medics 'fixing' problematic intersexed bodies (Hester 2006: 66). Rather than assuming that deaf people will hear in the new creation, we ought ask whether Jesus can sign (Lewis 2007: 133); rather than assuming intersexed bodies will be perfected to unambiguity, we ought ask what eschatologies of perfection suggest about our own body anxieties.

Questioning categories of 'goodness' and perfection for bodies is extremely important, for if the resurrection is linked unproblematically and uncritically with a capacity to perfect bodies, it might be argued that the salvation and redemption of the body is 'closer' for those who are already 'able' than those who are not. Conversely, as we have seen in Pailin, Hull, Lewis and others, it is necessary to query human standards of legitimacy and 'goodness' of bodies. An unproblematized account of perfection as ability and clear sex also fails to question the hegemonic stories of those who already have the power, status and prestige that are attached to being able-bodied, being non-intersexed, or whatever the particular privileged state is. In this way, redemption as conventionally accepted is 'closer' for the privileged and able because the definition of redemption is already coloured to their advantage. It is not that those who are 'more other' cannot be redeemed, but that they will have further to go and will be more changed from their initial selves in the process. It is not self-evident, though, that what is a disadvantage in this realm will be a disadvantage in the new one. If impaired and intersexed/DSD bodies are, in fact, neither less perfect or more in need of transformation than any other bodies, then the Church has no more right to make pronouncements over these bodies than over any other bodies – especially given the lack of strong assertion in the New Testament canon about what the actual physicality of the resurrection body will be like. There is a tantalizing vagueness and uncertainty surrounding what resurrected perfection will entail.

It matters, however, because within Christian theology the notion of the resurrection body is used to describe something about the destinies of present human bodies and, therefore, something about what is important about those bodies and their place within cosmic order and signification. It is therefore worthwhile to reflect here on the treatment of the resurrection body by Paul and Augustine in particular, since both have been so influential on later ideas about the resurrection body. If Christians are called to be heralds of the new order, to start living and building it here and now, we need to ask just what kind of world we are building, and what our various and irreducible bodies are to signify within it.

The Resurrection Body in Paul and Augustine

Paul and the Body Imperishable

Paul makes extensive use of the body as a metaphor for the Christian community, but when it comes to resurrection bodies he is less forthright about their constitution. The actual fleshliness of the resurrection body comes to be emphasized more overtly elsewhere in light of the Apostles' Creed, as, for example, in 2 Clement 9.1-5:

> And let not any one of you say that this our flesh is not judged nor raised again. Consider this: in what were you saved, in what did you recover your sight, if not in this flesh? We ought, therefore, to guard our flesh as the temple of God; for in the same manner as you were called in the flesh, in the flesh also shall you come. There is one Christ, our Lord who saved us, who being at the first spirit, was made flesh, and thus called us. So also shall we in this flesh receive the reward.

In his discussion of the resurrection body in 1 Cor. 15, by contrast, Paul is far less specific, stating rather enigmatically, 'There are both heavenly bodies and earthly bodies, but the glory of the heavenly is one thing, and that of the earthly is another' (verse 40). He continues,

> What is sown is perishable, what is raised is imperishable. It is sown in dishonour, it is raised in glory. It is sown in weakness, it is raised in power. It is sown a physical body, it is raised a spiritual body ... For the trumpet will sound, and the dead will be raised imperishable, and we will be changed. For this perishable body must put on imperishability, and this mortal body must put on immortality (1 Cor. 15.44, 52-53).

However, it is unclear to what extent Paul believes that the *essence* of the body will be altered, and whether the 'change' is one of kind or merely of persistence. John A.T. Robinson insists that 'whereas man as σάρξ cannot inherit the kingdom of God ... man as σῶμα can' (Robinson 1952: 31) and holds that the two descriptors which seem to be held in contrast merely refer to 'the whole man differently regarded – man as wholly perishable, man as wholly destined for

God' (Robinson 1952: 31–32) – but this does not address precisely what it is about the weakness and the 'perishability' of the *sarx* which will ebb away, and what will be retained in the *soma*. As Pheme Perkins observes, Paul perceives some sort of bond between the 'physical' and the 'spiritual' in the resurrection body but even he 'is hard put to describe the connection' (Perkins 1984: 319). It is thus not possible immediately or unequivocally to draw conclusions from the 'imperishability' of this body about the pathological or otherwise status of impairment or other 'blemishes'.

The Corinthians passages demonstrate a particular tension around the human earthly body and its part in the resurrection body. Perkins says,

> Paul presumes from the outset that the human, earthly body is a psychic one. It belongs to the realm of human life. What is gained in resurrection, then, is "spiritual body" ... Paul frequently presupposes that one thinks of "spiritual body" as the reality of resurrection. Thus, one may even wonder if he is able to consider seriously an alternate reading of human reality in terms of mind or soul as the central reality of the person (Perkins 1984: 299–300).

Paul accepts that there must be radical discontinuity between the earthly body-soul and the part of the human that reflects the divine mind (Perkins 1984: 303), but believes that the fact that the earthly body appears profoundly different from the divine mind does not preclude God from being able to make a resurrection body that *is* resurrectable yet still essentially a body (Perkins 1984: 304). It is thus not a case of *escaping* the body, as the Corinthians thought, but of accepting that it is through God's power in creating a new *kind* of body that one 'enters the realm of the immortal and incorruptible' (Perkins 1984: 308). Significantly, however, in 2 Corinthians 5, Paul strongly emphasizes that the heavenly body-dwelling is something to be 'put on' rather than stripped off the present body. Perkins says, 'Paul admits that the corruptible earthly dwelling is destroyed or swallowed up in the process. But his awkward concern with putting on rather than being unclothed can only be seen as a direct rejection of the alternative view of the soul's entry into heaven by shedding the body' (Perkins 1984: 309). So for Paul there is something eternal *already* inhering in bodies, and the persistence of bodies as bodies therefore matters, although there is also something still to come which is not yet realized.

The eschatological context in Paul, as simultaneously *already* and *not yet* realized is crucial, for without it, resurrection risks either being divorced from the body altogether, or rendered solely a psychic event in the disciples and not also a universal event. Resurrection for Paul is something in which the believer already participates, being grounded in the historical resurrection of Christ; but it is also delayed, in part, until the culmination of all things (Perkins 1984: 318). This ambiguity echoes the general character of Paul's assertions on the topic, which Perkins says are not particularly well-defined in their structure (Perkins 1984: 318). Holly E. Hearon suggests that Paul sees humanity as being at a turning point between two epochs, one foot rooted in what is passing away (and perishable bodies) and the other in the future reign of God but as a promise in Christ's resurrection:

> Flesh and blood belong to the perishable, that is, the present age; to the future belongs that which is incorruptible, the spiritual body that we receive through Christ ... The Corinthians have ... confounded the two by failing to recognize the fragility of their present existence and thereby jeopardizing their future (Hearon 2006: 612).

This might explain Paul's careful holding-apart of what is already and what is not yet realized in terms of resurrection – but Paul cannot describe, or perhaps does not feel the need to describe, the specificities of the actual bodiliness of the resurrection body. The 'putting on' of the resurrection body is important even within this uncertainty, however, for reasons emphasized by Robinson:

> The new creation is not a fresh start, but the old made new ... It is this very body of sin and death which, transformed, "must put on incorruption" ... The building up of the Church is not the gathering of an elect group *out of* the body of history, which is itself signed simply for destruction. It *is* the resurrection body of history itself (Robinson 1952: 82–83).

There is, then, at least an uncertainty around the extent to which attributes of present human bodies might be carried over into resurrected human bodies – yet as we see with the somewhat arbitrary measurements which define micropenis and clitoromegaly (Preves 2003: 55), there is sometimes a fine line between where what is considered benign variety ends and what is considered pathology begins.

Augustine and the Fathers

Theologians after Paul found it equally difficult to define the nature of the resurrection bodies of humans. Caroline Walker Bynum, in *The Resurrection of the Body* (1995), considers at length the shifts in understanding of the nature of resurrection in the patristic and medieval periods. Bynum notes that bodily resurrection was a pervasive and persistent idea from the earliest times of Christianity, despite its somewhat counterintuitive nature: bodies are, after all, sites of pain as well as pleasure (Bynum 1995: 9).

Some of the early patristic writers are happy enough to claim that matter might be 'resurrected' in another body. Clement of Rome, for instance, who may or may not be the author of 2 Clement, uses the analogy of the death and rebirth of the phoenix; although, as Bynum notes, this is problematic not least because there seem to be two birds here, rather than a resurrection of the one identical bird (Bynum 1995: 25–26). Others are adamant that one type of matter cannot 'become' another. This is partly influenced by the problem of chain consumption: 'If meat and drink do not merely pass through us but become us, there will be too much matter for God to reassemble; on the other hand, if people really eat other people, even God may have trouble sorting out the particles' (Bynum 1995: 33). Tertullian believes that it is the *structure* of the body which has to be resurrected to preserve its integrity, and, for him, 'Everything intrinsic to what we are must reappear in the resurrected body' (Bynum 1995: 37). This and other patristic assertions raise questions about *which* aspects of the pre-resurrection body are integral to the person, and which, by analogy, need not necessarily be 'healed' or eradicated out of what are now deemed 'imperfect' bodies. Although Tertullian claims that defects are healed and mutilations undone in the resurrection body, he also 'even argues that if cosmetics and jewellery were essential to women they would rise from the dead' (Bynum 1995: 37). It does not seem unreasonable to argue that any appurtenance which has become 'integral' to the personal identity of an individual might be present in the resurrection body: a person born with a leg missing whose prosthetic leg has become central to their personal identity might find in the resurrected body a leg present where there was none before. A female-to-male transsexual who has invested much in a 'phantom' penis might well find a penis present in his resurrected body, as more faithful to the integrity of his (psychosomatic) self.

Bodies which have had different configurations during their time on earth provoke questions about which particular configuration, if any, will be reflected in the resurrected body. Both male and female bodies have already undergone enormous changes, particularly at puberty, before reaching adulthood. The bodies of women who have carried and borne children also appear different afterwards: is it the pre- or post-motherhood body that is the more perfect and will be retained in the general resurrection? What body might we expect for someone shorn of an undersized penis and brought up as a girl, who has decided to make the best of a bad gender-assignment despite experiencing gender dysphoria? Quite simply, it is neither possible nor desirable to specify what resurrection bodies will be like; but the one thing they will all share will be a redeemed body *story* rather than an unproblematically 'perfected' body by human standards. The link between embodiment and temporality is essential, and a feature of the creation, not of some kind of fall. Conceivably, the pain and prejudice attached to a particular physical configuration will melt away without thereby erasing either the beauty of that specific configuration, or the genealogical importance of the life lived in this body in its joy and woundedness.

Augustine is not the only one of the fathers who discusses the nature of the resurrection body in detail, but I focus on him here because he influenced later work to such a great extent; it was readings of Augustine in particular which set the agenda for medieval discussion (Bynum 1995: 97). In book 23 of *The City of God* Augustine discusses at length whether physical eyes will be superfluous in the resurrection where humans will always be able to see perfectly with 'spiritual eyes' – for, he asserts, 'When the body, freed from corruption, offers no hindrance to the soul, the saints will certainly need no bodily eyes to see what is there to be seen' (Augustine 1984: 1083). Augustine assumes a duality of soul and body, understanding souls to be 'higher' than bodies. It is therefore unsurprising that Augustine has such a troubled and ambivalent relationship with his own body (and particularly his sexuality), and that he finds specific questions about the nature of the resurrection body, as raised by 'pagans', to be absurd. Given that his earthly flesh is a troublesome, second-best kind of incarnation for Augustine, his interest is more in rational mind and will. It is important to bear this in mind as we reflect on Augustine's assertions about the resurrection.

Augustine avows that God 'promises that what was already there [in the earthly body] would not be lacking [in the resurrection body]; but that does not deny that what was lacking will be supplied' (Augustine 1984: 1055). So in Augustine's logic, at least some earthly bodies *are* lacking. The dead infant, for instance, 'has not attained the limit of its potential stature' (Augustine 1984: 1055). 'Stature', of course, might well have a more than literal sense. In Augustine's own argument regarding whether the 'sharing in Christ's stature' of Eph. 4.13 means that everyone's resurrection body will physiologically resemble Christ's, he suggests, 'Christ's "full stature" is reached when, with Christ as the head, all the members of his body come to maturity, represented by the peoples who accept the Christian faith' (Augustine 1984: 1056). This renders 'stature' analogous to status: 'recognition of one's personhood by others', or self-esteem promoted by the knowledge of one's existence in community. We could therefore argue that physical 'perfection' in the resurrection body is less significant than right relationship and the eradication of inequity in bodies. This applies to variant sex and gender just as much as to impairment.

Augustine insists that 'while all defects will be removed from [resurrection] bodies, their essential nature will be preserved' (Augustine 1984: 1057): he is arguing here that the muliebrity of women is *not* a defect but a part of their nature, and will therefore not be erased. The question is whether this can be extended to other characteristics beyond dichotomous sex. Augustine was not unaware of the existence of hermaphrodites, and indeed believed that although they were 'monstrous' they must have been descended from Noah, thus made by God, thus redeemable (Augustine 1984: 663); but within the medical paradigm of his time he would have deemed them 'truly' one sex with extra material from the other added on. In other words, extraneous matter could be removed from hermaphrodites without affecting their 'real' nature (and sex). We now appreciate that certain intersex/DSD conditions, particularly those involving genetic mosaicism or the possession of ovotestes, are, potentially, far more problematic to the Augustinian notion of 'refinement' if human sexed nature must supervene on sexual biology.

Augustine says, '[I do not] think that anything will perish which is present in any body as belonging to the essential nature of that body; but ... anything in that nature that is deformed ... will be restored in such a way as to remove the deformity while preserving the substance intact' (Augustine 1984: 1060). It would not, however, be possible to remove what Augustine would have viewed as the 'deformity' of the person with mosaicism (the 'extraneous' material of the minority chromosomes) without compromising the substance. It is difficult to imagine how God could 'restore' the substance of a deaf person without removing the deafness, or indeed the substance of a genetic mosaic without removing the mosaicism. For many people, the persistence of personal identity is closely bound-up with the persistence of particular aspects of their bodiliness (such as deafness). Moreover, argues Pailin,

> If post-mortem existence were to involve transformations which result in the elimination of differences, what once were distinct individuals would become indistinguishable items. In that case the result would not be the perfecting of persons, whatever that may imply. It would be their destruction (Pailin 1992: 164–65).

Rather, says Moltmann,

> Everything that is bound up with a person's name ... is "preserved" in the resurrection and transformed ... What is meant here is not the soul, a "kernel" of the person's existence, or some inward point of identity, but the whole configuration of the person's life, the whole life history, and all the conditions that are meant by his or her name (Moltmann 1996: 75).

Of course, it may be that the elimination of only some, undesirable differences, would alter but not entirely threaten the uniqueness and particularity of individuals. However, this still leaves the difficulty of *which* characteristics are and are not deemed desirable and why. Some people 'corrected' of intersex/DSD-related anatomy in late childhood or adolescence have spoken of mourning their stolen anatomy and the pleasure it brought. Bynum notes that, in the revering of martyrs' relics in the thirteenth century, it was the body parts significant to the martyrdom that were believed to remain incorrupt, for God marked with the most glory those parts which had 'earned' them (Bynum 1995: 222–23). Conceivably, then, the body parts which have proven most troublesome in the present realm either in themselves or because of the negative attention they have solicited will also be the body parts most celebrated; because they are the parts which have been treated and responded to as weaker or less honourable, even if such assignment is arbitrary, they might also be the members which deserve more glory.

It is possible to reread the thrust of Augustine's argument through the lens of intersex/DSD. Importantly, Augustine is also keen to emphasize the fact that, in the new creation, 'a time will come when we shall enjoy one another's beauty for itself alone, without any lust' (Augustine 1984: 1074). He assumes a perfected will be associated with perfected control, but this is surely based on the maximization of a particular image of God as judge, ruler, commander and inspector. More than the libidinal lust to which Augustine refers, I propose, the lust which will not affect appreciation of one another's beauty in the new creation includes the patriarchal-capitalist lust to perfect, correct, regulate, manage, dominate and homogenize. In the new creation, body and will shall be loosed from the meanings which our conscious strivings assign to them. We shall also be freed from the apparently insatiable lust to know definitively what constitutes a good body, what bodies are 'supposed' to be like – and freed to embrace the fact that scars and stretch marks testify to the processes which have happened in and through bodies: pregnancies, injuries, fluctuations in weight and all. These stories tell of changed states, not unequivocal loss or gain.

Body parts, in the resurrection, shall also be freed from the constraint of particular functions (Augustine 1984: 1087): this includes the genitals from genitive function. Bynum notes that Bonaventure echoes the Augustinian view that genitals will be part of resurrected bodies because femaleness is not inherently unnatural (Bynum 1995: 255) – but the genitals' new functions may not be identical to their present ones. Just as impairments will not necessarily be impairing in the new creation, so atypically-sexed bodies will not be at a disadvantage. If there is to be no marriage in heaven, and no procreation either, there is no need for gametes to mean what they have meant in this realm, or for particular gender roles to reinscribe procreative sexed norms. Sexuality itself may not be erased, but it will no longer be tied to the economic complications of biological procreation (Goss 2006a: 539). This is significant read 'backwards' as well as 'forwards', as Matzko McCarthy shows: if the 'fecundity' of the Christian community transcends biological family relationships, then biological fecundity, and marriage, are actually secondary and subsidiary to broader household and social relations. Children are 'a symbol of a married couple's prior unity and vocation in community'(Matzko McCarthy 2007: 94), not the other way round. The unitive action of sexual intimacy, then, speaks to a fertility and mutual commitment which goes far beyond the procreative and thus should not be deemed to be 'for' biological procreation either.

This is the separation from concupiscence which Augustine envisages, but far more so than he could have known, for it is a separation from and letting-go of false bases of reason and legitimacy, not just from sexual lusts but from all lusts to control, concretize and oppress. The 'erotic domination' of men over women in Latin America, which Althaus-Reid sees as deeply ingrained in patterns of heteronormativity (Althaus-Reid 2000: 197), is always already more than merely sexual. A yearning for fulfilment can become a longing for possession, which then becomes a desire to control. Erotic domination, caught up in structures of access to wealth, education, healthcare, personal safety, and religious and conceptual legitimacy, will not pass away until binaries are blurred and each referent is freed into a future truly different and truly transformed.

Rejecting Erotic Domination in the New Creation

Erotic domination limits the dissemination of some types of knowledge; this has been very evident in medical attitudes toward intersex/DSD and the level of information patients and families should be given. Parents have been given misleading or incomplete information (Karkazis 2008: 184–85), coerced into agreeing to surgical intervention (Arana et al., 2005: 19), advised not to speak to their children about their conditions (Karkazis 2008: 188–89), and denied the authority to decide what is best for their infant child where any surgery could be deferred. For example, the parents of Betsy Driver, born with CAH in the 1960s, were told that if she did not have her large clitoris removed she would 'grow up with gender problems, become a lesbian or commit suicide' (Arana et al., 2005: 31). Parents whose children have vaginoplasty are not always told that they will have to undertake or oversee regular dilation of the vagina, which may be 'distasteful or painful' (Liao and Boyle 2004: 460). Older individuals have not always been allowed full access to their medical records, or have had their specific diagnoses concealed from them (Arana et al., 2005: 19–24; Morris 2003). One woman with AIS says, 'At around 13, 14, I asked the surgeon again what he'd done to me ... I was so angry and upset that I'd been kept in the dark. But all he would still say was, "You don't need to know. It's not important. You'll find out when you're old enough to get married"' (Melissa, speaking in Mortimer 2002). The protocols Fausto-Sterling noted in 2000 still persist in some places:

> Medical manuals and original research articles almost unanimously recommend that parents and children not receive a full explanation of an [intersexed] infant's sexual status ... Physicians are to allege that the intersex child is clearly either male or female, but that embryonic development has been incomplete ... An intersexed child assigned to become a girl ... should understand any surgery she has undergone not as an operation that turned her into a girl, but as a procedure that removed parts that didn't belong to her as a girl (Fausto-Sterling 2000: 64–65).

But if impaired, intersexed and other bodies cannot partake in their own direction, agency and redemption; if this redemption cannot begin here and now; if those in these dead structures of erotic domination are not raised: then not even Christ is raised; and if Christ is not raised, our faith is worthless. If, however, our transformation out of our slavery to erotic domination *is* already beginning and has already begun, then we do have hope; and, in and through this hope, it is imperative that – as Pailin has suggested – bodies are understood as *already* showing forth the glory of their creator and co-creators, those who exist in and as them. Augustine muses,

> Perhaps God will be known to us and visible to us in the sense that he will be spiritually perceived by each one of us in each one of us, perceived in one another, perceived by each in himself; he will be seen in the new heaven and the new earth, in the whole creation as it then will be; he will be seen in every body by means of bodies (Augustine 1984: 1087).

For God to be seen 'in *every* body by means of bodies', and for God to be seen 'by each in himself', is a radically empowering vision. God-reflectiveness is not only for male bodies, for potent bodies, for able or independent bodies, even for human bodies. It is for the *whole* creation in its diversity and insubordination.

Humans cannot know for certain the nature of the bodily resurrection. However, it *is* possible to realize that the existence of bodies that still suffer and die prompts seeking their redemption as far as possible here on earth, an earth where the buds of the new creation have begun to open in the early sunshine of the eschaton. Impaired bodies, like other bodies, have prosaic, bodily needs; their redemption entails improvements in accessibility, pain control, and the provision of good-quality care, as well as the grander projects of changing assumptions about which bodies are considered full members of general and ecclesiastical society (see Lewis 2007; Anderson 2003; Nichols 2002; Eiesland 1994; Mairs 1996). In providing for the needs of people with disabilities, and making them visible in the fabric of public buildings and facilities, society openly acknowledges the reality of the impaired world. Moreover, the resurrection of human bodies is always profoundly linked with the resurrection of the rest of the creation too; Moltmann comments that the expression 'the resurrection of the flesh', as it echoes formulae about 'all flesh' in the Hebrew Bible, encompasses animals' flesh too (Moltmann 1996: 69–70). The new creation is thereby for the whole cosmos (Moltmann 1996: 70).

The transformation of excluded bodies in the new creation need not preclude their retaining some of the characteristics which have seemed the most problematic in their present circumstances, but these characteristics will be interpreted differently, just as signals of gender and sexuality need not forever be tied to their present meanings. The woundedness of Christ even after his resurrection figures significantly in the disability theology of Nancy Eiesland. Eiesland depicts Jesus as a disabled God 'who embodied both impaired hands and feet and pierced side and the imago Dei' (Eiesland 1994: 99). She says,

> God is revealed as tangible, bearing the representation of the body reshaped by injustice and sin into the fullness of the Godhead … Jesus, the resurrected Savior, calls for his frightened companions to recognize in the marks of impairment their own connection with God, their own salvation (Eiesland 1994: 99–100).

If Christ himself has a wounded body even after his resurrection, other instances of physical impairment and atypicality can also persist in resurrected human bodies. If God has come to inhabit this, Jesus' unexpected, non-dominant body, the way is opened for other unexpected, non-dominant bodies to reflect and live God too. The resurrected Jesus, with impaired hands and feet, *is* God's revelation of a new humanity – 'underscoring the reality that full personhood is fully compatible with the experience of disability' (Eiesland 1994: 100). The impaired Jesus' wounds are not to be vilified, nor to be pitied; they are marks of life experience, and signposts to a new kind of life too.

This imagery of God as impaired sets up a disjunction with the complete, powerful, independent God as espoused in the traditional philosophical perfections. It is not therefore possible to suppose that God's perfection and wholeness is like human perfection and wholeness (or what humans consider to be perfection and wholeness) but more so. God's ability, God's ableness, is not human ableness writ large. It is in God's limitedness as human that we encounter God, in the specific and limited body of Jesus. It is in and through other specific, limited bodies that we go on encountering God. Intersexed/DSD and impaired bodies exist on a conceptual cusp, and mean that notions of health, illness, goodness, legitimacy, pathology and perfection must continue to be problematized and reframed. For Eiesland, then, Jesus' wounds render impaired bodies far less 'other' than they are often perceived to be by those who are currently able; it is extremely significant, she suggests, that the risen Jesus invites people to touch his wounds, for this speaks of helping people to overcome their fear of coming into contact with 'distorted' bodies lest they should somehow 'catch' the impairment, or be tainted by association with someone who lacks conventional status (Eiesland 1994: 101). Other impaired bodies, too, 'announce the presence of the disabled God for us and call the church to become a communion of struggle' (Eiesland 1994: 115). (For further reflection on God/Christ as disabled, see Hull 2003b; Rappmann 2003; Swinton 2003; Tan 1998.)

Some Conclusions

The structures which have oppressed and excluded impaired and intersexed bodies are not unique, although impaired and intersexed people might have experienced and interpreted them uniquely because of their own particular social and historical circumstances. Importantly, as noted by Koyama (2006) and Dreger (2004), the types of medical paternalism criticized by intersex/DSD activists and by some people with disabilities are not limited to these particular conditions or situations. However, argues Eiesland, 'People with disabilities have been encouraged to see our needs as unique and extraordinary, rather than as society-wide issues of inclusion and exclusion' (Eiesland 1994: 28). This has led to the further alienation and 'othering' of people with disabilities from the rest of society. The Church's history of almsgiving and an acknowledgement of its duty to provide for marginalized people have come from good motives but, says Eiesland, have sometimes led to further segregation rather than to inclusion, because they have failed to emphasize the need of people with disabilities for political engagement, and have not encouraged people to full social and religious participation even in their 'nonconventional bodies' (Eiesland 1994: 74). Charity can and sometimes has emphasized the sense that the disabled person or group is there to be the grateful, passive recipient of a good, kind or generous act, rather than part of a whole community which reciprocally gives and receives good, kind and generous acts. This contrasts with the *mutual* concern between the members of the Body of Christ emphasized in 1 Cor. 12.12–31 (Horne 1998: 96).

Eiesland maintains, 'Many religious bodies have continued to think of and act as if access for people with disabilities is a matter of benevolence and goodwill, rather than a prerequisite for equality and the foundation on which the church as model of justice must rest' (Eiesland 1994: 67). Promoting the welfare of those marginalized for any reason is thereby seen by some church bodies as an optional extra, ethically supererogatory to the 'real business' of saving souls. Inclusion of people with disabilities, and other excluded groups, is understood as 'kindness' rather than righteousness. This may stem from a failure to see people with disabilities or other 'differences' (intersex/DSD conditions, homosexual orientations, and so on) as 'really' the church or the speaking group. These implicit ecclesiologies are insidious, further affecting who is and is not figured as part of the legitimate, conceivable mainstream. As we saw in Chapter 3, however, each human inhabits a single, unique body, but is also figured by participation in the Body and co-figures the Body too. Barbara Patterson thereby insists, 'If embodied symbols of Christian redemption are to be authentically inclusive, they must contain those other/silenced/hidden exemplars whose bodystories have been excluded. We must correct traditional misunderstandings of what kinds of bodies are appropriate sites for God's redeeming work' (Patterson 1998: 137). This includes intersexed bodies and *their* excluded stories, not generally discussed or even acknowledged despite the relative frequency of intersex/DSD conditions. To fail to engage with these stories and testimonies is to fail to engage with the stories and testimonies of a significant segment of our human community. This will always involve tension; intersex activist Thea Hillman writes, 'You and I have bodies that make people pray ... Oh God, my mother said, please make my daughter normal ... We have fallen so many times ... You and you and you and I are our mothers' worst nightmares. And yet they thank God each day for our perfection' (Hillman 2008: 19–20). Theologies which are theologies only of the privileged and those considered (overtly or otherwise) decent or legitimate cannot tell the whole tale of how humans have related and continue to relate to God. To repeat, disseminate and legitimate only the theological stories of those who have found a heterosexual binary model of sex and gender adequately represents them is to construct a theology made solely in our own image, rather than also in that of a God who is multiple, discomfiting and pluriform.

We have seen that healing a particular condition or state of being does not necessarily equal eradicating it. This is particularly important for intersex/DSD. Healing might be figured more usefully as reframing or resisting a particular narrative in order to claim one's own world as legitimate and good, and to query the incontrovertibility of a more dominant or accepted one. Hester comments,

> By addressing the strategies that have fostered illness, many intersex people develop counter-strategies of healing that include confronting slence and isolation by speaking out and/or creating communities of support ... Rhetorics of healing emphasize truth-telling ... and reject pathological labels and practices that have dominated the discourse (Hester 2006: 49).

Such a pluriform, discomfiting, resisting stance has been part of what has characterized much queer theology; it is this to which I turn in the next chapter, in order to explore to what extent the shifting, provisional methodologies and conclusions attached to queer might chime with the specific challenges of thinking with intersexed people and formulating theologies from intersex/DSD.

Chapter 6

RESISTING AND REAPPROPRIATING: INTERSEX/DSD AND QUEER THEOLOGIES

> "To queer"means to make strange – and Queer Interpretation is precisely a practise of making strange that which has been assumed to be familiar. [It] challenges domesticated constructions and interpretations ... and wonders about who such constructions and interpretations have closeted. As a strategy of liberation, Queer Interpretation seeks to expose and to challenge the violence that such constructions and interpretations have done to people's identities, experiences and bodies (Goss and Krause 2006: 684).

Many of the tensions acknowledged thus far in different readings of bodies and the concerns of different groups are repeated in the multiplicity, provisionality and open-endedness of queer theologies. It is these very tensions, however, which make queer theologies important resources for thinking theologically about intersex/DSD – since intersexed bodies are themselves loci of a plethora of simultaneous perceived oppositions (male/female, healthy/ pathological, normal/abnormal, natural/unnatural, powerless/ powerful, and so on). Queer theologies have the potential to be simultaneously 'about' more than one thing. As such, they may provide an important site of positionality for those people who find that their bodies or sex-gender identities cannot easily be categorized or demarcated – and whose bodies may be described as 'coming into being', not objects but *events* (Roen 2008: 51). Importantly, too, queer theologies are often categorized by their resisting attitudes to oppressive or abusive socio-political norms. Resisting is, as Goss and Krause note above, a project of 'making strange that which has been assumed to be familiar'. Seeking to resist the male-and-female picture of human sex which does not tell the full story of human experience might entail resisting theologies based in uncritical, unproblematized notions of gender complementarity.

I begin by grounding queer theologies in their genealogies from queer theory, and showing how differences and variations across queer theologies and queer theories create both problems and potential for using queer methodologies in considering intersex/DSD.

Problematizing Terms: Queer and Heteronormativity

Queer theory has been characterized in large part by a desire to challenge and contest sexual boundaries and essentialist portrayals of sex, and to stand in contrast to heteronormativity. This term began to be used in the early 1990s; Michael Warner, in a 1991 *Social Text* essay, writes of 'a new style of "queer" politics that ... has begun to challenge the pervasive and often invisible heteronormativity of modern societies' (Warner 1991: 3). Heteronormativity denotes a hegemony based in the overarching assumption that all humans are either male or female, that males who are sexually or erotically active should only be sexually or erotically active with females and vice versa, and that non-heterosexual activities and eroticisms are illegitimate or even pathological. A privileging of heterosexuality in society means that non-heterosexual relationships and activities have often come to be figured as 'unnatural'. This has sometimes been based on the fact that they are not procreative. The privileging of heterosexuality within Christianity specifically continues to be well-examined elsewhere. However, argues David M. Halperin,

> The heterosexual/homosexual binarism is itself a homophobic production, just as the man/woman binarism is a sexist production. Each consists of two terms, the first of which is unmarked and unproblematized – it designates "the category to which everyone is assumed to belong" ... – whereas the second term is marked and problematized: it designates a category of persons whom *something differentiates* from normal, unmarked people. The marked (or queer) term ... functions not as a means of denominating a real or determinate class of persons but as a means of delimiting and defining – by negation and opposition – the unmarked term (Halperin 1995: 44).

Heteronormativity assumes that heterosexuality is the natural, *a priori* default to which everyone should adhere; but, ironically, as Halperin notes, 'Heterosexuality defines itself implicitly by constituting itself as the negation of homosexuality ... Heterosexuality ... *depends* on homosexuality to lend it substance – and to enable it to acquire *by* default its status *as* a default, as a *lack of difference* or an *absence of abnormality'* (Halperin 1995: 44). Since heterosexuality perceives itself as unremarkable and the norm, it is continually figured as a locus from which to study 'other' or 'different' modes of socio-sexual behaviour – which deflects attention from heterosexuality's own incoherence (Halperin 1995: 47). As we have seen, people with intersex/DSD conditions, and particularly those with ambiguous genitalia, continue to be seized upon in their difference from the norms they have failed to meet. This exacerbates intersex/DSD's otherness in contrast with a supposed coherence or *a priori* self-evidence in non-intersexed bodies.

Heteronormativity also causes certain body parts – and *only* those body parts – to be ascribed with meaning thick enough to 'show' and to 'tell' a particular, immovable story of sex. Much heteronormative discourse relies on body parts being imbued with particular meanings which are then fixed as meanings so they can come to mean nothing else – which, in turn, results in particular configurations of body parts being taken as evidence for 'truths' about an individual, especially about the individual's legitimate gender and what that should mean for their upbringing and for appropriate expressions of their personality and identity.

Like heteronormative ideologies, mainstream Christian theologies, too, have tended to essentialize body parts, making claims that genitals, gonads and chromosomes unproblematically add up to a picture of sex on which gender and sexuality must also rest (as we saw in some of the reactions to transgender discussed in Chapter 4). This insistence on a conceptual either/or binary is belied and disrupted, however, by liminal or 'crossing' phenomena, whose implications are often read through the lens of methodologies, as in the social sciences, which quite deliberately 'do not rely on comparing polarised categories' (Kitzinger 2004: 454). Queer's propensity to disrupt binaries in this way can be clearly traced back to Foucault's and Derrida's work in the conceptual deconstruction of binary tropes such as oppressor/oppressed. Christian theology itself has important resources for challenging exclusion and alienation, and for the uncritical acceptance of would-be overarching metanarratives like those of compulsory heterosexuality. Queer theologies' particular acceptance of their own liminality and diglotic nature place them well to be in solidarity with bodies and entities existing on conceptual boundaries. Binary categories of sex and gender will not necessarily stand in God's new order; they are constructed in a context of dominance and exclusion, and, says Elizabeth Stuart, 'grate against the sign of baptism' (Stuart 2003: 108). She says, 'The Church as the community of the redeemed must play out gender and sexuality in such a way as to reveal their lack of eschatological significance' (Stuart 2003: 114).

Acknowledging the *provisionality* of human sex and gender must be a central conceit of theology done in solidarity with intersex/DSD and other unusual sexual or physical configurations. It stands in sharp contradistinction to theological anthropologies said to foreshadow the redeemed and perfected nature of humanity in relation to its God, and in which heterosexuality in particular is endowed with almost soteriological significance. As evidence for the mainstream fetishization of heteronormativity, Stuart cites 'conservative Christian resistance to inclusive language and gender-neutral imagery for God', for, she says, this opposition 'is based upon awareness that if God is not male then the social construction of gender, the heterosexual family, and gender theology cannot stand' (Stuart 2003: 93).

Positionality, Not Positivity: The Problems of Defining Queer

Queer, as marginalized by heteronormativity, is figured by Halperin as 'by definition, *whatever* is at odds with the normal, the legitimate, the dominant. *There is nothing in particular to which it necessarily refers* ... "Queer" ... demarcates not a positivity but a positionality vis-à-vis the normative – a positionality that is not restricted to lesbians and gay men' (Halperin 1995: 62). Queer, in these terms, is less about certainty and more about possibility – about exploring opportunities beyond those afforded within a heteronormative hegemony. Although this might make it very attractive as a locus of identity for those who have felt themselves excluded from restrictive forms and structures of social acceptance, such liminality or looseness of boundary also raises problems. As Halperin says, it is exactly queer's lack of specificity, which he identifies as its major advantage, which 'has also become its most serious drawback' (Halperin 1995: 64), since it might be appropriated by people who have not experienced the 'unique political disabilities and forms of social disqualification from which lesbians and gay men routinely suffer in virtue of our sexuality' (Halperin 1995: 64–65). This affects queer theologies too; Goss, responding to criticisms that queer theology risks eliding the 'hard fought differences' (Goss 1999: 52) rooted in maleness or femaleness, gayness or lesbianism, admits that 'queer does muddy the distinctions' (Goss 1999: 52). Guest claims that queer is a 'safe option' when compared to radical lesbian and gay theory, and that it might come to be 'applied by trendy straight-identified academics to bring a new dimension to their modules' (Guest 2005: 236) without necessarily having to address any of the more controversial or recalcitrant elements of lesbian and gay politics.

Queer has come to signify more than homosexual, but for many people its rootedness in LGBT history is crucial, and this in particular, they argue, must not be erased or forgotten through a broadening-out of definitions surrounding queer. It is worth remembering that homosexual activity is still illegal in over 80 countries, in some of which it is punishable by death (Baird 2004: 7, 36). Boone says, 'Envisioning future frontiers depends … on recognizing the pioneering efforts of lesbian feminist and gay pioneers working on the front lines and at the outposts of early gay activism, since the future frontiers envisioned by current queer theory and practice depend on knowing how we got to where we are … today' (Boone 2000b: 10).

Iain Morland and Annabelle Willox hold that it was HIV-AIDS which catalyzed queer into being a political *strategy* rather than an *identity*, through demonstrating that other socially- and biologically-based identities were no barrier to contracting HIV. They say, 'Queer activism's necessity and urgency lay in its challenge to the notion that identities could classify people, keep them safe, and keep them alive' (Morland and Willox 2005b: 2). In a sense, then, to speak of a 'queer identity' is counter-intuitive. Morland and Willox say, 'Queerness calls … for a celebration of a diversity of identities, but also for a cultural diversity that surpasses the notion of identity' (Morland and Willox 2005b: 3). Guest concurs, 'The idea of "being queer" is something of a misnomer given that queer theory problematizes identity categories and labels. Thus one "is" queer only insofar as one contests the confining labels that have been applied' (Guest 2005: 45). Queer thus is the discomfiting position of questioning categories of identity *per se* whilst simultaneously building on the political will and experiences of people for whom asserting the right to have a publicly visible and legal identity as lesbian or gay (for example) has been a long struggle.

Discussing possible definitions and understandings of queer in relation to formulating queer commentaries on the Bible, however, Ken Stone concludes that a broader use of queer than a lesbian or gay approach is expedient and that even the non-lesbian and non-gay contributors to his 2001 edited volume provide queer commentary 'inasmuch as they challenge conventional ways of bringing sexuality and the Bible into relation with one another' (Stone 2001b: 28). This also comes across in work by Loughlin and others (below).

Provisional, Multiple, Eschatological: Is Intersex/DSD Queer?

To what extent might there already exist affinities between queer and intersex/DSD? It has been suggested that 'as long as surgeons seek to (re)produce the reality of binary sexes' through corrective surgeries, medics 'inevitably keep producing queer embodied subjects' (Roen 2008: 48). In this account, queer is, ironically, almost an inescapable consequence of *reinforcing* the heteronormative binary. ISNA and Accord Alliance founder Cheryl Chase [Bo Laurent] argues,

> The value of the word "queer" is that it talks about difference that's stigmatized or transgressive without defining exactly what that difference is ... When intersexed people say "my body is OK like this" and "my identity is OK like this", those are queer things to do and to think (in Hegarty and Chase 2005: 79).

Whereas gay/lesbian, homo/hetero and similar either/or terms may be rooted in binary sex-gender expressions, intersex shakes up the terminology through being less prescriptive (Hegarty and Chase 2005: 80). It thus resonates with a concept of queer deliberately transcendent of exclusively homosexual concerns, and holds together apparent opposites as well as their interim shades of grey. Queer can encompass differing sexualities, sexes, genders and bodies without reducing any of them to sameness or enforced amorphousness with the others. Some people with intersex/DSD conditions have found it politically expedient to align themselves with LGBT groups:

> I recently graduated from U[niversity] of Mississippi, where I was on the campus Gay-Straight Alliance ... I was able to support diversity issues all across the board, and ... to educate others in intersex issues. I know some do not agree with intersex being included in Gay and Lesbian issues; however, being in Mississippi, intersex does not have a strong backing alone (I would have essentially been the only person) (Amy, at http:// home.vicnet.net.au/~aissg/amy.htm).

Others do not identify at all with homosexual and LGBT groups or with the queer label, even as a temporary or preliminary step.

Like transgender, intersex/DSD has sometimes been figured as *necessarily* queer, which risks homogenizing and misrepresenting intersexed people who do not identify in this way. J. David Hester argues that intersex/DSD effectively continues the queer project even better than queer itself can: 'The bodies of intersexed people expose the limits of the sex-gender dichotomy in ways not anticipated by gender constructionists and queer theorists' (Hester 2004: 217). Hester asserts that the very existence of intersexed bodies demonstrates that there are not one or two sexes, but hundreds. He argues that much gender and queer theorizing is still based in the notion of two stable, immovable sexes, negating the particularity of 'other' bodies. He concludes that 'multiple, pluriform, abundant sexes ... are the end of gender' (Hester 2004: 221), and comes to figure intersexed bodies as 'postgender'. This 'postgender' state might be considered, positively or negatively, as queering *all* gender. But Hester's assertion that 'intersexed bodies ... raise a threat to gender altogether' (Hester 2004: 223) might be a problematic one. ISNA, for example, insisted that claiming an intersexed identity does *not* necessarily entail situating oneself within a liminal or third gender (Herndon 2006), although some people with intersex/DSD conditions do identify as androgynous. What Hester's argument actually implies is that intersexed/DSD bodies are post*sex*, not postgender. ISNA's point was that it *is* possible to have a clear gender (which is not necessarily the same as a permanent gender) without having an 'unambiguous' binary sex. Just as it is not the sole 'job' or purpose of transsexuals to subvert non-transsexual, binary categories of sex and gender, so people with intersex/DSD conditions cannot, in and of themselves, stand for the 'end' of gender for all other persons.

Some intersexed individuals, then, do not identify as queer precisely *because* of its potential to blur borders. There has been a suspicion amongst some intersexed people that sympathy for a queer political project might entail assimilation into a homogenous conglomerate which cannot fully acknowledge the distinct concerns faced by its various sub-groups. As we have seen, this may be one reason for endorsing the use of 'DSD' rather than 'intersex' if this means that the emphasis will be on healthcare rather than politics: Preves notes, 'Identity-based political movements, such as the intersex movement, are problematic in that they simplify social categories as unified and generalized phenomena' (Preves 2003: 147). Preves found in 2003 that many of her subjects, despite their membership of intersex support groups, did not even identify as (politically) intersexed, let alone queer (Preves 2003: 7). Lih-Mei Liao, a clinical psychologist who works with individuals who have AIS and other intersex/DSD conditions, comments, 'My conversations with intersexed women ... have sensitized me to the possibility that criticism of [heteronormative socio-medical] discourses is at risk of being misunderstood as criticism of individuals who feel bound by them' (Liao 2007: 391–92). There are plenty of intersexed women who simply want to be 'normal', which they often understand as involving penetrative vaginal sex and marriage (Liao 2007: 398; Harper 2007: 34, 118), and they may not always find a welcome from lesbian and gay groups (Robinson 2006).

However, Morgan Holmes suggests that one aspect of the value of queer for intersex/DSD is that it might help to articulate the difference of intersexed bodies and experiences from those of others *despite* the fact that there may not be any very obvious difference between intersexed and non-intersexed anatomy to a lay onlooker – and despite the fact that some individuals with intersex/DSD conditions may not perceive a very great difference between their own bodily histories and those of other (non-intersexed, non-queer) people. Holmes says, 'It is my hope that in a future perfect world, queers will not question the validity of calling oneself "queer" even if no-one can *see* their difference' (Holmes 1998: 225). Holmes' comment draws upon the hope that queer can be a *positionality* – the outside to heteronormativity's inside – rather than a descriptor.

It is not heterosexuality in itself which is problematic, then, but unquestioned heterosexual *ideology* – or heteronormativity. Even Halperin acknowledges that it is not just homosexuals who can be marginalized by their sexual practices, and that queer might also embrace some heterosexual married couples (Halperin 1995: 62). Stone notes that some individuals involved in sexual practices which are not non-heterosexual *per se* but which are unconventional in other ways – like polyamory and S/M – have also claimed the terminology of queer for themselves (Stone 2001b: 27–8). Guest concurs that 'queer readings of scripture are potentially open to any persons who would apply the insights of queer theory and have relevant knowledge … or anyone who perceives that their marginalized or non-normative status could be usefully examined via the filter of queer theory' (Guest 2005: 45). Even if they do not feel an initial affinity with queer political activity, then, straight, heterosexual people with intersex/DSD conditions might also find it beneficial to reflect on queer's potential for querying the norms of sexuality – *not* because they are 'intersexed' (and may not wish to claim this as an identity), but because queer questions and critiques *all* structures of relation and sex-gender construction.

Butler asserts in *Bodies That Matter* that critiquing and thereby expanding the term queer might 'open up new possibilities for coalitional alliances' (Butler 1993: 229). She warns,

> If identity is a necessary error, then the assertion of "queer" will be necessary as a term of affiliation, but it will not fully describe those it purports to represent. As a result, it will be necessary to affirm the contingency of the term: to let it be vanquished by those who are excluded by the term but who justifiably expect representation by it (Butler 1993: 230).

In other words, if queer does not adequately represent intersex/DSD interests, this is a good and inevitable thing. As soon as it were possible to pin down and homogenize queer, it would already be limiting and useless. Rather, argues Butler, those who seek to reclaim 'queer' (particularly as a linguistic reaction to an initially shaming, accusatory term) exist *always already* in this oppositional context. Crucially, she says, 'queer' must be recognized as a profoundly contingent term, which must be allowed to take on meanings beyond those anticipated by people for whom it carries specific and limited political meaning; to 'become … a discursive site whose uses are not fully constrained in advance … [and] to expose, affirm, and rework the specific historicity of the term' (Butler 1993: 230).

Queer Theologies

The expansion of queer (particularly within queer theologies) in the last decade to include models and sites of subversion not specifically located in lesbian and gay discourse is the revision mooted by Butler. It is profoundly eschatological: ongoing, self-constituting (Hall 2003: 67), transformative and transforming, provisional, its meaning always being made and remade, done and undone. It is the 'already and the not yet'. It might be that queer's 'finality' will simply be its eventual existence as part of a world where even subversion and resistance to oppressive hegemonies and narratives have become commonplace; where successful hermeneutics no longer need to be extraordinarily suspicious, because the transformation of renewed human minds means that *every* hermeneutic strategy incorporates (literally) an awareness of its own story and backstory. Queer theologies might be sites for multiplicity and for diversities held in tension. Just as no real penis can ever live up to the mythic phallus emblematic of social agency and religious identity (Brenner 1997: 34–35), so no individual 'normal' body can meet every ideal. By their very nature, bodies are abnormal. Queer's promise lies in its capacity to demonstrate the *a priori* transgressive nature of bodies – crucial in refiguring and re-examining metaphors of perfection and completion as morally good.

Katrina Roen and others have shown that queer identity for people who have undergone surgical intervention on their bodies is, at least in part, a *production* of medical discourses. Where bodies 'corrected' by surgery are deemed 'monstrous' either before or after intervention, the monster can be read not solely as an excluded, stigmatized category, but also 'as a sign, a warning, a reminder that where health practices seek to police the bounds of normativity, danger lies ahead' (Roen 2008: 48). It is thereby society itself which becomes teratological. Similarly, 'queer theologies' not only involve positively reclaiming queer identities, but also implicate narrowly heteronormative theologies as the ones which are *really* hideous and grotesque.

Many theologians writing out of a queer socio-political setting have largely used 'queer' as a synonym for lesbian, gay and bisexual. I wish to focus in particular on Marcella Althaus-Reid's 'indecent' liberating-queer theology, as it employs a broader sense of queer not just rooted in LGBT. However, it is interesting to note some of the points brought out in other scholars' work in order to trace a trajectory through these fairly gay-centric queer theologies into wider socio-economic concerns. I am particularly concerned to draw out the strands which are not solely 'sexual' ones; Tat-siong Benny Liew has commented that 'queer theory, despite its emphasis on queering more than just the norm of heterosexuality, tends to inherit ... the centrality of sex and sexuality' (Liew 2001: 186). Liew fears other issues, such as race and ethnicity, have been pushed aside.

Some scholars, such as Grace Jantzen and Daniel T. Spencer, have explicitly expressed a desire to employ queer approaches which address ecological and political liberationist concerns too (Jantzen 2003; Spencer 2001: 196–97). For Jantzen, for example, queer theology is characterized by emphases on immanence, process, beauty and flourishing. This is in contrast to what Jantzen says have been the major themes of Christendom and of the secular West which is its legacy – namely, a deity outside, beyond and remote from humans, and a soteriology based in Jesus' swooping down to rescue humanity without being intimately involved with or affected by humans. The sacramental natures of trees, rocks and other elements of the created world have been sacrificed in favour of a God who pronounces laws and unbending truths from outside it (Jantzen 2003: 353; cf. Ruether 1993: 21). However, like Stuart, Jantzen believes that queer theology must still be rooted in theological history – for, although the latter is flawed, it can also be redeemed. Jantzen comments, 'Christendom has not only been the worst of my personal past but also the best of it; and the need to deal with the former requires a reappropriation and transformation of the latter. I will not become a more flourishing person by cutting off my roots' (Jantzen 2003: 345). Jantzen uses the image of the 'lesbian rule', a flexible piece of metal used by architects and builders to measure curved or irregularly-shaped forms, and suggests that such a philosophical device should be employed in queer processes of discourse. She explains, 'Though flexible, [the lesbian rule] is still a device for measurement. Not just anything goes ... Criteria are needed, even though not the straight criteria that set creed upon creed and consider any curves or queer angles an invitation for chipping away and bashing into conformity' (Jantzen 2003: 346). Truth, then, is still necessary for Jantzen, even in a queer theology; but the project of a queer theology must be to uncover *whose* truths have been negated or ignored by Christendom. She continues, 'By deliberately adopting a lesbian rule, the mirror we hold up to our culture, religious and secular, is a mirror of curves and corners that reveals the multiple distortions of discursive and material reality' (Jantzen 2003: 351). Jantzen believes that this will help to prevent our becoming simply 'flat mirrors of our contexts' (Jantzen 2003: 351), rather than drawing out the full possibility of our flourishing and becoming – becoming divine – from within. Jantzen's reading is invaluable in formulating a broad queer theology which is holistic and in considering how heteronormativity has linked with other oppressive and violent modes of thought to do with humans' relationships with other animals, with the environment and so on.

Similarly, Ken Stone's study on food, sex and the Bible in queer perspective (Stone K. 2005) demonstrates that it is neither possible nor desirable to think queerly about sex in distinction from thinking queerly about all kinds of other things. To ensure that queer theologies do not become tied into the sexual concern alone is especially important when considering the application of queer theological methods and concerns to intersex/DSD, given the way in which intersex/DSD has in the past sometimes been reduced to an adjunct to reflection on homosexuality rather than examined in its own right as an issue which affects far more than just sexuality.

The contributors to Loughlin's 2007 edited volume *Queer Theology: Rethinking the Western Body* cover a number of angles on queer theology: specific reflection on homosexuality (as in essays by Alison and Rudy); exploring possible flashes of 'queerness' across the tradition, in figures such as Gregory of Nyssa, the Beguines, St John of the Cross, and von Balthasar (Burrus, Hollywood, Hinkle, Muers); queer perspectives on ecclesiology, theological anthropology, Mariology and other issues of doctrine (Stuart, Ward, Beattie); and more besides. What is particularly interesting about this collection is the wide range of backgrounds and positions of the authors, both denominationally and in terms of political-sexual identity. Although several identify publicly as gay or queer, others are married heterosexuals – yet there is no sense here that they cannot also reflect 'queerly' on these matters. Loughlin holds in his introduction that *theology itself* has always been profoundly queer, even when it was culturally dominant, 'for it sought the strange; it sought to know the unknowable in Christ' (Loughlin 2007b: 7). For Loughlin, theology is therefore inherently counter-cultural, and 'relativizes all earthly projects'; when it does not do so, it becomes idolatry. 'Queer' has a specific history, in terms of insult given and insult turned; it is exactly for this reason, however, that it has potential beyond solely homosexual concerns. Queer readings will find that variant gender and sexuality are less alien to the tradition than the tradition would like to suppose; even so, Loughlin argues, 'unlike gay, [queer] names more than erotic interests ... and ... marginal, minority interests' (Loughlin 2007b: 8). Although the authors of this volume do not specifically discuss intersex, then, and despite the fact that some of the essays are strikingly apolitical, their queer reflections on issues such as Barth's understanding of human sex and gender (Ward 2007) and the more-than-biological meaning of fecundity in marriage (Matzko McCarthy 2007), are highly pertinent and fruitful reframings of the tradition which may prove useful tools in constructing specific theologies from intersex.

More overt links with intersex may be seen in Guest, Goss, West and Bohache's 2006 volume, *The Queer Bible Commentary*. Several of the contributors have explicitly begun to consider how queer readings of the biblical narratives might open conceptual space for considering intersex/DSD embodiment. In his entry on Genesis, Michael Carden uses Gross' work on intersex and scripture (Gross 1999) in his discussion of the 'primal androgynous unity' (Carden 2006: 25) traceable in the creation stories, and comments that 'the hermaphrodite inhabits the intermediate world of the ancient gender hierarchy' (Carden 2006: 28). Gross discusses a rabbinic tradition which suggests that Abraham and Sarah were both intersexed (Gross 1999: 71–73). Another rabbinic text suggests that Adam was originally two-sexed before the two halves were separated. It is fascinating to note that at least some rabbis 'did not see intersex conditions as falling under the condemnation of the canon of Hebrew Scripture' (Gross 1999: 73). This is why, claims Carden, 'to become one flesh, a man must give up his gender privilege and with his wife descend to the intermediate level, neither male nor female' (Carden 2006: 28). David Tabb Stewart also claims a more-than-binary stream elsewhere in the Hebrew Bible, saying that 'what appears to be a binary gender system in the D-source (Deut. 22.5) and P-source (Gen. 1.27) ... looks like a three-gender system in the J-source (Gen. 2.20–21): male, female and androgyne or *ha-'adam*, "the human"' (Stewart 2006: 92).

Queer theologies, then, might have the potential to overcome some of the binaries entrenched in mainstream theology and in Western heteronormative discourse in general. This liminality is important in exploring queer theologies in their broader sense, located not just in lesbian and gay discourse but in a broader project of subverting sexual and social norms. For Althaus-Reid, such a queering of the norms in which theology has been located and which it has bolstered is vital because it disrupts 'heterosexual ideology ... as a central discourse of authority', and 'liberates the assumed reference of theology and therefore liberates [God] from assumptions and ideological justifications' (Althaus-Reid 2004b: 143). She says, 'The Queer God is the God who went into exile with God's people and remained there in exile with them' (Althaus-Reid 2004b: 146). Althaus-Reid stresses repeatedly that queer theologies must comprise theological reflection that does not negate or gloss over the sexuality and sexual activity of those who formulate it (Althaus-Reid 2000: 28), for to compartmentalize sex out of the rest of one's lives is to remain closeted, and risks 'duplicity between the realms of a public and a private theology' (Althaus-Reid 2000: 88). But queer theologies have the potential to interrupt not only obviously sexual understandings of God and humanity but also those, for example, which emphasize the epistemic distance between God and humanity and insist that God cannot suffer or change. Queer readings and traditions are not *exclusively* sexual – it is simply that they do not *negate* the sexual. They are sexual and non-sexual at the same time; they are more than one thing at once, just like the deity to whom they appeal.

Stuart gives a particularly interesting queer reading of scripture in her entry on Proverbs in *The Queer Bible Commentary* (Stuart 2006). She argues that the fairly banal, unremarkably patriarchal, workaday set of guidelines in this book is suddenly broken into by the irruption of the figure of Wisdom (also called Sophia or Hochma) in Proverbs 8. Stuart says, 'Hochma is wisdom in drag. She is the excessive performance of the wisdom outlined in the main body of the text, and so excessive is the performance that previous understandings of wisdom are blown apart' (Stuart 2006: 328). This aspect of the divine is 'at the heart of human activity':

> She has built her house among the people and prepared a feast to which she invites all (9.1–6). She is the expression of the divine delight in humanity (8.31). This is a God who is ... at the heart of

human experience, the most difficult and dangerous God of all, who becomes tangled (sometimes hopelessly) in our own hopes and desires (Stuart 2006: 328).

Hochma is thus 'a subversive performance of divinity, a God of the streets' (Stuart 2006: 328). Whereas Hochma or Wisdom has traditionally been held up in contrast to the 'strange woman' (often translated, tenuously, 'loose woman') or 'Dame Folly' who seduces young men with her wiles (as in Prov. 7.6-7), in fact, proposes Stuart, the 'strange woman' could simply be Hochma perceived from a radically different angle. They have striking similarities: perhaps Hochma is actually 'acting up', parodying the representation of herself as a prostitute. The 'strange woman' seduces a young man; Hochma seductively 'offers the divine ... to all and at the heart of human life' (Stuart 2006: 330-31). Both figures are 'loud, bold, challenging and demanding' (Stuart 2006: 329). Hochma 'undoes' God, disrupting God's assumed gender, making God immanent to human experience but not thereby 'any less easy to grasp or any less mysterious' (Stuart 2006: 328). Stuart concludes,

> We sense that Hochma will confront us with Otherness and foreignness and with ideas that will challenge and undo our own ... In the figure of Hochma (and the Strange Woman) God refuses to be easily named or understood and therefore ultimately avoids manipulation and control ... There is a greater point than social transformation for queerness and an ultimate target for it and that is the divine life. The divine is queer and summons us all into queerness (Stuart 2006: 336-37).

God is *at once* Hochma and the Strange Woman, seductress and Spirit, immanent to human concerns such as sex and beyond them. God turns over the social norms and constructions which God is often invoked to endorse and maintain. A God as queer as Stuart's Hochma might profoundly inhabit theologies of intersex/DSD where difference cannot be homogenized or erased and where God by definition breaks out of human models.

Stuart's work points to the queer in other aspects of Christianity too. Just as the Trinity is not strictly procreative, in that the Spirit is not the 'child' of the Father and Son despite 'proceeding' from them both (at least in Western orthodoxy), so not every human relationship need be biologically procreative (Stuart 2003: 97). Actually, reproduction and dissemination in this new order is about hospitality to strangers, those outside the biological kinship group, rather than care only for biological children and 'insiders' (Stuart 2003: 95). So queer theologies possess the conceptual tools to refuse the idolization of the family and heterosexual, procreative relations (Stuart 2003: 91), which should stand them in good stead to explore other non-heteronormative structures of family and relationship. The objection that non-heterosexual or otherwise non-normative relationships are 'unnatural' – often invoked in opposition to non penis-in-vagina or at least non-reproductive sexual activity – is also subverted in some strands of the Christian tradition, says Stuart, for even God is portrayed (in Rom. 11.24) as transcending what is 'natural' by admitting non-Jews into salvation history (Stuart 2003: 96). Christians, too, 'are called to imitate their God in acting *para phusin*, in excess of nature' (Stuart 2003: 106). Whether or not an action or event is 'natural' thus cannot be appealed to as the be-all and end-all of whether it is legitimate, for nature itself is disrupted as a category. For this reason, demarcations of righteousness and unrighteousness are also disturbed: Bohache comments that Matthew's Gospel says Joseph was a righteous man, but that actually, if Mary had become pregnant as the result of an affair (likely Joseph's initial assumption), the strictly 'righteous' thing according to the Law would have been to put her and her child to death (Bohache 2006: 495). Joseph thus does what is technically *un*righteous in marrying her, but this act of unrighteousness prompts Matthew to call him righteous. Bohache says,

> In this way Joseph subverts heteropatriarchal expectation; he spoils the spoiled system of sexual double-standard that would demand a woman's life. As a result of his queer act, Mary and Jesus are neither ostracized nor put to death, but allowed to live and prosper: God's Messiah is born because of a man who acts outside of his heteronormative role (Bohache 2006: 496).

Such holy recalcitrance is queer indeed.

Thus far I do not know of any work which specifically explores the religious beliefs and experiences of people with intersex/ DSD conditions. Such work is long overdue, particularly since, anecdotally, at least some intersexed individuals have felt rejected and dehumanized by heteronormative Christian churches. However, we might conjecture that reflecting on the spiritualities of people who identify as queer will shed light on the experience of relating to God and religious communities as people whose sex-gender-sexuality configurations are deemed deviant or imperfect in at least one respect.

Christophobia, Violence, and Birthing the Divine

Peter Sweasey, in *From Queer to Eternity,* draws on interviews with lesbian, gay and bisexual people who identify as religious or spiritual, and broadly queer. Although the interviewees' beliefs and attitudes toward religion are diverse, it is possible to trace some recurring tendencies. For example, Sweasey believes that many queer people have tended to reject *all* religion as oppressive, or 'not for queers', simply because their experience of *some* aspects of religion has been negative. Having battled not to allow one crucial aspect of their identity – their sexuality – to be negated, it would be ironic, says Sweasey, if queer people have subsequently colluded with their 'oppressors' in keeping spirituality hidden, leading to the subsuming of another, equally momentous aspect of identity (Sweasey 1997: 24). Rather, suggests Sweasey, 'If the ranks of religious believers include not only homophobes but also queers, we steal their trump card. Instead of saying we don't want to play your stupid game, we're saying, we're already playing, and what makes you think you can set the rules here?' (Sweasey 1997: 79). This is echoed in a later essay, by Bohache, who attempts specifically to trace a queer Christology. Bohache says,

> There is ... [a] deep-seated feeling among many gays and lesbians that Jesus Christ is not an option for them, that he, as the embodied representative of God, hates them, and that they have no place in either Christ's church or the Kingdom of God ... This is a mindset that I call "christophobia". It is as factually bankrupt as homophobia and just as pernicious, for it separates many spiritually focused and religiously gifted individuals from a path that could bring them the fulfilment they have sought and been unable to find elsewhere (Bohache 2003: 12–13).

The Christophobia of the queer community and the homophobia of the non-gay Christian community must therefore *both* be overcome. Bohache compares the development of a queer image of Christ with that of portrayals of Jesus which transcend historical maleness and historical race, so that abused women might find affinity with a Christa or Chinese people with an ethnically Chinese

Christic.[1] Moreover, he states, 'The queer consciousness ... seeks to critique heteronormativity and heteropatriarchal patterns of domination. This is where a queer Christology intersects with biblical studies, for we can discern from Jesus' recorded words and deeds how he felt about power relations' (Bohache 2003: 19). Since, says Bohache, the 'Christ-presence' dwells in *all* people (Bohache 2003: 21), it is not limited to one historical figure, and therefore is not exclusively epitomized by that one historical figure. He argues that if every human is created in God's image, then God *is* every race, age, ability, sex and sexuality – and yet is also more than these, for God still continues to create (Bohache 2003: 22).

Bohache's queer Christology also resonates with D'Costa's view that, as Mary carried Christ in her body, so all humans can be co-sustainers of the divine (D'Costa 2000: 36). Bohache says,

> God calls us to do great things. For Mary, that great thing is conceiving the Christ in her body. For queers, that great thing ... means conceiving of our self-worth, our creativity, and our birthright as children of God ... who can give birth to the Christ. This is good news for every oppressed person, but especially for queers, who are often led to believe that we cannot and should not give birth to anything (Bohache 2003: 26).

Birthing is important symbolically as a gateway through which new ideologies and social structures are brought about; it is not coincidental that much panic and secrecy around bodies with intersex/DSD conditions takes place soon after birth, since the inability of parents and doctors to identify sex easily in the case of genital ambiguity is really a case of an inability to initiate the child seamlessly into a particular social and ideological story. Control of birthing is control of what is and is not allowed to move through into membership of the legitimate conceptual community, but the separation of 'birthing' from procreation in Bohache's narrative means that 'birthing' is no longer limited to those who can or will have fertile, contraception-free penis-in-vagina sex. The privileges afforded nuclear families and their leadership, so often a foot in the door of leadership in churches and in wider society (despite what might charitably be called an ambivalence toward biological

---

1. See Clague 2005a and 2005b, and Murphy 1990, for fascinating explorations of the problems and potential attached to representations of the female Christ. See also Cornwall 2008b.

family in Jesus and Paul, and Christianity's strong tradition of monastic and non-kinship communities), are not, in this account, the domain of heterosexuals alone – and thus not the domain of clearly-sexed people alone either. This should resonate strongly with a Christian tradition whose children have been gained through adoption as well as birth, who are born again when already old, whose founder himself transgressed biological kinship loyalties (as in Mt. 12.46–50). Clear sex and biologically fertile relationships are less necessary in this new kind of economy, which renders intersex/DSD far less problematic on both these counts.

Truth-telling

Ken Stone appeals to queer's tendency to break down divisions between what have been traditionally considered public and private modes of discourse and 'realms of intimacy' (Stone K. 2005: 69–70) so that matters of sex and sexuality need not be hushed up in queer discourse, or kept out of the public sphere. Similarly, Robert Hamilton Simpson warns that cognitive dissonance 'between theological reflection and lived sexual experience' leads to 'flawed pastoral practice' (Simpson 2005: 99), fatal if the church is to care for the whole person. Gay people in particular tend to be demonized as a group solely on the basis of this one aspect of their identities, their 'tendency to commit acts considered to be gravely objectively disordered' (Alison 2002: 400).

This resonates with the experiences of some people with intersex/DSD conditions in church settings; one Southern Baptist ex-pastor in the US reports losing his pastorate of five years because people did not understand his chromosomal make-up as a genetic chimera, and because of opposition to his web-based ministry to intersexed and transgender individuals. This man was told by his Director of Missions that he needed counselling to rid himself of his 'female side'. Other pastors, whom he had considered friends, cancelled his preaching engagements at their own churches. Sally Gross reports that her superior in the Dominican order while she was a Roman Catholic priest seemed to connect her intersex/DSD condition with paedophilia and sexual abuse, and 'was almost determined to see this as a perverse moral choice' (speaking in van Huyssteen 2003). Although it is important to recognize that intersex/DSD conditions are, for many people, first and foremost *medical* conditions rather than sexual identity conditions; and that some church communities may be more likely to accept individuals whose difference stems from a biological condition like Klinefelter's syndrome than from what appears to be a 'chosen' or otherwise non-biologically-caused state; this distinction is not in fact a particularly helpful one. It is not that people with intersex/DSD conditions must be welcomed as full members *because* their condition is biological and unchosen; it is more that a disruption is needed of the binarization of what biological/non-biological, chosen/unchosen, and normal/pathological are and imply in the first place. To figure intersex/DSD as non-ethically-reprehensible because it is biological does not aid a subversion of the norms which render other disruptive states such as transgender pathological or ethically perverse. Moreover, other unchosen physical states such as impairment have not, as we have seen, entirely escaped being figured as having an underlying moral implication, so to call something ethically non-problematic simply on the grounds that it is biological does not go far enough.

As we saw in the testimonies of people who had undergone surgery, being lied to and kept in the dark was often felt to be more harmful than knowing more fully about an intersex/DSD condition. In this way, too, the truth-telling bent of queer theories and queer theologies might inform future models of best practice for responding to intersex/DSD. It might be retorted that queer theology is no more bound to tell the 'truth' about God than are the traditions it critiques; however, what is crucial about the kind of queer theology exhorted by Althaus-Reid and others is that it stands in the liberating-prophetic tradition, with its 'plumb-line' of justice, explicitly focusing on issues of marginality and poverty, not only difference. Ward comments that 'theology ... needs to understand how time-conditioned is its language and thought; how what it assumes it knows needs to be critically assessed. It needs to understand also the kinds of bodies its own discourse has been implicated in producing' (Ward 2004: 74). This is what it really means to speak truth in love.

Counter-Cultural Embodiment and Transgressive Sex

As we have seen, it has sometimes been argued that existence as man or as woman is the only authentic expression of human existence, and that any other configuration should not be embraced. However, as we have also seen, such assertion may belong more to heterosexual norms than to more inherent truths about humanity. Embracing the reality of one's body as it is – as intersexed or as impaired, for example – might be an important aspect of building a positive identity. The truth of embracing a body which does not bolster heteronormative standards is profoundly counter-cultural and even prophetic.

Another possible advantage of coming to religion out of a queer positionality, suggests Sweasey, is that many queer people claim to have what might be considered an unusually strong sense of being embodied, and a lack of shame about bodies and sexual encounter which contrasts, they assert, with that found in society at large (Sweasey 1997: 101). Hearon concurs that 'GLBTI communities revel in bodies. They know, in a way that heterosexuals can often ignore, that you cannot really know who you are until you come to grips with who you are in your body' (Hearon 2006: 612). Theologies which endorse and celebrate even bodies which have been problematic in other contexts (such as socio-medical constructions of sickness and health) might provide a welcoming home for people who feel ambivalent about their own bodies – including many people with impairments or intersex/DSD conditions. People with intersex/DSD conditions who have not undergone surgical intervention and who do not like their bodies in their natural states might be encouraged that their bodies need not be typical in order to be beautiful or celebrated; those who feel alienated from their bodies as a direct result of surgery or other medical intervention might be encouraged to mourn or grieve the loss of their erstwhile bodies as an ongoing process even as they come to inhabit their present ones more peacefully.

In general, suspects Sweasey, queer people may be less likely than others to 'close off' possible areas of experience, or of belief, before having explored them. The embracing by queer people of unusual sexual lifestyles and activities can either be perceived as nihilistic decadence lacking benchmarks for what is desirable, respectable (or, indeed, moral) activity, or, more positively, as a refusal to be limited by many of the arguably arbitrary inhibitions which quash non-queer people. There might still, and always, be aspects of some behaviours held to be incompatible with certain tenets of Christianity: it would be difficult to argue that any kind of non-consensual sex, such as rape or sex with children, could be deemed just or pleasurable for everyone concerned. However, in the questioning of heterosexual norms there is potential for at least considering the possible spiritual and theological merits of non-'vanilla' sexual activity. For example, Rudy holds that communal sexual activity, as in some gay settings, need not be demonized as impersonal, non-relational or entirely alien to Christian ideals, but can in fact speak deeply of initiation, hospitality and welcome in ways that marriage-centred families (often deemed the only legitimate arena for sexual activity) do not always manage (Rudy 1996). Goss makes a particularly interesting reading of the gender codes in Ephesians 5 in light of polyamory:

> When the church is understood as a collective of countless men and women, married and unmarried, with a variety of sexual orientations and gender expressions, then Christ becomes the multi-partnered bridegroom to countless Christian men and women ... Christ is polyamorous in countless couplings and other erotic configurations ... The lover is a sexual outlaw, not a bridegroom as the sanitized Jewish and Christians read the text (Goss 2004: 61).

Of course, the erotic need not (and should not) be inevitably conflated with the genital; it is possible to envisage sexual and erotic loves for multiple persons without necessarily engaging in genito-sexual activity with all these persons. A reading like Goss's, though, at least exposes the *oddness* of the one-body-many-parts imagery for the Church, and what its logical extension might imply for the bridegroom/bride imagery too.

'Lazarus, Come Out!': Friendly Strands

Such readings as those which appear in *The Queer Bible Commentary* flesh out another tendency identified by Sweasey – that is, the working by queer individuals to draw out 'friendly' strands from a largely unfriendly tradition, sometimes reclaiming phrases, pronouncements, poems or stories which resonate with their own particular experiences (Sweasey 1997: 32; Simpson 2005: 103; Althaus-Reid 2000: 114; West 1999: 33–34). However, the exercise of tracing queer-friendly strands in scripture is also, often, about a simple acknowledgement that they are not there; Timothy R. Koch stresses that his homoerotic approach to reading scripture does not mean insisting that 'the Bible ... really likes us!' (Koch 2001: 11). Robin Hawley Gorsline, in his commentary on 1 and 2 Peter (Gorsline 2006) comments,

> What queers may not do is take this text [1 Peter] as a sourcebook
> for strategy and tactics to achieve liberation. Instead, we may
> read it with profit if our goal is to learn what not to do, how not
> to be in alliance or solidarity with the oppressed ... Queers
> recognize the author of 1 Peter as one of the "don't rock the
> boat" types, but thanks to the author's address to others in his
> community we also recognize our fellow boat-rockers (Gorsline
> 2006: 732).

Carden concurs that to depatriarchalize or homosexualize a text
like Genesis would be to negate the extent to which it simply *is*
ancient, alien, and strange to modern sensibilities (Carden 2006:
25). Similarly, says Schneider, queer female exegetes might 'have
to face the very real possibility that the Bible is simply not a source
for imagining female homoeroticism in the divine-human
relationship except through extrapolation by example from the male
tales read queerly here' (Schneider 2001: 220).

However, this does not necessarily negate the value of using
such a 'queer' methodology – of reading *into* a biblical text more
than is strictly there as well as reading *out* of it. Even the former
kind of reading, though it transcends the text itself, might 'yield
[fruit] for our contemporary thoughts about a divine being whose
founding tales *could* include such a deed' (Schneider 2001: 215).
Moreover, whilst it might be argued that some queer readings of
certain traditions are inappropriate or anachronistic, it is also
important to be mindful of the fact that modern heteronormative
readings may be no more faithful to the spirit of the text. Quero
argues that the process of queering the past via historical texts 'is a
double process that implies the opening up of the space of the
historical event to new discourses as well as the opening up of the
methods and procedures of the sciences attempting to analyse that
case' (Quero 2004: 27). He argues, 'To queer the past is not to
transplant *gays*, *lesbians*, *bisexuals* or *transsexuals* into the past, but to
disrupt monolithic discourses that oppress historical periods' (Quero
2004: 28). So it is *possible* that David and Jonathan were lovers, as is
sometimes claimed on the basis of passages such as 1 Sam. 18.1–5
and all that ensues; it is also *possible* that their ardent, passionate
friendship was just that, with no specifically sexual or 'romantic'
element. Stone remarks that it would be anachronistic to assume
that, in the social world of the Hebrew Bible, the persons with
whom one experienced the greatest closeness and intimacy were

the same persons with whom one engaged in sexual activity (Stone K. 2006: 208). However, he also notes that it is clear that the author of Samuel clearly does not assume all the sexual regulations of Leviticus, so that there was not necessarily a blanket prohibition on male-male sexual activity (Stone K. 2006: 207). Stone comments that, although 'love' in the ancient context could mean a political relationship, not just a sexual one, 'the specific comparison that David makes between Jonathan's "love" and "the love of women"… is somewhat unusual even within the framework of those ancient Near Eastern political "love" relations' (Stone K. 2006: 206). Stone concludes that, whilst it is not possible to arrive at any definitive answer about the exact nature of David and Jonathan's relationship, the very fact that it has multiple interpretations can be read as 'queer' (Stone K. 2006: 208).

More than taking on the biblical narratives wholesale, then, it may be useful when formulating queer and intersex/DSD theologies to employ what Althaus-Reid terms 'textual poaching' (Althaus-Reid 2000: 112; see also Sugirtharajah 2003: 82–84). She notes, for example, that 'one element which people at the margins usually "poach" is that elusive fluidity of Jesus, that fluidity which … presents round edges and becomes ambiguous' (Althaus-Reid 2000: 112). This also chimes with Koch's suggestion that 'cruising' the Scriptures might be more instructive or realistic for queers than some of the other apologetic methodologies which have tended to be employed (Koch 2001). It is possible that people with intersex/DSD conditions might also be able to draw on some of these strands, not necessarily in identical ways to LGBT people (which might erase the specificity of all their particular situations) but in ways appropriate to themselves. As R.S. Sugirtharajah notes in his reflection on textual poaching as a postcolonial reading strategy, texts 'derive their meaning in their encounter with context and reader. They are like sojourners who hardly ever go back to the habitat they left behind' (Sugirtharajah 2003: 84).

Autobiography and Incarnation

Isherwood and Althaus-Reid argue that queer theology must be profoundly autobiographical, drawing on and giving import to 'experiences which traditionally have been silenced in theology' (Isherwood and Althaus-Reid 2004: 6). These might include sexual experiences, particularly those from outside the heteronormative stable, but an appreciation of multiple sexual experiences is also a way into an appreciation of multiple human locations and experiences generally (Isherwood and Althaus-Reid 2004: 6). As we have seen, autobiographical writings are also particularly important in considering the experiences of people with intersex/DSD conditions, especially given that under the early surgery paradigm these voices have often been negated or undervalued. The work of Morland is an important reminder that the voices narrating intersex/DSD are always multiple, that there is no such thing as monolithic intersex/DSD experience any more than there is monolithic female or black experience. Engaging with polyphonic narratives means engaging with this tension, the 'queerness' of what may appear to be a lack of cohesion or consensus in intersex/DSD history, which will also feed into intersexed theologies.

We have seen that notions of incarnation, and engagements with bodiliness which may be simultaneously positive and problematic, are central to theologies from impairment and transgender. Intersex/DSD, too, can be a site for embodied theologies which refuse to downplay the real and recalcitrant qualities of bodies – bodies which may be deemed problematic either by individuals or by communities, but which are also loci for God's solidarity and interaction in and with human beings. Isherwood and Althaus-Reid say,

> [Queer theology] identifies moments of sexual resistance in church traditions, or even alternative church traditions; it exposes the profound homophobia of theology and the sexual assumptions in doctrines; and finds neglected areas of attention in theological discussions. More than anything else, queer theology is an incarnated, body theology (Isherwood and Althaus-Reid 2004: 6).

Incarnation is crucial to this theology, they argue, because in the incarnation of Christ is held the tension between human and divine which opens the way to transcend other seemingly gaping chasms of signification and difference too. This occurred and occurs in a bodily body, one made of flesh, one born messily and bloodily (Isherwood and Althaus-Reid 2004: 7) – which means that other messy, bloody, fleshly, libidinous and rejected bodies can also be part of this human-divine story. The claim that 'male theologians have preferred to distance themselves from these all too earthy moments' (Isherwood and Althaus-Reid 2004: 7) is not quite a fair one, but the point stands that, wherever theology tends unproblematically to elevate the spiritual over the carnal, it also tends to displace real bodies with their real needs and desires (including sexual needs and desires) (Althaus-Reid 2004a: 99).

The embracing of uncertainty and provisionality in queer and marginal theologies, particularly their acceptance of multiple genders and sexualities, is often uncomfortable for a Church which has tended to thrive on givenness, singularity and grand metanarratives (Isherwood and Althaus-Reid 2004: 5). But the most dearly-held doctrines of theology have taken decades and centuries to be thrashed out, although the Church may behave today as if the Nicene Creed had been found neatly written out and folded inside the grave-clothes in the empty tomb. Messiness in the tradition should not be cleaned-up, sanitized or bowdlerized, for to do so is to make neat and safe what is actually recalcitrant and profoundly risky and to limit the spheres 'appropriate' for human encounter with the divine. Like queer theologies, theologies from intersex/DSD might be considered very dangerous, threatening heteronormative structures and economies based on exclusion and lack. But this is a good danger, for it is a danger which comes in admitting the contingency and limitedness of human constructs. Part of embracing the 'danger' in queer theologies, then, must also always acknowledge that even dearly-held productions of God, Jesus and the Virgin rest in particular (usually heteronormative) sexual narratives (Althaus-Reid 2000: 96); giving up 'beloved' sexual/theological ideologies which one has come to realize are based in injustice might be as painful and complicated as leaving an abusive lover (Isherwood and Althaus-Reid 2004: 3). But even formulations of the Godhead *must* be 'indecented', for even God has been 'genderized' through prayers and proclamations.

There have, as Althaus-Reid owns, already been multiple theological reflections and enquiries surrounding the femininity of Christ and God (Althaus-Reid 2004a: 104), which might be said to have exposed and undermined the 'masculinist' bent of much classical theology. However, importantly, argues Althaus-Reid, these various enquiries have not successfully destabilized the category of *sex itself* (Althaus-Reid 2004a: 106). She says, 'Not only is there an important theological contribution to the formation of heterosexual ideologies in the history of the churches, but ... sexual ideological formation is constitutive of the theological praxis itself' (Althaus-Reid 2004a: 106). In fact, it is possible to go beyond Althaus-Reid, and to say that theology has been part of formulating not only heterosexual ideology but the ideology of *any* fixed and prescriptive categories in sex. These are rooted in heteronormativity, but have extended to encompass norms which extend beyond heterosexual acts and social structures in themselves. To be clearly sexed has come to be part of the theological definition of perfection; male and female bodies are the grounds for masculine and feminine cosmically-echoing identities in Barth, and in Augustine post-resurrection bodies still have at least their secondary sexual markers.

To learn to think in different, other, indecent ways, then, is to allow people 'to develop their own identities outside the closure and boundaries of theo/social systems' (Althaus-Reid 2000: 175). The 'decentralizing' effect of acknowledging multiple narratives will also help to challenge the more broadly homogenizing effects of globalization (Althaus-Reid 2000: 192), where community traditions and practices are often subsumed to systematization. Indecent theology requires 'perversion', or the taking of different 'roads' from those which have been taken before, in order to examine the true nature of that which has become so entrenched as to be invisible. Brazilian theologian Claudio Carvalhaes appeals to 'limping' or 'a/theological' thought which 'tries to slip away from the ontotheological structures of theological discourse' (Carvalhaes 2006: 52); which is prepared to down the tools of power and certainty and to be improper, provisional, to see in a glass darkly and realize reality is opaque (Carvalhaes 2006: 58–59).

Such a 'bricolage' theology might seem arbitrary or groundless, but actually it is crucial that Christianity recognizes its nomadic, shifting history. Gorringe points out that the Bible itself is made up of a variety of different kinds of literature representing different periods and cultural concerns, and thus 'represents a palimpsest of ideologies ... This means that this text is not in a position to tout for any one particular ideology' (Gorringe 2004: 117). Does the text's 'mish-mash' status mean it cannot be called the Word of God? No, says Gorringe, for – as Barth held – it is the Bible's very mixed-up nature which renders it 'the possibility of dissonance with and resistance to ... general ideology' (Gorringe 2004: 118). Crucially, 'To call a collection of texts "the Word of God" is to say that such a possibility of dissonance is permanent and thorough going, that these texts resist every attempt at colonization and all forms of hegemony' (Gorringe 2004: 118). The Bible is still constantly pushed and pulled by the proponents of particular ideologies to suit their agenda, but the silence also evident in the texts mean that it resists being appropriated in this way. This silence is complex and multi-faceted; it is itself dissonant and multiple, but its existence in scripture means that the scriptural witness is always Other than 'the deafening clamours of conflicting ideologies' (Gorringe 2004: 120), and thus testifies to the fact that God also cannot be subsumed to any one human ideology (Gorringe 2004: 120). It is in this way that even a flawed, compromised tradition can be queered, and in this way that flashes of God can be found in it. The tension, difference and conspicuous silences remain, but it is in and through these that God is found. God *is* queer (Althaus-Reid 2003).

Some Conclusions

Stone comments that 'feminist projects and queer projects, while not reducible to one another, are likely to remain intertwined due to the fact that both sets of projects have a stake in exploring, and contesting, hegemonic notions of proper gendered behaviour' (Stone 2005: 112). Similarly, it seems to me, queer projects and intersex/DSD projects, particularly theological ones, are also likely to remain intertwined. Although they will never be reducible to the same thing, there are areas of commonality and affinity by which they might continue mutually to inform each other, and where there might be individuals who identify with some or all parts of each 'identity' (acknowledging that the very category of identity has been questioned and disrupted). One of the strengths of queer political activism has lain in its insistence that it not be fobbed-off, that people who have been excluded from signification on various grounds deserve to be heard. This is important in considering intersex/DSD, too, for exclusion on the grounds of bodily configuration or an identity rooted in being intersexed is just as problematic as exclusion on the grounds of sexuality.

Even the ethics of treating intersex/DSD might be considered profoundly queer, given that they appear uncertain, unfinished, continually in flux. We should not, says Morland, 'rush to pronounce the single right way to manage intersex, but admit uncertainty, replace dogma with discussion' (Morland 2006: 331). There are no easy answers to questions, like that posed by Sytsma, about whether Western surgeons who have come to oppose what is essentially cosmetic genital surgery on intersexed children should agree to perform it at the request of parents whose children appear in European or North American clinics but will be brought up in different cultures where variant sex-gender may be strongly opposed (Sytsma 2006c; see also Karkazis 2008: 115). Some parents' conservative religious beliefs may make them less likely to be happy with a genitally-atypical child (Feder 2002: 312). It might be deemed colonial to refuse surgery on the grounds that the enlightened Western doctrine is 'better' than that of the parents' religion or country of origin; but, on the other hand, carrying out surgery might be deemed to violate the child's rights and physical integrity, just as for any other intersexed child. There are no easy answers here.

Resisting and reappropriating for intersex/DSD will necessitate ongoing engagements with work from related disciplines such as sociology and gender studies, but it is important that specifically theological resistance and reappropriation also occurs. Resisting means exposing and challenging violent cultural-ecclesial constructions and interpretations; reappropriating means looking back to the strands of love and justice which run through the tradition alongside those which are abusive. Theology is always already self-queering, since it contains within itself tools for hermeneutical suspicion, for overturning religious and cultural practices which do not meet the demands of love, justice and *shalom* (a 'wholeness' about far more than 'completeness'). Importantly, too, theology also already contains within its tradition flashes of acknowledgement that male-and-female is not the whole story of humanity; that there is something irreducible and profoundly holy about bodies since they are the mediators of all our encounters with the divine; that perfection and integrity in God's order does not always coincide with that deemed perfect and whole in human definition; that God does not always appear or behave as humans might expect or desire.

Although people with intersex/DSD conditions do not always or necessarily align themselves with the politically queer, there is, then, a sense in which intersex/DSD is, unavoidably, *theologically* queer. Even alongside the oppressive, sexist aspects of its legacy, there are throughout the Christian tradition instances of the problematizing of unproblematized norms. This begins with the

Bible itself. A clear strand of concern for justice and the marginalized also survives in the tradition: heteronormativity and the exclusion of homosexual, queer, transgender, intersex/DSD and impaired people always have repercussions for economic and social well-being, and thus cannot persist in a just order. The voices of Bo Laurent and other pioneers of intersex/DSD rights are prophetic ones, and these prophets have had the distinction of beginning to be recognized in their own times. However, intersex/DSD and queer theologies are also eschatological, so along with the progress that has already been made in reforming surgical and related practices, there is still much to be done. The voices of theologians who work in solidarity with those with intersex/DSD conditions, and, it is to be hoped, of those who themselves have intersex/DSD conditions, must continue to query and critique the social and religious norms which curb the multiplicity and possibility of the sexed bodies which make up the Body of Christ.

Chapter 7

REALIZING AND REMAKING: CONCLUSIONS

> My body and the bodies of the people I love are the most intimate
> sites of American imperialism ... Normal is a weapon of mass
> destruction ... Every time we choose an option that wasn't offered,
> every time we question, we make it safer to be in between ... I'm
> tired of resisting love. Love will never be safe, but we've seen the
> alternative (Hillman 2008: 95-96).

> I really have a place in the world ... It's just wonderful. I am very
> proud to come out as an [intersex] person. The world has tried
> to make us feel like freaks ... I felt like a freak most of my life, but
> look at me. I'm just a human being like everybody else (Barbara,
> in Preves 2003: 133).

Barbara, interviewed by Sharon Preves for the latter's sociological
study into intersex and identity, speaks of finding her place in a
world from which she had felt excluded. Barbara's eventual
discovery of her 'place' was sited in a realization that she was 'a
human being like everybody else', despite her difference. Dreger
has shown that to treat intersex/DSD humanely means to treat the
person with an intersex/DSD condition as 'a full-fledged member
of the human race':

> If you wouldn't slice into the genitals of a non-intersex child
> because her parents wanted it ... then you ought not to do it to
> an intersex child. If you would not obfuscate the medical history
> of a person who was born without intersex, then you ought
> not to do so when dealing with a person born intersex (Dreger
> 2006a: 81).

Simultaneously, it might be said that to be a human *like* everybody
else is simultaneously to be a human *un*like everybody else: unique,
distinct, matchless. To be rendered freakish is to be rendered
meaningless – to be excluded from the signification which 'normal'
people share, because one's difference is deemed to have deeper or
more threatening import than that of others. Throughout this book

I have sought to render intersex/DSD theologically meaningful, and to query the strands within theology which have privileged heteronormativity and unambiguous sex. A lack of knowledge about intersex/DSD has contributed to the hegemonic nature of heteronormativity in churches, affecting not just sexual moralities but Church teaching about gender, marriage, the family, economics and much more. These have fed back into the norms of societies which cannot recognize intersex/DSD as anything but aberration, somehow a failure to make sense.

A project of education on and engagement with issues of intersex/DSD and otherwise atypical physicality or sex-gender configuration in the Church would enable appropriate pastoral care and non-hysterical debate. Statistically, people with intersex/DSD conditions are in a minority, but intersex/DSD is more than a minority issue for theology. Appreciating the complexity and diversity of human embodiment, biology and sex identity has implications for male-and-female heterosexual norms deeply naturalized across theological discourse. The frequency or commonality of a given bodily state should not necessarily correspond with the amount of consideration given it: it is not that the more intersexed people there are, the more their stories and voices deserve to be heard. Rather, it should be possible for theology to accept that intersex/DSD is statistically far less common than XX-female and XY-male births (though not as uncommon as it may at first appear), but to retain conceptual and pastoral tools for engaging with it nonetheless.

Reflection on the existence of bodies which differ from the expected physiological norms may break down theology's investment in the cult of all-encompassing male-and-female in a way that homosexuality and transgender – sometimes explained away as 'chosen' identities which can be further marginalized as 'sinful' or 'perverse' – have not. Unusually-sexed bodies have been and continue to be sites of tension about autonomy and self-direction, contested goods, and the nature of sex itself. Some of the ostensible 'truths' about bodies in which theology has had particular ideological investment – such as the 'truth' that every human body is solely and ineluctably either male or female – are on shaky ground in light of both the existence of intersex/DSD, and of theology's fundamental responsibility to resist or queer systems and structures of injustice and exclusion. Theologies which claim an immovable male-and-female model, with no conceptual or pastoral space for exceptions, likewise protect and fetishize a non-existent truth, shifting allegiance from God to human ideology. However, theology has helped to construct discourse around goodness and legitimacy for bodies, and can help to change it too. Feder quotes Ruby, the mother of two daughters with CAH: 'I had pastors who told me that they didn't know how to pray for me. And I told them I know how you can pray for me. You imagine a God who is bigger than all of these problems' (in Feder 2006: 195). Theology's resistance of ideology must involve accepting the *provisionality* of human sex, and of human systems generally, whilst at the same time acknowledging that since humans partake in building and constituting the new creation, what we do in, to and through bodies profoundly matters.

Sex is bolstered by the customs and standards of society, which are provisional human standards despite having been co-opted to back-up 'overarching' theological models. Since biological reproduction is necessary for the continuation of the species, some sexed characteristics do persist: it is male-and-female as a socially-limiting construct, not male and female as gamete possibilities (among a range of other possibilities), which pass away in Christ. However, if male-and-female is passing away, then it need not stand for or encompass everyone; human bodies need not be altered to 'fit' it. There is no need for gametes or gender roles to universally reinscribe procreative sexed norms. Anticipating this state of affairs through the transforming love of God will enable a ceding of the desires to control, to concretize, to oppress – and, for theology, to speak over, sanction and discipline various kinds of bodies. The Church must speak *with* those whose bodies and souls are written out of legitimacy, rather than propounding models of sex and sexuality which only favour decent, heteronormative bodies and lives. This is a *real* and *realizable* prospect: getting beyond male-and-female as a system of privilege is possible in the new order, the eschatology-come-to-fruit which is humanity's *telos*. The end of male-and-female, 'no more male-and-female in Christ', means the end of exclusivity, heteronormativity, and a model of complementarity which erodes difference even as it prescribes it. This also means no more taxonomies of goodness or perfection attached to how a body meets heteronormative criteria for maleness or femaleness, and no more annexations of bodies by misplaced moralistic pronouncements about how a small, decent clitoris or a large, powerful penis should look.

As I showed in Chapter 3, the connotations of human bodies are made and emblazoned by socio-cultural narratives, and in turn constitute, propagate, appraise and contest such narratives. Bodies which are both socially-constructed and self-directing were identified as *ecstatic* bodies, which belied any finality or fixity of meaning for themselves. We saw that this created tensions around autonomy and the extent to which bodies may 'legitimately' direct and identify themselves, as with debates over the legitimacy of technological intervention for transsexualism. I argued that this is of particular ethical acuteness when considering intersex/DSD, since people with such conditions have found their agency, responsibility and subjectivity unusually eroded by social responses to their bodily states. I suggested that the ecstatic body is also the Eucharistic body, the Body of Christ which, through the participation of multiple bodies, is remade in a new way each time it is re/membered (put back together) in Eucharist. As such, Eucharist might be a particularly important site of solidarity for stigmatized bodies, with its connotations of disrupted and critiqued political power and a breaking-in of a new cosmic order. Since human bodies are already part of the new creation, and also have the capacity to shape and direct it, the bodies which call themselves the Church have an especial responsibility to model this new order by looking beyond even apparently self-evident patterns of human being and intercourse. This must be done even where, and especially where, it will entail a shake-up and re-examination of its own foundational assumptions. For example, I argued (after Iain Morland) that it may be those whose bodies are considered *un*remarkable in terms of a sex-gender harmony who must be prepared to relinquish the (unsolicited) power and status currently attached to this state. *Kenosis* for non-intersexed/DSD people thereby necessitates thinking ourselves beyond male-and-female, and reflecting this both in our theory and in ecclesiological praxis.

Norms about sex and gender, procreation, consummation and complementarity, which have become theological *a prioris*, must be tested against whether they promote love, justice and fullness of being. Queer theologies in particular have the capacity to refigure and re-examine metaphors of perfection and completion as morally good, and might be valuable in formulating theologies from intersex/DSD *even where* people with such conditions do not identify politically as queer. Liberative theologies from intersex/DSD will be incarnational theologies which refuse to quash the obstinate and intractable bodiliness of bodies. These theologies, like queer theologies, will inform mainstream theological tradition and critique it from their liminal perspective. They will be multiple, not single; heterogeneous, not systematic. If we do not talk about bodies as they really are, including bodies in their variation and transgression from demarcation as male or female, then we are not really talking about bodies at all. Embodiment is about concentric circles of similarity and difference; about the limitedness of being a unique organism, and the capacity, through perichoretic relationship, to change the definition of 'body' *per se*. The message that the image of God is not reflected more perfectly in some (able, clearly-sexed, unremarkably-gendered) human bodies than in other (impaired, unusually-sexed, atypical or queer) human bodies is a crucial one. God is a creator who has created a world with freedom in it. This means a freedom for things to go 'wrong' – mutation is necessary for the way the process has unfolded. God is not an inherently heterosexual, respectable God, so Christians should not hide behind this identity either. As humans we are also inventive, ingenious co-creators of the new and better world.

An acknowledgement that the bodies of people with intersex/ DSD conditions are not unproblematicallybodies which have 'gone wrong' is crucial to disturbing heteronormativity. Realizing that sex is more complex than male-and-female, and that this is not inherently pathological or 'fallen', provides a way into exploring the more-than-binary character of human gender and sexuality too. This matters soteriologically, as it disturbs the meaning of fallenness and imperfection. What we really need to be saved from is unjust power-structures, along with our own fears and the arbitrary limits of our own creation. The fear of attack or violence if our bodies, sexualities or sex-gender identities are deemed deviant is a very real fear, but it is one from which we as humans can save ourselves by making a society where difference is not stigmatized or attacked, and where individuals do not need to demonize other groups in order to feel secure in their own identity. The fact that we also need to be 'saved' from physical pain, suffering and death remains, but this does not mean bodies should be devalued even in their awkwardness and dyingness. The things about bodies considered troublesome or undesirable by outsiders may not always be the things considered troublesome by those who live in them. Erasing pain and indignity is not the same as erasing variation.

Although it is problematic to use intersex/DSD as a 'tool' or 'weapon' to wield against phenomena which I, a non-intersexed theologian, find distasteful, it is true – as John Hare (2007) has begun to consider – that a wider knowledge and understanding of intersex/DSD may also help provide a way forward in the rapidly-stultifying impasse surrounding homosexuality, particularly within the Anglican Communion. Formulating theologies openly informed by 'controversial' sexual identities has not always been easy because of Church hierarchies which have devalued and demonized non-heterosexuality, but the existence of biological intersex/DSD conditions may enable some people to recognize that the universality of male-and-female is an illusion. Rendering something legitimate because it is 'biological' is in itself far too simplistic and would not, in any case, go far enough in breaking down the prejudices and fears surrounding homosexuality in the Church; calling for an acceptance of homosexuality on the grounds that it is a 'mental' form of intersex would be misleading and would rather miss the point. However, intersex/DSD does at least open up discussion of difference and variation, and may, *precisely because* it is a medical issue and not just a 'sexual' one, be a less threatening way into exposing the hegemony of heteronormativity for what it is than discussion of homosexuality would be.

Resistance to the twin idols of male-and-female and heteronormativity necessitates a heightened awareness and engagement with issues stemming from atypical bodies in local church settings as well as throughout Church hierarchies. Critical Bible reading which will acknowledge the alien cultural setting in which texts were produced, disseminated and redacted, and show that even the biblical picture of humanity is already more complicated than the male-and-female picture which it is has been convenient for much theology to perpetuate, is therefore also fundamental. Contextual Bible study and reader-response criticism can be anti-ideological tools, recognizing systems of subordination and oppression (like heteronormativity) within the texts but resisting complicity with them. Reflection on intersex/DSD can sharpen the focus on those strands of the Judaeo-Christian tradition which are already anti-imperial, anti-idolatrous and anti-monolithic. The implications of intersex/DSD thus profoundly impact other aspects of theology than the specific area of ethics: hermeneutic strategies, eschatologies, anthropologies, ecclesiologies, Christologies. Intersex/DSD can provide a lens through which to examine the more-than-heteronormative status of human sex, and to re-evaluate the non-genital eroticism and sensuality sometimes lost where heterosexual intercourse and patriarchal social and familial structures are apotheosized.

Intersex/DSD is a kaleidoscope, a tube of mirrors reflecting society's assumptions about the nature of sex and gender back at itself and showing them up as the artifices they are. Consideration of intersex/DSD must always turn the viewer back to considering the norms which appear self-evident but are actually shifting and impermanent like the kaleidoscope's coloured shapes. Although theology contains important resources for engaging with the elusive and unexpected shape of God, and of what it means to be humans who also reflect God, it has often preferred to fall back on prescriptive (and proscriptive) 'certainties' which privilege the *status quo*. The erasure of a whole swathe of bodies and experiences demands a theological response motivated not by fear but by a desire to expand the ways in which human lives and bodies tell stories. Until theologians, medics and others accept that the male-and-female world is not the only 'real' world, and that the normalizing procedures of surgery and signification which bolster it are themselves grounded in something partial and arbitrary, the silencing and devaluing of otherness in human bodies will go on. This cannot, and must not, be justified.

GLOSSARY: A SUMMARY OF SOME INTERSEX/DSD CONDITIONS AND RELATED TERMINOLOGY

Intersex has been used as an umbrella term encompassing a range of conditions, some of which cause ambiguous external genitalia. However, as Bo Laurent and others have pointed out, it was never well-defined. There has been much disagreement about whether particular conditions should or should not be considered intersex conditions (Dreger and Herndon 2009). Contentious as it is, then, the term 'disorder of sex development' may be a more useful broad term than intersex, given that it can encompass a wide range of developmental variations of the chromosomes, reproductive and endocrine systems, not all of which were ever considered 'intersex' conditions. In this glossary I continue to use the construction 'intersex/DSD conditions', whilst acknowledging that there is still disagreement about whether certain physical occurrences should or should not be counted as instances of intersex/DSD. Some of the more well-known intersex/DSD conditions are outlined below for reference; a fuller list appears in Consortium on the Management of Disorders of Sex Development 2006a: 5-7.

Estimates put the frequency of ambiguous genitalia at around 0.1–0.2% of births, but the prevalence of hormonal and chromosomal variants is higher, possibly around 2% (Preves 2003: 2). Some conditions are not diagnosed until much later, which may skew the figures. This renders intersex/DSD conditions about as frequent as Down's syndrome or cystic fibrosis (Preves 2003: 3). Sax (2002) is particularly keen to refute Fausto-Sterling's figures on the prevalence of intersex (1993, 1997, 2000). Sax argues that Fausto-Sterling is wrong to include within her statistics conditions other than those where either the phenotype is not classifiable as male or female, or the phenotype and karyotype do not match. He suspects that she does so in order to make intersex appear far more common than it actually is (Sax 2002: 177). These 'controversial' conditions include those outlined below; ISNA's Consortium on the Management of Disorders of Sex Development does count them as DSDs (Consortium on the Management of Disorders of Sex Development 2006a: 2).

Androgen Insensitivity Syndrome (AIS)

Every foetus initially has both Wolffian ducts, which could develop into male-related organs and features, and Müllerian ducts, which could develop into female-related organs and features. Foetuses which will become male and those which will become female look identical until around six weeks' gestation (Preves 2003: 23–25). Which structures develop largely depends on the ability of the foetus to respond to androgens, but each foetus has the nascent physiological capability to develop either way, or somewhere in between. Sometimes an XY foetus cannot respond to androgens produced by the gonads, largely due to a variant SRY gene on the Y chromosome (Roughgarden 2004: 291), so external genitalia develop along female-related lines. The internal organs develop along male-related lines, as Müllerian Inhibiting Factor from the testes atrophies the primitive female-related internal organs (Gard 1998: 134). In Complete AIS, the external genitalia appear female, with a clitoris and labia, though the vagina itself may be shallow or absent. In Partial AIS, some ambiguity of the external genitalia may be present. Internally there are testes rather than ovaries, and no uterus. Complete AIS is not usually detected at birth because there is no external ambiguity. However, the undescended testes often result in hernias in infancy – which leads to about half of cases being diagnosed. Otherwise, AIS is often not discovered until puberty when absent menstruation prompts medical investigation. Pubescent girls with AIS develop breasts and hips (the testes produce oestrogen as well as testosterone, and AIS does not prevent response to oestrogen) but no pubic or underarm hair. The vast majority of individuals known to have AIS identify as women, and report sexual attraction to men rather than women (Hines 2004: 457). It is not possible to know the extent to which this is a result of having been treated as girls from birth because of their external morphology. The parents of Ilizane Broks and her half-sister Xenia, featured in the *Secret Intersex* documentary, have consciously told both children that they are 'inters' (rather than girls) and have sought to follow their daughters' own cues as to gender identity. At the time of the film, 16-year-old Ilizane said, 'I see myself as more female than male', and 6-year-old Xenia said 'I'm half girl and half boy' (in Godwin 2004). Their mother commented, 'It doesn't matter to me if they see themselves as superwomen, or girls with AIS, or as intersexual beings. I'm happy to go along with whatever makes them feel comfortable about themselves' (in Godwin 2004).

Frequency

Frequency for Complete AIS is given variously as 1 in 13,000 births to 1 in 20,000 births. Partial AIS is said by Roughgarden to affect 1 in 130,000 births (Roughgarden 2004: 291).

Cause

Inherited from a maternal carrier (66%), or from a spontaneous mutation in the egg (33%).

Congenital Adrenal Hyperplasia (CAH)

In CAH the body's production of cortisol (essential to survival, regulating energy, blood sugar levels, blood pressure and response to injury) is low due to the absence of a gene called CYP21 which converts progesterone to cortisol (Roughgarden 2004: 289). As the body pushes the adrenal gland harder trying to correct the low cortisol level, more and more testosterone is also made. In XX foetuses with 'classic' (prenatal-onset) CAH, the excess in testosterone can cause unusual genital development before birth – a large clitoris and, sometimes, fused labia. Increasing the levels of cortisol through substitute therapy means the body no longer needs to produce excessive amounts of testosterone. As many people with CAH also lack aldosterone (which helps maintain adequate salt levels in the body), if the hormone imbalance is not treated with steroids then life-threatening salt-wasting can occur. Not all individuals with CAH have enlarged clitorises or fused labia; the genital presentation of some XX infants is a side-effect of the condition. It is the surgery on infants' genitals that is the contentious issue, not the treatment of CAH itself. Salt-wasting CAH in girls and boys requires immediate intervention to replace salts and glucose in the blood, but this need not entail surgery to reduce the size of the clitoris in girls. Surgery to create a vaginal opening *is* sometimes necessary, and must occur before menstruation begins; but a pre-pubertal girl does not need a vaginal opening (although obviously does require urethral and anal openings) (Roen 2008: 56; Creighton 2004: 329). If it is suspected that a pregnant woman may be carrying a child with CAH (because CAH already exists in the family), she may undergo steroid treatment to prevent 'masculinization' of the child's genitals if the child is a girl. However, to be effective, the steroid therapy must begin several weeks before it is possible to tell whether or not the child does actually have CAH (Fausto-Sterling 2000: 55), and indeed before it is known whether the foetus is male or female (Sytsma 2006b: 241). Only one in eight children at risk of CAH will actually benefit from prenatal treatment by the drug dexamethasone, and in half of the cases where the drug's use *is* beneficial, children will still be considered to be in need of genital surgery anyway (Sytsma 2006b: 247). Sytsma comments,

> Prenatal [dexamethasone] therapy to prevent virilization requires subjecting at least seven out of eight fetuses ... to the risks of [dexamethasone] treatment even though they do not stand to benefit from it. They are being subjected to those risks in order to prevent a child from being born with ambiguous genitalia and to spare the parents the burden of raising such a child. Therefore, they are being treated as a means only (Sytsma 2006b: 250).

Both the steroid therapy and the prenatal diagnostic tests for CAH can create undesirable side-effects for the mother and foetus, including miscarriage (Fausto-Sterling 2000: 55; Sytsma 2006b). Sytsma argues, 'At minimum, prenatal [dexamethasone] administration should be considered an experimental treatment rather than the standard of care, but ... even as an experimental treatment, prenatal [dexamethasone] administration requires further justification' (Sytsma 2006b: 241).

Frequency

1 in 10,000 people have CAH; ranging from 1 in 300 people among Yupik Native Alaskans to 1 in 40,000 in mainland USA (Roughgarden 2004: 290); unusual genital appearance related to CAH affects 1 in 20,000 to 1 in 36,000 births overall.

Cause

Inheritance of the affected gene from both parents (those who inherit it from one parent only will become carriers themselves).

5-Alpha Reductase Deficiency (5-ARD)

People with 5-ARD have XY chromosomes but cannot, as infants, convert testosterone into dihydrotestosterone (DHT) (which has more potent 'masculinizing' effects), due to an absence of the enzyme 5-alpha-reductase, usually found in the cytoplasm (Gard 1998: 133). As a result, they develop externally along female-related lines. However, the uterus and fallopian tubes are absent because the body has still inhibited the growth of the Müllerian structures as in a 'normal' male foetus. The testes, epididymis, vas deferens and seminal vesicles are present, though the testes may be hidden inside the body. Although people with 5-ARD lack the tissues which would convert testosterone to DHT, they are still responsive to testosterone itself (Gard 1998: 137), so when increased levels of testosterone are produced at puberty, secondary male-related sexual characteristics still develop. These include enlarging of the penis, deepening of the voice, increased body hair (including facial hair) (Preves 2003: 29), increased height and muscle mass. If the condition is discovered before puberty and a feminine gender role is preferred, then oestrogen therapy will be recommended at puberty (the testes will be removed to prevent 'masculinization', but without replacement oestrogen, osteoporosis would be a risk later in life). However, it is becoming more common for the condition to be discovered early and for parents to be advised to raise the child as a boy, despite the feminine phenotype in childhood; the influence of androgens on the foetal brain is now being emphasized (as by Diamond and Sigmundson). The testes of people with 5-ARD may remain undescended and, if so, there is an increased risk of testicular cancer, so monitoring is required. 5-ARD was the condition experienced by Cal, protagonist of Jeffrey Eugenides' 'intersex novel' *Middlesex* (Eugenides 2002), which raised awareness of intersex issues despite being criticized by some people with intersex/DSD conditions.

Frequency

Unclear. Some newborns with 5-ARD are known to have been misdiagnosed as having AIS. 5-ARD has been found to be relatively frequent in some communities where consanguine reproduction is prevalent. Well-known examples are communities in Turkey, the Dominican Republic and Papua New Guinea. 5-ARD individuals in the Dominican Republic are known as *guevedoche* –'balls at 12'– and among the Sambia people in Papua New Guinea as *kwolu-aatmwol* – 'changing from a female thing into a male thing'. In fact, whilst *kwolu-aatmwol* share social characteristics of both boys and girls, their eventual social standing is identical neither with that of adult women nor of adult men. There is a specific role for *kwolu-aatmwol* within the community (Herdt 1994c).

Cause

A deficiency of 5-alpha-reductase in the cytoplasm.

Genetic Mosaics and Chimeras

Mosaic bodies have a mixture of chromosomes in their cells: this could be a combination of, for example, XX and XY, or XY and XO (with only one sex chromosome). Many people may be mosaics and never realize it because they experience no physical sex ambiguity. However, those with a relatively large minority of 'different' cells may experience some extent of genital ambiguity. Technically, mosaics are any individuals who have 'patches' of cells which differ from the majority of cells in their body, which could have arisen as the result of mutations within a single embryo; chimeras are those whose tissues originally belonged to two separate embryos. It should be noted that the term 'chimera' may carry negative connotations of exoticism and monstrosity.

Frequency

Unknown. However, an increase in IVF treatment may lead to a greater instance of chimerism because it is common to implant multiple foetuses in the uterus, and two foetuses may then fuse (Strain, Dean, Hamilton and Bonthron 1998).

Cause

XX/XY chimeras occur when two early embryos fuse to form one individual (Dreger 1998: 37); mosaicism happens when an interruption to the cell division in the early embryo either prevents the expected number of chromosomes from dividing, or creates a mutation in a single gene. The earlier in cell division this occurs, the higher the number of cells which will eventually be affected.

Ovotestes ('true hermaphroditism')

Individuals with this condition have both ovarian and testicular cells – either having both a complete or partial testis and a complete or partial ovary, or having all or part of one ovotestis or two ovotestes. The external genitalia may show a huge variation of ambiguity at birth. Testicular tissue in ovotestes is thought to be at increased risk of gonadal cancer, so the testicular portion may be removed. 'True hermaphroditism' was a term commonly used when it was also usual to speak of other conditions as male pseudo-hermaphroditism (e.g. AIS) and female pseudo-hermaphroditism (e.g. CAH), but this is now considered stigmatizing. ISNA campaigned for terms with the root 'hermaphrodite' to be dropped from medical parlance and this is being continued by Accord Alliance and the medics with whom they are working (see Lee *et al* 2006).

Frequency

1 in 85,000 people.

Cause

Sometimes ovotestes may be the result of genetic chimerism; in many cases there is no known medical cause.

Klinefelter's syndrome (KS)

In this condition, chromosomes can be 47-XXY (80%), 48-XXXY, 49-XXXXY, 48-XXYY, or mosaic combinations (http://www.ksa-uk.co.uk/Introduction.htm). Adult men with Klinefelter's Syndrome usually have a very small penis and testes (they do not increase in size at puberty, and puberty may be much delayed) and are often infertile due to very low or non-existent sperm production. Like Down's syndrome, Klinefelter's syndrome may be more common in children of older mothers (Godwin 2004), and the extra chromosome may be discovered if prenatal screening for Down's syndrome takes place (http://www.ksa-uk.co.uk/Introduction.htm). Otherwise, many people may have the condition their whole lives without knowing it. Some boys with KS begin to grow breasts and to lay down fat in a more 'feminine' pattern at puberty because of their low levels of testosterone. There is also a tendency for people with KS to be taller and to have longer limbs than average (Godwin 2004;http://www.ksa-uk.co.uk/ Introduction.htm#Physical). When KS is discovered after the age at which puberty would typically take place in males, regular testosterone injections may be offered to help increase or maintain penis size and libido. Bone density scans are also recommended, as people with KS are at increased risk of osteoporosis. The Klinefelter's Syndrome Association states that KS is not an intersex condition and that people with KS are unequivocally male (Harper 2007: 156), but this is refuted by individuals such as Andrea Marshall, Paula Ryder and Steph Tonner (in Godwin 2004).

Frequency

1 in 500 to 1 in 1,000 males; the majority of cases probably go undiagnosed (http://www.ksa-uk.co.uk/Introduction.htm).

Cause

May result from a variation during the division of a parent's sex cells, when the parental chromosomes have not finished pairing up before fertilization is complete. The extra X chromosome or chromosomes may have come from either parent.

Turner's syndrome (TS, XO, 45XO, 45X)

Females usually have XX chromosomes. Individuals with Turner's syndrome are missing one sex chromosome and are therefore sometimes described as XO. Their external genitalia usually appear unambiguously female, but their gonads may be extremely underdeveloped or effectively absent. Where gonads are present, they may stop functioning early in life. However, the other internal female-related organs will be present. The missing genetic information from the X chromosome leads to several distinctive features and possible health complications: girls with TS may have very short stature; absent puberty (which can lead to bone problems such as osteoporosis if replacement oestrogen is not given); a narrow palate and crowded teeth; a receding lower jaw; widely-spaced, possibly inverted nipples; arms which turn out at the elbow; a funnel chest; a thick, short neck; prominent ears; or narrow fingernails and toenails that point upwards. Girls with TS may also be more prone to problems with spatial awareness and non-verbal reasoning. Cardiovascular and renal problems, sight and hearing complications, and obesity are also risks. Some individuals with TS may be genetic mosaics, with a mixture of XY/XO chromosomes, and may appear externally 'male', with some male-related internal organs such as testes. Nonetheless, the majority of people with TS identify as girls and women (Harper 2007: 171).

Frequency

1 in 2,000 to 1 in 3,000 female births. Roughly 50% of people with Turner's syndrome have only one X chromosome (XO). 30% have two X chromosomes but one is incomplete. Others are genetic mosaics.

Cause

Uncertain, but may result from an error during the division of a parent's sex cells; the missing or incomplete chromosome could be the mother's X or the father's Y, as the complete X chromosome could have come from either parent.

Hypospadias

In hypospadias the urinary meatus opens up somewhere along the underside of the penis rather than at the tip. Boys with hypospadias usually have to sit to urinate. First-degree hypospadias, where the meatus is located somewhere on the glans, is not usually corrected. However, where the opening is further underneath along the shaft, surgery is sometimes performed to relocate it. Complications from surgery are fairly common and include infection, hair growth inside the penis (Kessler 1998: 70), stenosis (narrowing of the urethra), pain during sexual intercourse, and difficulty with ejaculation. Hypospadias is a fairly common aspect of the anatomy of people with 5-ARD and extreme CAH. More severe hypospadias may be associated with undescended testes.

Frequency

Reports of frequency vary widely, from 1 in 125 to 1 in 4,000 boys. Various degrees of hypospadias are among the most common conditions affecting the genitalia of young boys. Many boys who would not be considered to have an intersex/DSD condition have some degree of hypospadias, but hypospadias can also be present alongside conditions such as CAH.

Micropenis

Micropenis is where the penis is considered to fall below the acceptable range of size at birth – that is, under 2.4cm (Preves 2003: 55). The pre-pubescent child can be treated with testosterone to increase penis size, but this means that no further growth will take place at puberty (Kessler 1998: 19). In the past it was sometimes felt that as it was difficult to construct an erectile penis, boys with micropenis would be better off reassigned as girls. This occurred even when there was no other specific intersex condition present.

Vaginal Agenesis (MRKH)

Vaginal agenesis is also known as Mayer Rokitansky Kuster Hauser Syndrome or Müllerian Agenesis. It comprises congenital absence of the vagina, fallopian tubes, cervix and uterus in an XX individual. Some individuals have uterine remnants. The external genitalia are typically female. Some individuals undergo surgery to enlarge their vaginas; others use non-surgical methods such as the insertion of dilators. However, dilation can be painful and some people resent the idea that a 'functional' vagina is necessarily one which can receive an erect penis.

Frequency

MRKH is believed to affect around 1 in 5,000 females.

BIBLIOGRAPHY

Adams, Carol J., (ed.), *Ecofeminism and the Sacred* (New York: Continuum, 1993).

Adrenal Hyperplasia Network UK, www.ahn.org.uk

Ahmed, S.F., S. Morrison and I.A. Hughes, 'Intersex and Gender Assignment; The Third Way?', *Archives of Disease in Childhood* 89 (2004), pp. 847–50.

Alderson, Julie, Anna Madill and Adam Balen, 'Fear of Devaluation: Understanding the Experience of Intersexed Women with Androgen Insensitivity Syndrome', *British Journal of Health Psychology* 9 (2004), pp. 81–100.

Alison, James, 'Theology Amidst the Stones and Dust', in Eugene F. Rogers (ed.), *Theology and Sexuality: Classic and Contemporary Readings* (Oxford: Blackwell, 2002), pp. 387–408.

_____ 'The Gay Thing: Following the Still Small Voice', in Gerard Loughlin (ed.), *Queer Theology: Rethinking the Western Body* (Oxford: Blackwell, 2007), pp. 50–62.

Althaus-Reid, Marcella, *Indecent Theology* (London and New York: Routledge, 2000).

_____ *The Queer God* (London and New York: Routledge, 2003).

_____ 'Queer I Stand: Lifting the Skirts of God', in Marcella Althaus-Reid and Lisa Isherwood (eds), *The Sexual Theologian: Essays on Sex, God and Politics* (London and New York: T&T Clark, 2004a), pp. 99–109.

_____ *From Feminist Theology to Indecent Theology: Readings on Poverty, Sexual Identity and God* (London: SCM Press, 2004b).

_____ (ed.), *Liberation Theology and Sexuality* (Aldershot: Ashgate, 2006a).

_____ "Let Them Talk..!' Doing Liberation Theology from Latin American Closets', in Marcella Althaus-Reid (ed.), *Liberation Theology and Sexuality* (Aldershot: Ashgate 2006b), pp. 5–17.

_____ 'Mark', in Deryn Guest, Robert E. Goss, Mona West and Thomas Bohache (eds), *The Queer Bible Commentary* (London: SCM Press, 2006c), pp. 517–25.

Althaus-Reid, Marcella and Lisa Isherwood (eds), *The Sexual Theologian: A Primer in Radical Sex and Queer Theology* (London and New York: Continuum, 2005).

Althaus-Reid, Marcella and Lisa Isherwood (eds), *Controversies in Body Theology* (London: SCM Press, 2008).

Anderson, Robert C. (ed.), *Graduate Theological Education and the Human Experience of Disability* (Binghampton, NY: The Haworth Pastoral Press, 2003).

Androgen Insensitivity Syndrome Support Group, http://www.aissg.org

Androgen Insensitivity Syndrome Support Group Australia, http://home.vicnet.net.au/~aissg

Arana, Marcus de María *et al*, 'A Human Rights Investigation into the Medical "Normalization" of Intersex People: A Report of a Public Hearing by the Human Rights Commission of the City and County of San Francisco', 2005, online at http://www.sfgov.org/site/uploadedfiles/sfhumanrights/Committee_ Meetings/Lesbian_Gay_Bisexual_Transgender/SFHRC%20 Intersex%20 Report(1).pdf

The Archbishops' Council, *Some Issues in Human Sexuality, A Guide to the Debate: A Discussion Document from the House of Bishops' Group on* Issues in Human Sexuality (London: Church House Publishing, 2003).

Ashley, David J.B., *Human Intersex* (Edinburgh and London: E&S Livingstone Ltd., 1962).

Atkins, Dawn (ed.), *Looking Queer: Body Image and Identity in Lesbian, Bisexual, Gay, and Transgender Communities* (New York and London: Harrington Park Press, 1998).

Atkinson, Rebecca, 'I Hoped our Baby Would be Deaf', *The Guardian* 21 March 2006, online at http://www.guardian.co.uk/g2/story/0,,1735544,00.html

St. Augustine, *Concerning the City of God, Against the Pagans* (Henry Bettenson, trans; London: Penguin, 1984).

Baird, Vanessa, *Sex, Love & Homophobia: Lesbian, Gay, Bisexual and Transgender Lives* (London: Amnesty International UK, 2004).

Balen, Adam H., Sarah Creighton, Melanie C. Davies, Jane MacDougall and Richard Stanhope (eds), *Paediatric and Adolescent Gynaecology: A Multidisciplinary Approach* (Cambridge: Cambridge University Press, 2004).

Barbin, Herculine, *Herculine Barbin: Being the Recently Discovered Memoirs of a Nineteenth-Century French Hermaphrodite* (introduction, Michel Foucault, Richard McDougall, trans; New York: Pantheon Books, 1980).

Barth, Karl, *Church Dogmatics III/1: The Doctrine of Creation* (G.T. Thomson et al., trans; Edinburgh: T&T Clark, 1958).

_____ *Church Dogmatics III/4: The Doctrine of Creation* (A.T. Mackay et al., trans; Edinburgh: T&T Clark, 1961).

Beardsley, Christina, 'Taking Issue: The Transsexual Hiatus in *Some Issues in Human Sexuality*', *Theology* 58.845 (Sept–Oct 2005), 338–46.

Beattie, Tina, 'Sexuality and the Resurrection of the Body: Reflections in a Hall of Mirrors', in Gavin D'Costa (ed.), (1996), *Resurrection Reconsidered* (Oxford: Oneworld Publications, 1996), pp. 135–49.

_____ (2007), 'Queen of Heaven', in Gerard Loughlin (ed.), *Queer Theology: Rethinking the Western Body* (Oxford: Blackwell, 2007), pp. 293–304.

Beck, Max, 'Hermaphrodites With Attitude Take to the Streets', 1996, online at http://www.isna.org/books/chrysalis/beck

_____ 'My Life as an Intersexual', 2001, *Nova* online at http://www.pbs.org/wgbh/nova/gender/beck.html

Berinyuu, Abraham, 'Healing and Disability', *International Journal of Practical Theology* 8.2 (Nov. 2004), pp. 202–11.

Billings, Dwight B. and Thomas Urban, 'The Socio-Medical Construction of Transsexualism: An Interpretation and Critique', *Social Problems* 29.3 (Feb. 1982), pp. 266–82.

Bird, Phyllis A., 'Male and Female He Created Them': Gen 1.27b in the Context of the Priestly Account of Creation', *Harvard Theological Review* 74.2 (April 1981), pp. 129-59.

Blevins, John, 'Broadening the Family of God: Debating Same-Sex Marriage and Queer Families in America', *Theology & Sexuality* 12.1 (Sept. 2005), pp. 63-80.

Bloom, Amy, *Normal: Transsexual CEOs, Crossdressing Cops, and Hermaphrodites With Attitude* (London: Bloomsbury, 2002).

Bodies Like Ours Intersex Information and Peer Support Forums. http://www.bodieslikeours.org/forums/

Bohache, Thomas, 'Embodiment as Incarnation: An Incipient Queer Christology', *Theology & Sexuality* 10.1 (2003), pp. 9-29.

_____ 'Matthew', in Guest, Deryn, Robert E. Goss, Mona West and Thomas Bohache (eds), *The Queer Bible Commentary* (London: SCM Press, 2006), pp. 487-516.

Boone, Joseph A. *et al* (eds), *Queer Frontiers: Millennial Geographies, Genders, and Generations* (Madison, WI: University of Wisconsin Press, 2000a).

Boone, Joseph A. (2000b), 'Go West: An Introduction', in Joseph A. Boone *et al* (eds), *Queer Frontiers: Millennial Geographies, Genders, and Generations* (Madison, WI: University of Wisconsin Press, 2000a), pp. 3-20.

Brawley, Robert L. (ed.), *Biblical Ethics and Homosexuality: Listening to Scripture* (Louisville, KY: Westminster John Knox Press, 1996).

Brenner, Athalya, *The Intercourse of Knowledge: On Gendering Desire and 'Sexuality' in the Hebrew Bible* (Leiden, New York and Cologne: Brill, 1997).

Brown, Peter, *The Body and Society: Men, Women, and Sexual Renunciation in Early Christianity* (New York: Columbia University Press, 1988).

Burrus, Virginia, 'Queer Father: Gregory of Nyssa and the Subversion of Identity', in Gerard Loughlin (ed.), *Queer Theology: Rethinking the Western Body* (Oxford: Blackwell, 2007), pp. 147-62.

Butler, Judith, *Gender Trouble: Feminism and the Subversion of Identity* (New York and London: Routledge, 1990).

_____ *Bodies That Matter: On the Discursive Limits of 'Sex'* (New York and London: Routledge, 1993).

_____ 'Performative Acts and Gender Constitution: An Essay in Phenomenology and Feminist Theory', in Katie Conboy, Nadia Medina and Sarah Stanbury (eds), *Writing on the Body: Female Embodiment and Feminist Identity* (New York: Columbia University Press, 1997), pp. 401-17.

_____ 'Doing Justice to Someone: Sex Reassignment and Allegories of Transsexuality', *GLQ* 7.4 (2001), pp. 621-36.

Bynum, Caroline Walker, *The Resurrection of the Body in Western Christianity, 200-1336* (New York: Columbia University Press, 1995).

Campbell, Douglas A. (ed.), *Gospel and Gender: A Trinitarian Engagement with Being Male and Female in Christ* (London: T&T Clark, 2004).

Carden, Michael, 'Genesis / Bereshit', in Deryn Guest, Robert E. Goss, Mona West and Thomas Bohache (eds), *The Queer Bible Commentary* (London: SCM Press, 2006), pp. 21-60.

Carvalhaes, Claudio, 'Oh, Que Sera, Que Sera... A Limping A/Theological Thought in Brazil', in Marcella Althaus-Reid (ed.), *Liberation Theology and Sexuality* (Aldershot: Ashgate, 2006a), pp. 51–69.

Central Board of Finance of the Church of England, *Issues in Human Sexuality: A Statement by the House of Bishops* (London: Church House Publishing, 1991).

_____ *Common Worship: Standard Edition* (London: Church House Publishing, 2000).

Chase, Cheryl [Bo Laurent], 'Intersexual Rights', Letter to the Editor, *The Sciences* 33.4 (Jul–Aug 1993), p. 25.

_____ (director) *Hermaphrodites Speak!*, Rohnert Park, CA: Intersex Society of North America, 1996.

_____ 'Surgical Progress is Not the Answer to Intersexuality', *Journal of Clinical Ethics* 9.4 (Winter 1998a), pp. 385–92.

_____ 'Affronting Reason', in Dawn Atkins (ed.), *Looking Queer: Body Image and Identity in Lesbian, Bisexual, Gay, and Transgender Communities* (New York and London: Harrington Park Press, 1998b), pp. 205–19.

_____ 'What is the Agenda of the Intersex Patient Advocacy Movement?', *The Endocrinologist* 13.3 (May–June 2003), pp. 240–42.

_____ 'Disorders of Sex Development Similar to More Familiar Disorders', Letter to the Editor, *Archives of Disease in Childhood*, 22 August 2006, online at http://adc.bmj.com/cgi/eletters/91/7/554#2546

Clague, Julie, 'The Christa: Symbolizing My Humanity and My Pain', *Feminist Theology* 14.1 (Sept. 2005a), pp. 83–108.

_____ 'Divine Transgressions: The Female Christ-Form in Art', *Critical Quarterly* 47.3 (Autumn 2005b), pp. 47–63.

Clarke, Victoria and Elizabeth Peel (eds), *Out in Psychology: Lesbian, Gay, Bisexual, Trans and Queer Perspectives* (Chichester: John Wiley & Sons Ltd., 2007).

Climb Congenital Adrenal Hyperplasia Support Group. http://www.livingwithcah.com

Coakley, Sarah, *Powers and Submissions: Spirituality, Philosophy and Gender* (Oxford: Blackwell, 2002).

Coan, Stephen, 'The Journey from Selwyn to Sally', *The Natal Witness*, 21 February 2000a, http://www.intersex.org.za/publications/witness1.pdf

_____ 'Shunned by the Church', *The Natal Witness*, 22 February 2000b, http://www.intersex.org.za/publications/witness2.pdf

_____ 'The Struggle to be Sally', *The Natal Witness*, 25 February 2000c, http://www.intersex.org.za/publications/witness3.pdf

Cohen, Andrew (producer), *The Boy Who Was Turned Into a Girl*, BBC Horizon, broadcast BBC2 (UK), 7 December 2000.

Cohen, Andrew and Stephen Sweigart (producers/directors), *Sex: Unknown*, PBS, 2001.

Colapinto, John, 'The True Story of John/Joan', *Rolling Stone*, 11 December 1997, pp. 54–97, online at http://www.pfc.org.uk/node/905

_____ *As Nature Made Him: The Boy Who Was Raised As A Girl* (New York: HarperCollins, 2001).

_____ 'Gender Gap: What Were The Real Reasons Behind David Reimer's Suicide?', *Slate*, 3 June 2004, online at http://www.slate.com/id/2101678

Colson, Charles, 'Blurred Biology: How Many Sexes Are There?', 1996, online at http://www.breakpoint.org/listingarticle.asp?ID=3054

Combe, Victoria, 'Sex-Change Vicar Tells How Her Prayers Have Been Answered', *The Daily Telegraph* 29 November 2000, online at http://www.telegraph.co.uk/news/uknews/1376173/Sex-change-vicar-tells-how-her-prayers-have-been-answered.html

Committee for Ministry Among Deaf People for the General Synod of the Church of England's Advisory Board of Ministry, *The Church Among Deaf People* (London: Church House Publishing, 1997).

Conboy, Katie, Nadia Medina and Sarah Stanbury (eds), *Writing on the Body: Female Embodiment and Feminist Theory* (New York: Columbia University Press, 1997).

Consortium on the Management of Disorders of Sex Development, *Clinical Guidelines for the Management of Disorders of Sex Development in Childhood* (Rohnert Park, CA: Intersex Society of North America, 2006a).

_____ *Handbook for Parents* (Rohnert Park, CA: Intersex Society of North America, 2006b).

Cornwall, Susannah, 'The *Kenosis* of Unambiguous Sex in the Body of Christ: Intersex, Theology and Existing "for the Other"', *Theology & Sexuality* 14.2 (Jan 2008a), pp. 181–200.

_____ 'Ambiguous Bodies, Ambiguous Readings: Reflections on James M. Murphy's "Christine on the Cross", in Zowie Davy et al (eds), *Bound and Unbound: Interdisciplinary Approaches to Genders and Sexualities* (Newcastle: CSP, 2008b), pp. 93–110.

_____ '"State of Mind" versus "Concrete Set of Facts": The Contrasting of Transgender and Intersex in Church Documents on Sexuality', *Theology & Sexuality* 15.1 (2009a), pp. 7–28.

_____ 'Theologies of Resistance: Intersex, Disability and Queering the "Real World"', in Morgan Holmes (ed.), *Critical Intersex* (Aldershot: Ashgate, 2009b).

Countryman, L. William, *Dirt, Greed and Sex: Sexual Ethics in the New Testament and their Implications for Today* (London: SCM Press, 1989).

Coventry, Martha, 'Making the Cut', *Ms Magazine* (Oct–Nov 2000), online at http://www.msmagazine.com/oct00/makingthecut.html

Craig, Olga, 'We Are Not What We Seem', *Sunday Telegraph* Review, 29 February 2004, pp. 1–4.

Crasnow, Sharon L., 'Models and Reality: When Science Tackles Sex', *Hypatia* 16.3 (Summer 2001), pp. 138–48.

Crawford, Jennifer M., Garry Warne, Sonia Grover, Bridget R. Southwell and John M. Hutson, 'Results from a Pediatric Surgical Centre Justify Early Intervention in Disorders of Sex Development', *Journal of Pediatric Surgery* 44.2 (February 2009), pp. 413–16.

Creamer, Deborah, 'Toward a Theology That Includes the Human Experience of Disability', in Robert C. Anderson (ed.), *Graduate Theological Education and the Human Experience of Disability* (Binghampton, NY: The Haworth Pastoral Press, 2003), pp. 57–67.

Creighton, Sarah, 'Long-term Sequelae of Genital Surgery', in Adam H. Balen, Sarah Creighton, Melanie C. Davies, Jane MacDougall and Richard Stanhope (eds), *Paediatric and Adolescent Gynaecology: A Multidisciplinary Approach* (Cambridge: Cambridge University Press, 2004), pp. 327–33.

Creighton, Sarah and Lih-Mei Liao, 'Changing Attitudes to Sex Assignment in Intersex', *BJU International* 93 (2004), pp. 659–64.

Creighton, Sarah and Catherine Minto, 'Managing Intersex: Most Vaginal Surgery in Childhood Should be Deferred', *British Medical Journal* 323 (2001), pp. 1264–65.

Creighton, S.M., C.L. Minto and S.J. Steele, 'Objective Cosmetic and Anatomical Outlines at Adolescence of Feminizing Surgery for Ambiguous Genitalia done in Childhood', *The Lancet* 358 (2001), pp. 124–25.

Crouch, Robert A., 'Betwixt and Between: the Past and Future of Intersexuality', *Journal of Clinical Ethics* 9.4 (Winter 1998), pp. 372–84.

D'Costa, Gavin (ed.), *Resurrection Reconsidered* (Oxford: Oneworld Publications, 1996).

_____ *Sexing the Trinity: Gender, Culture and the Divine* (London: SCM Press, 2000).

Devore, Howard, 'Growing Up in the Surgical Maelstrom', in Alice Domurat Dreger, *Intersex in the Age of Ethics* (Hagerstown, MD: University Publishing Group, 1999), pp. 78–81.

Diamond, Milton and H.K. Sigmundson, 'Sex Reassignment at Birth: Long Term Review and Clinical Implications', *Archives of Pediatrics and Adolescent Medicine* 151 (March 1997a), pp. 298–304.

_____ 'Management of Intersexuality: Guidelines for Dealing with Persons with Ambiguous Genitalia', in *Archives of Pediatrics and Adolescent Medicine* 151 (October 1997b), pp. 1046–1050

Diamond, Milton and Hazel Glenn Beh, 'The Right to be Wrong: Sex and Gender Decisions', in Sharon E. Sytsma (ed.), *Ethics and Intersex* (Dordrecht: Springer, 2006), pp. 103–13.

Dormor, Duncan and Jeremy Morris (eds), *An Acceptable Sacrifice? Homosexuality and the Church* (London: SPCK, 2007).

Douglas, Mary, *Purity and Danger: An Analysis of the Concepts of Pollution and Taboo* (London: Routledge & Kegan Paul, 1966).

Downing, F. Gerald, 'The Nature(s) of Christian Women and Men', *Theology* 58.843 (May–June 2005), pp. 178–84.

Dreger, Alice Domurat, *Hermaphrodites and the Medical Invention of Sex* (Massachusetts and London: Harvard University Press, 1998).

_____ (ed.), *Intersex in the Age of Ethics* (Hagerstown, MD: University Publishing Group, 1999).

_____ 'Intersex Treatment as Standard Medical Practice, or, How Wrong I Was', 2004, online at http://www.isna.org/articles/howwrongiwas

_____ 'Intersex and Human Rights: The Long View', in Sharon E. Sytsma (ed.), *Ethics and Intersex* (Dordrecht: Springer, 2006a), pp. 73–86.

_____ 'My Identity/Politics', 2006b, online at http://www.alicedreger.com/identity_politics.html

Dreger, Alice Domurat and April M. Herndon, 'Progress and Politics in the Intersex Rights Movement', *GLQ* 15.2 (Jan 2009), pp. 199–224.

Dreifus, Claudia, 'A Conversation with Anne Fausto-Sterling: Exploring what makes us Male or Female', *The New York Times*, 2 January 2001, F3.

Dussel, Enrique, *Ethics and the Theology of Liberation* (Bernard F. McWilliams trans; Maryknoll, NY: Orbis Books, 1978).

_____ *Philosophy of Liberation* (Aquilina Martinez and Christine Morkovsky trans; Maryknoll, NY: Orbis Books, 1985).

Eiesland, Nancy L., *The Disabled God: Towards a Liberatory Theology of Disability* (Nashville, TN: Abingdon Press, 1994).

Eiesland, Nancy L. and Don E. Saliers (eds), *Human Disability and the Service of God: Reassessing Religious Practice* (Nashville, TN: Abingdon Press, 1998).

Ellingson, Stephen and M. Christian Green (eds), *Religion and Sexuality in Cross-Cultural Perspective* (New York and London: Routledge, 2002).

Eugenides, Jeffrey, *Middlesex* (London: Bloomsbury, 2002).

Evangelical Alliance Policy Commission, *Transsexuality* (London: Evangelical Alliance, 2000).

Evangelical Alliance and Parakaleo Ministry, *Gender Recognition: A Guide for Churches to the Gender Recognition Act (UK)* (London: Evangelical Alliance and Parakaleo Ministry, 2006).

Fausto-Sterling, Anne 'The Five Sexes: Why Male and Female Are Not Enough', *The Sciences* 33.2 (Mar–Apr 1993), pp. 20–24.

_____ 'How to Build a Man', in Vernon A. Rosario (ed.), *Science and Homosexualities* (London and New York: Routledge, 1997), pp. 219–25.

_____ *Sexing the Body: Gender Politics and the Construction of Sexuality* (New York: Basic Books, 2000).

Feder, Ellen K., 'Doctor's Orders: Parents and Intersexed Children', in Eva Feder Kittay and Ellen K. Feder (eds), *The Subject of Care: Feminist Perspectives on Dependency* (Lanham, MD: Rowman and Littlefield, 2002), pp. 294–320.

_____ '"In Their Best Interests": Parents' Experience of Atypical Genitalia', in Erik Parens (ed.), *Surgically Shaping Children: Technology, Ethics, and the Pursuit of Normality* (Baltimore, MD: The Johns Hopkins University Press, 2006), pp. 189–210.

_____ 'Imperatives of Normality: From "Intersex" to "Disorders of Sex Development"', *GLQ* 15.2 (Jan 2009), pp. 225–47.

Feder, Ellen K. and Katrina Karkazis, 'What's in a Name? The Controversy over "Disorders of Sex Development"', *Hastings Center Report* 38.5 (Sept-Oct 2008), pp. 33–36.

Fiddes, Paul S., 'The Status of Woman in the Thought of Karl Barth', in Janet Martin Soskice (ed.), *After Eve: Women, Theology and the Christian Tradition* (London: Marshall Pickering, 1990), pp. 138–55.

Fontaine, Carole R., 'Response to Elly Elshout, Roundtable Discussion: Women with Disabilities: A Challenge to Feminist Theology', *Journal of Feminist Studies in Religion* 10.2 (Fall 1994), pp. 108–14.

Ford, David F., *Self and Salvation: Being Transformed* (Cambridge: Cambridge University Press, 1999).

Gale, Porter and Laleh Soomekh (producers/directors) *XXXY*, Stanford University Department of Communications, 2000.

Gard, Paul, *Human Endocrinology* (London: Taylor & Francis, 1998).

Gilbert, Ruth, *Early Modern Hermaphrodites: Sex and Other Stories* (Basingstoke: Palgrave, 2002).

Godwin, Nick (producer/director), *Secret Intersex*, broadcast Channel 4 (UK), 5-6 April 2004.

Gorringe, T.J., *Karl Barth: Against Hegemony* (Oxford: Clarendon Press, 1999).

_____ *The Education of Desire: Towards a Theology of the Senses* (London: SCM Press, 2001).

_____ *Furthering Humanity: A Theology of Culture* (Aldershot: Ashgate, 2004).

Gorsline, Robin Hawley, '1 and 2 Peter', in Deryn Guest, Robert E. Goss, Mona West and Thomas Bohache (eds), *The Queer Bible Commentary* (London: SCM Press, 2006), pp. 724-36.

Goss, Robert E., 'Queer Theologies as Transgressive Metaphors: New Paradigms for Hybrid Sexual Theologies', *Theology & Sexuality* 10 (1999), pp. 43-53.

_____ 'Proleptic Sexual Love: God's Promiscuity Reflected in Christian Polyamory', *Theology & Sexuality* 11.1 (2004), pp. 52-63.

_____ 'Luke', in Deryn Guest, Robert E. Goss, Mona West and Thomas Bohache (eds), *The Queer Bible Commentary* (London: SCM Press, 2006a), pp. 526-47.

_____ 'John', in Deryn Guest, Robert E. Goss, Mona West and Thomas Bohache (eds), *The Queer Bible Commentary* (London: SCM Press, 2006b), pp. 548-65.

_____ 'Ephesians', in Deryn Guest, Robert E. Goss, Mona West and Thomas Bohache (eds), *The Queer Bible Commentary* (London: SCM Press, 2006c), pp. 630-38.

Goss, Robert E. and Deborah Krause, 'The Pastoral Letters: 1 and 2 Timothy, and Titus', in Deryn Guest, Robert E. Goss, Mona West and Thomas Bohache (eds), *The Queer Bible Commentary* (London: SCM Press, 2006), pp. 684-92.

Grabham, Emily, 'Knitting the Nation: Intersex Surgeries and Time', paper presented at Critical Sexology seminar, London South Bank University, 3 September 2008.

Greenberg, Blu, *How to Run a Traditional Jewish Household* (New York: Simon & Schuster, 1985).

Gross, Sally, 'Intersexuality and Scripture', *Theology & Sexuality* 11 (1999), pp. 65-74.

Groveman, Sherri A., 'Sex, Lies and Androgen Insensitivity Syndrome', Letter to the Editor, *Canadian Medical Association Journal* 154.12 (June 1996), pp. 1829-30.

_____ 'The Hanukkah Bush: Ethical Implications in the Clinical Management of Intersex', *Journal of Clinical Ethics* 9.4 (Winter 1998), pp. 356-59.

Guest, Deryn, *When Deborah Met Jael: Lesbian Biblical Hermeneutics* (London: SCM Press, 2005).

_____ 'Deuteronomy', in Deryn Guest, Robert E. Goss, Mona West and Thomas Bohache (eds), The *Queer Bible Commentary* (London: SCM Press, 2006), pp. 122-43.

Guest, Deryn, Robert E. Goss, Mona West and Thomas Bohache (eds), *The Queer Bible Commentary* (London: SCM Press, 2006).

Halperin, David M., *Saint Foucault: Towards a Gay Hagiography* (New York and Oxford: Oxford University Press, 1995).

Hampson, Daphne, *Theology and Feminism* (Oxford: Blackwell, 1990).

_____ (ed.), *Swallowing a Fishbone? Feminist Theologians Debate Christianity* (London: SPCK, 1996a).

_____ 'Response', in Daphne Hampson (ed.), *Swallowing a Fishbone? Feminist Theologians Debate Christianity* (London: SPCK, 1996b), pp. 112–24.

_____ 'On Power and Gender', in Adrian Thatcher and Elizabeth Stuart (eds), *Christian Perspectives on Sexuality and Gender* (Leominster: Gracewing, 1996c), pp. 125–40.

Hare, John, '"Neither Male Nor Female": The Case of Intersexuality', in Duncan Dormor and Jeremy Morris (eds), *An Acceptable Sacrifice? Homosexuality and the Church* (London: SPCK, 2007), 98–111.

Harmon-Smith, Helena, '10 Commandments', *Journal of Clinical Ethics* 9.4 (Winter 1998), p. 371.

Harper, Catherine, *Intersex* (Oxford and New York: Berg, 2007).

Harvey, Susan A., 'Embodiment in Time and Eternity: A Syriac Perspective', in Eugene F. Rogers (ed.), *Theology and Sexuality: Classic and Contemporary Readings* (Oxford: Blackwell, 2002), pp. 3–22.

Hauerwas, Stanley, 'Suffering the Retarded: Should we Prevent Retardation?', in John Swinton (ed.), *Critical Reflections on Stanley Hauerwas' Theology of Disability: Disabling Society, Enabling Theology: Journal of Religion, Disability and Health,* Special Issue, 8.3/4 (2004a), pp. 87–106.

_____ 'The Retarded, Society, and the Family: The Dilemma of Care', in John Swinton (ed.), *Critical Reflections on Stanley Hauerwas' Theology of Disability: Disabling Society, Enabling Theology, Journal of Religion, Disability and Health,* Special Issue, 8.3/4 (2004b), pp. 161–79.

Hearon, Holly E., '1 and 2 Corinthians', in Deryn Guest, Robert E. Goss, Mona West and Thomas Bohache (eds), *The Queer Bible Commentary* (London: SCM Press, 2006), pp. 606–23.

Hegarty, Peter and Cheryl Chase [Bo Laurent], 'Intersex Activism, Feminism and Psychology', in Iain Morland and Annabelle Willox (eds), *Queer Theory* (Basingstoke: Palgrave Macmillan, 2005a), pp. 70–80.

Herdt, Gilbert (ed.), *Third Sex, Third Gender: Beyond Cultural Dimorphism in Culture and History* (New York: Zone Books, 1994a).

_____ 'Third Sexes and Third Genders', in Gilbert Herdt (ed.), *Third Sex, Third Gender: Beyond Cultural Dimorphism in Culture and History* (New York: Zone Books, 1994b), pp. 21–81.

_____ 'Mistaken Sex: Culture, Biology and the Third Sex in New Guinea', in Gilbert Herdt (ed.), *Third Sex, Third Gender: Beyond Cultural Dimorphism in Culture and History* (New York: Zone Books, 1994c), pp. 419–45.

Herndon, April, 'Why Doesn't ISNA want to Eradicate Gender?', 2006), online at http://www.isna.org/faq/not_eradicating_gender

Hester, J. David, 'Intersexes and the End of Gender: Corporeal Ethics and Postgender Bodies', *Journal of Gender Studies* 13.3 (Nov 2004), pp. 215–25.

_____ 'Eunuchs and the Postgender Jesus: Matthew 19.12 and Transgressive Sexualities', *Journal for the Study of the New Testament* 28.1 (Sept 2005), pp. 13–40.

_____ 'Intersex and the Rhetorics of Healing', in Sharon E. Sytsma (ed.), *Ethics and Intersex* (Dordrecht: Springer, 2006a), pp. 47–71.

Heyward, Carter, *The Redemption of God: A Theology of Mutual Relation* (Lanham, MD: University Press of America, 1982).

_____ 'Godding', in Lisa Isherwood and Dorothea McEwan (eds), *An A to Z of Feminist Theology* (Sheffield: Sheffield Academic Press, 1996), p. 85.

Hillman, Thea, *Intersex (For Lack of a Better Word)* (San Francisco, CA: Manic D. Press, 2008).

Hines, Melissa, 'Neuroscience and Intersex', *The Psychologist* 17.8 (Aug 2004), pp. 455-58.

Hinkle, Christopher, 'Love's Urgent Longings: St John of the Cross', in Gerard Loughlin (ed.), *Queer Theology: Rethinking the Western Body* (Oxford: Blackwell, 2007), pp. 188-99.

Hird, Myra J., 'Gender's Nature: Intersexuality, Transsexualism and the "Sex"/ "Gender" Binary', *Feminist Theory* 1.3 (2000), pp. 347-64.

Hird, Myra J. and Germon Jenz, 'The Intersexual Body and the Medical Regulation of Gender', in Kathryn Backett-Milburn and Linda McKie (eds), *Constructing Gendered Bodies* (Basingstoke: Palgrave, 2001), pp. 162-78.

Hoad, T. F., *The Concise Oxford Dictionary of English Etymology* (Oxford and New York: Oxford University Press, 1986).

Holder, Rodney, 'The Ethics of Transsexualism, Part 1: The Transsexual Condition and the Biblical Background to an Ethical Response', *Crucible* 37 (April-June 1998a), pp. 89-99.

_____ 'The Ethics of Transsexualism, Part 2: A Christian Response to the Issues Raised', *Crucible* 37 (July-Sept 1998b), pp. 125-36.

Hollywood, Amy, 'Queering the Beguines: Mechthild of Magdeburg, Hadewijch of Anvers, Marguerite Porete', in Gerard Loughlin (ed.), *Queer Theology: Rethinking the Western Body* (Oxford: Blackwell, 2007), pp. 163-175

Holmes, Morgan (1998), 'In(to)Visibility: Intersexuality in the Field of Queer', in Dawn Atkins (ed.), *Looking Queer: Body Image and Identity in Lesbian, Bisexual, Gay, and Transgender Communities* (New York and London: Harrington Park Press, 1998), pp. 221-26.

_____ 'Rethinking the Meaning and Management of Intersexuality', *Sexualities* 5.2 (2002), pp. 159-80.

_____ 'Locating Third Sexes', *Transformations* 8 (July 2004), online at http:// transformations.cqu.edu.au/journal/issue_08/article_03.shtml

_____ 'Mind the Gaps: Intersex and (Re-productive) Spaces in Disability Studies and Bioethics', *Journal of Bioethical Inquiry* 5.2-3 (2008), pp. 169-81.

Horne, Simon, '"Those Who Are Blind See": Some New Testament Uses of Impairment, Inability and Paradox', in Nancy L. Eiesland, and Don E. Saliers (eds), *Human Disability and the Service of God: Reassessing Religious Practice* (Nashville, TN: Abingdon Press, 1998), pp. 88-101.

Hrabovszky, Zoltan and John M. Hutson, 'Surgical Treatment of Intersex Abnormalities: A Review', *Surgery* 131.1 (Jan 2002), pp. 92-104.

Hull, John M., *In the Beginning There Was Darkness: a Blind Person's Conversations with the Bible* (London: SCM, 2001).

_____ '"Sight To The Inly Blind"?: Attitudes to Blindness in the Hymnbooks', *Theology* 105:827 (Sept-Oct 2002), pp. 333-41.

_____ 'A Spirituality of Disability: The Christian Heritage as both Problem and Potential', *Studies in Christian Ethics* 16:2 (2003a), pp. 21-35.

_____ 'The Broken Body in a Broken World: A Contribution to a Christian Doctrine of the Person from a Disabled Point of View', *Journal of Religion, Disability and Health* 7.4 (2003b), pp. 5-23.

Hutson, John M., 'Clitoral Hypertrophy and Other Forms of Ambiguous Genitalia in the Labour Ward', *Australian and New Zealand Journal of Obstetrics and Gynaecology* 32.3 (1992), pp. 238-39.

Intersex Initiative, www.intersexinitiative.org

Intersex Society of North America, www.isna.org

Intersex Support Group International, www.xyxo.org/isgi/index.html

Intersex Pride, http://www.intersexpride.blogspot.com

Irigaray, Luce *Speculum of the Other Woman* (trans. Gillian C., Gill; Ithaca, NY: Cornell University Press, 1985).

Isherwood, Lisa and Marcella Althaus-Reid, 'Queering Theology: Thinking Theology and Queer Theory', in Marcella Althaus-Reid and Lisa Isherwood (eds), *The Sexual Theologian: Essays on Sex, God and Politics* (London and New York: T&T Clark, 2004), pp. 1-15.

Jantzen, Grace M. 'Contours of a Queer Theology', in Janet Martin Soskice and Diana Lipton (eds), *Feminism & Theology* (Oxford: Oxford University Press, 2003), pp. 344-55.

Jardine, Cassandra, 'It Sounds Silly But I've Nothing To Wear', in *The Daily Telegraph*, 23 June 2000, online at http://www.pfc.org.uk/node/720

Jasper, Alison, 'Theology at the Freak Show: St Uncumber and the Discourse of Liberation', *Theology & Sexuality* 11.2 (Jan 2005), pp. 43-54.

Johnson, Katherine, 'Transsexualism: Diagnostic Dilemmas, Transgender Politics and the Future of Transgender Care', in Victoria Clarke and Elizabeth Peel (eds), *Out in Psychology: Lesbian, Gay, Bisexual, Trans and Queer Perspectives* (Chichester: John Wiley & Sons Ltd., 2007), pp. 445-64.

Jones, Sarah, interview with Martha Kearney, *Woman's Hour*, BBC Radio 4, broadcast 1 November 2005.

Jordan, Mark D., 'God's Body', in Gerard Loughlin (ed.), *Queer Theology: Rethinking the Western Body* (Oxford: Blackwell, 2007), pp. 281-92.

Jung, Patricia Beattie, 'Christianity and Human Sexual Polymorphism: Are They Compatible?', in Sharon E. Sytsma (ed.), *Ethics and Intersex* (Dordrecht: Springer, 2006a), pp. 293-309.

Karkazis, Katrina, *Fixing Sex: Intersex, Medical Authority, and Lived Experience* (Durham, NC and London: Duke University Press, 2008).

Kessel, Edward L., 'A Proposed Biological Interpretation of the Virgin Birth', *Journal of the American Scientific Affiliation* 35 (Sept 1983), pp. 129-36.

Kessler, Suzanne J., *Lessons from the Intersexed* (New Brunswick, NJ and London: Rutgers University Press, 1998).

Kessler, Suzanne J. and Wendy McKenna, *Gender: An Ethnomethodological Approach* (Chicago, IL: University of Chicago Press, 1978).

Kipnis, Kenneth and Milton Diamond, 'Pediatric Ethics and the Surgical Assignment of Sex', *Journal of Clinical Ethics* 9.4 (Winter 1998), pp. 398-410.

Kirk, Jenny, 'After My Sex Change I Felt a Huge Weight Had Been Lifted. It Was Like Being Reborn', *The Independent on Sunday*, 4 February 2007, p. 57.

Kitzinger, Celia, 'The Myth of the Two Biological Sexes', *The Psychologist* 17.8 (August 2004), pp. 451-54.

Klinefelter Organization, http://www.klinefelter.org.uk/

Klinefelter's Syndrome Association UK, http://www.ksa-uk.co.uk

Koch, Timothy R., 'A Homoerotic Approach to Scripture', *Theology & Sexuality* 7.14 (March 2001), pp. 10–22.

Kolakowski, Victoria S., 'Toward a Christian Ethical Response to Transsexual Persons', *Theology & Sexuality* 6 (1997a), pp. 10–31.

_____ 'The Concubine and the Eunuch: Queering Up the Breeder's Bible', in Robert E. Goss and Amy Adams Squire Strongheart (eds), *Our Families, Our Values: Snapshots of Queer Kinship* (New York and London: The Haworth Press, 1997b), pp. 35–50.

Koyama, Emi, 'Suggested Guidelines for Non-Intersex Individuals Writing About Intersexuality & Intersex People', in Emi Koyama (ed.), *Teaching Intersex Issues: A Guide for Teachers in Women's, Gender and Queer Studies* (Portland, OR: Intersex Initiative, 2003a, 2nd edn), pp. 32–33.

_____ (ed.), *Teaching Intersex Issues: A Guide for Teachers in Women's, Gender and Queer Studies*, (Portland, OR: Intersex Initiative, 2003b, 2nd edn).

_____ 'From "Intersex" to "DSD": Toward a Queer Disability Politics of Gender', 2006, online at http://intersexinitiative.org/articles/intersextodsd.html

Laqueur, Thomas, *Making Sex: Body and Gender from the Greeks to Freud* (Cambridge, MA and London: Harvard University Press, 1990).

Laurent, Bo, 'Why a Focus on Surgery Can't Improve Health Care Services for Disorders of Sex Development', paper presented at Genital Cutting in a Globalized Age: A Forum for Interdisciplinary Debate conference, Royal Society of Medicine, London, 4 July 2008.

Lebacqz, Karen, 'Difference or Defect? Intersexuality and the Politics of Difference', in *Annual of the Society of Christian Ethics* 17 (1997), pp. 213–29.

Lee, Peter A., Christopher P. Houk, S. Faisal Ahmed and Ieuan A. Hughes, in collaboration with the participants in the International Consensus Conference on Intersex 'Consensus Statement on Management of Intersex Disorders', *Pediatrics* 118 (2006), e488–e500.

Lehrman, Sally, 'Sex Police', in *Salon.com*, (1999), online at http://www.salon.com/health/feature/1999/04/05/sex_police/index.html

Lewis, Hannah, *Deaf Liberation Theology* (Aldershot: Ashgate, 2007).

Liao, Lih-Mei, 'Towards a Clinical-Psychological Approach to Address the Heterosexual Concerns of Intersexed Women', in Victoria Clarke and Elizabeth Peel (eds), *Out in Psychology: Lesbian, Gay, Bisexual, Trans and Queer Perspectives* (Chichester: John Wiley & Sons Ltd., 2007), pp. 391–408.

Liao, Lih-Mei and Mary Boyle, 'Surgical Feminising: The Right Approach?', *The Psychologist* 17.8 (August 2004), 459–62.

Liew, Tat-siong Benny, '(Cor)Responding: A Letter to the Editor', in Ken Stone (ed.), *Queer Commentary and the Hebrew Bible* (Sheffield: Sheffield Academic Press, 2001), pp. 182–92.

Long, Lynnell Stephani, 'DSD vs Intersex', Letter to the Editor, *Archives of Disease in Childhood*, 23 August 2006, online at http://adc.bmj.com/cgi/eletters/91/7/554#2549

Loughlin, Gerard, 'Sex After Natural Law', *Studies in Christian Ethics* 16.1 (2003), pp. 14–28.

_____ *Alien Sex: The Body and Desire in Cinema and Theology* (Oxford: Blackwell, 2004).

_____ (ed.), *Queer Theology: Rethinking the Western Body* (Oxford: Blackwell, 2007a).

_____ 'Introduction: The End of Sex', in Gerard Loughlin (ed.), *Queer Theology: Rethinking the Western Body*, Oxford: Blackwell, 2007b, pp. 1–34.

Looy, Heather, 'Male and Female God Created Them: The Challenge of Intersexuality', *Journal of Psychology and Christianity* 21.1 (2002), pp.10–20.

Looy, Heather and Hessel Bouma III, 'The Nature of Gender: Gender Identity in Persons who are Intersexed or Transgendered', *Journal of Psychology and Theology* 33.3 (2005), pp. 166–78.

MacDonald, Mairi, 'Intersex and Gender Identity', at United Kingdom Intersex Association website, (2000), http://www.ukia.co.uk/voices/is_gi.htm

MacDougall, Jane and Sarah Creighton, 'Surgical Correction of Vaginal and Other Anomalies', in Adam H. Balen, Sarah Creighton, Melanie C. Davies, Jane MacDougall and Richard Stanhope (eds), *Paediatric and Adolescent Gynaecology: A Multidisciplinary Approach* (Cambridge: Cambridge University Press, 2004), pp. 120–30.

Mairs, Nancy, *Carnal Acts* (Boston: Beacon Press, 1996).

Matzko McCarthy, David, 'Fecundity: Sex and Social Reproduction', in Gerard Loughlin (ed.), *Queer Theology: Rethinking the Western Body* (Oxford: Blackwell, 2007), pp. 86–95.

_____ 'Christ's Body in its Fullness: Resurrection and the Lives of the Saints', in Gavin D'Costa, (ed.), *Resurrection Reconsidered* (Oxford: Oneworld Publications, 1996), pp. 102–17.

McKim, Chris (producer/director), *Sex Change Hospital*, World of Wonder, broadcast More4 (UK), August 2007.

Meeks, Wayne A.,'The Image of the Androgyne: Some Uses of a Symbol in Earliest Christianity', *History of Religions* 13.3 (Feb 1974), pp. 165–208.

Meyer, Marvin, *The Gospel of Thomas: The Hidden Sayings of Jesus* (San Francisco, CA: HarperSanFrancisco, 1992).

Meyerowitz, Joanne, *How Sex Changed: A History of Transsexuality in the United States* (Cambridge, MA: Harvard University Press, 2002).

Mollenkott, Virginia Ramey *Omnigender: A Trans-Religious Approach (Revised and Expanded Edition),* (Cleveland, OH: Pilgrim Press, 2007).

_____ Untitled lecture given at Religion and the Feminist Movement conference, Harvard Divinity School, November 2002, online at http://www.hds.harvard.edu/wsrp/scholarship/rfmc/video/speakervid3_3.htm

Mollenkott, Virginia Ramey and Vanessa Sheridan *Transgender Journeys* (Cleveland, OH: Pilgrim Press, 2003).

Moltmann, Jürgen, *The Coming of God: Christian Eschatology* (trans. Margaret Kohl, London: SCM Press, 1996).

_____ 'Liberate Yourselves By Accepting One Another', in Nancy L. Eiesland, and Don E. Saliers (eds), *Human Disability and the Service of God: Reassessing Religious Practice* (Nashville, TN: Abingdon Press, 1998), pp. 105–22.

Moltmann-Wendel, Elisabeth, *I Am My Body: New Ways of Embodiment* (London: SCM Press, 1994).

Money, John, *Love and Love Sickness: The Science of Sex, Gender Difference, and Pair-Bonding* (Baltimore and London: The Johns Hopkins University Press, 1980).

_____ 'The Development of Sexuality and Eroticism in Humankind', *The Quarterly Review of Biology* 56.4 (Dec 1981), pp. 379–404.

_____ *Gay, Straight and In-Between: The Sexology of Erotic Orientation* (New York and Oxford: Oxford University Press, 1988).

_____ *Gendermaps: Social Constructionism, Feminism and Sexosophical History* (New York: Continuum, 1995).

Money, John and Anke A. Ehrhardt, *Man & Woman, Boy & Girl: The Differentiation and Dimorphism of Gender Identity from Conception to Maturity* (Baltimore and London: The Johns Hopkins University Press, 1972).

Moore, Stephen D., *God's Beauty Parlor: And Other Queer Spaces In and Around the Bible* (Stanford, CA: Stanford University Press, 2001).

Moreno, Angela, 'In Amerika They Call Us Hermaphrodites', in Alice Domurat Dreger (ed.), *Intersex in the Age of Ethics* (Hagerstown, MD: University Publishing Group, 1999), pp. 137–39.

Morland, Iain, 'Is Intersexuality Real?', *Textual Practice* 15.3 (2001a), pp. 527–47.

_____ 'Feminism and Intersexuality: A Response to Myra J. Hird's "Gender's Nature"', *Feminist Theory* 2.3 (2001b), pp. 362–66.

_____ 'Thinking With The Phallus', *The Psychologist* 17.8 (Aug 2004), 448–50.

_____ 'Narrating Intersex: On the Ethical Critique of the Medical Management of Intersexuality, 1985–2005', PhD thesis, Royal Holloway: University of London, 2005a.

_____ ''The Glans Opens Like a Book': Writing and Reading the Intersexed Body', *Continuum: Journal of Media and Culture Studies* 19.3 (2005b), pp. 335–48.

_____ 'Postmodern Intersex', in Sharon E. Sytsma (ed.), *Ethics and Intersex* (Dordrecht: Springer, 2006), pp. 319–32.

_____ 'Ways of Reading the Intersex Controversy', paper presented at Critical Sexology seminar, London South Bank University, 3 September 2008.

_____ 'What can Queer Theory do for Intersex?', *GLQ* 15.2 (Jan 2009), pp. 285–312.

Morland, Iain and Annabelle Willox (eds), *Queer Theory* (Basingstoke: Palgrave Macmillan, 2005a).

_____ 'Introduction', in Iain Morland and Annabelle Willox (eds), *Queer Theory* (Basingstoke: Palgrave Macmillan, 2005b), pp. 1–5.

Morris, Esther, 'The Missing Vagina Monologue', (2003), online at http://www.intersexinitiative.org/vday/missingvagina.pdf

_____ 'The Self I Will Never Know', *New Internationalist* 364: Equality (Jan–Feb 2004), pp. 25–27.

Morris, Jan *Conundrum* (London: Faber & Faber, 2002).

Morris, Sherri Groveman, 'DSD and Identity', Letter to the Editor, *Archives of Disease in Childhood*, 22 August 2006, (2006a), online at http://adc.bmj.com/cgi/eletters/91/7/554#2540

_____ 'Twisted Lies: My Journey in an Imperfect Body', in Erik Parens (ed.), *Surgically Shaping Children: Technology, Ethics, and the Pursuit of Normality* (Baltimore: The Johns Hopkins University Press, 2006b), pp. 3–12.

Mortimer, Roz (producer/director), *Gender Trouble*, Wonderdog Productions/Wellcome Trust, 2002.

Mottet, Lisa and Justin Tanis, *Opening the Door to the Inclusion of Transgender People: The Nine Keys to Making Lesbian, Gay, Bisexual and Transgender Organizations Fully Transgender-Inclusive* (New York: National Gay and Lesbian Task Force Policy Institute and the National Center for Transgender Equality, 2008).

MRKH Organization, http://www.mrkh.org/

Muers, Rachel, 'A Question of Two Answers: Difference and Determination in Barth and von Balthasar', *Heythrop Journal* 40.3 (July 1999), pp. 265–79.

_____ 'The Mute Cannot Keep Silent', in Janet Martin Soskice and Diana Lipton (eds) *Feminism & Theology* (Oxford: Oxford University Press, 2003), pp. 109–20.

_____ 'A Queer Theology: Hans Urs von Balthasar', in Gerard Loughlin, (ed.), *Queer Theology: Rethinking the Western Body* (Oxford: Blackwell, 2007), pp. 200–11.

Murphy, James M., 'A Female Christ for Men and Women', unpublished document (1990).

Nanda, Serena, 'The Hijras: An Alternative Gender in Indian Culture', in Stephen Ellingson and M. Christian Green (eds), *Religion and Sexuality in Cross-Cultural Perspective* (New York and London: Routledge, 2002), pp. 137–63.

Nataf, Zachary I., *Lesbians Talk Transgender* (London: Scarlet Press, 1996).

Natarajan, Anita, 'Medical Ethics and Truth Telling in the Case of Androgen Insensitivity Syndrome', *Canadian Medical Association Journal* 154.4 (February 1996), pp. 568–70.

Newell, Christopher, 'Disabled Theologies and the Journeys of Liberation to Where our Names Appear', *Feminist Theology* 15.3 (May 2007), pp. 322–45.

Nichols, Bridget, 'The Picture of Health: Liturgical Metaphors of Wholeness and Healing', *Studies in Christian Ethics* 15:1 (2002), pp. 40–53.

Nixon, David, '"No More Tea, Vicar". An Exploration of the Discourses which Inform the Current Debates about Sexualities within the Church of England', *Sexualities* 11.5 (Oct 2008), pp. 595–620.

O'Donovan, Oliver, *Transsexualism and Christian Marriage* (Nottingham: Grove Books, 1982).

O'Neill, Sean, 'Vicar Can Carry on Preaching after Sex Change', *The Daily Telegraph*, 20 June 2000, online at http://www.telegraph.co.uk/news/uknews/1344012/Vicar-can-carry-on-preaching-after-sex-change.html

Organisation Intersex International, http://www.intersexualite.org/

Pailin, David, *A Gentle Touch: From a Theology of Handicap to a Theology of Human Being* (London: SPCK, 1992).

Parens, Erik (ed.), *Surgically Shaping Children: Technology, Ethics, and the Pursuit of Normality* (Baltimore, MD: The Johns Hopkins University Press, 2006).

Parlagreco, Joseph (producer/director), *Call Me Malcolm*, Filmworks/United Church of Christ, 2005.

Patterson, Barbara A.B., 'Redeemed Bodies: Fullness of Life', in Nancy L. Eiesland and Don E. Saliers (eds), *Human Disability and the Service of God: Reassessing Religious Practice* (Nashville, TN: Abingdon Press, 1998), pp. 123-43.

Pauly, Ira, 'Terminology and Classification of Gender Identity Disorders', *Journal of Psychology and Human Sexuality* 5.4 (1992), pp. 1-14.

Pazeraite, Aušra, '"*Zakhar* and *neqêvah* He created them": Sexual and Gender Identities in the Bible', *Feminist Theology* 17.1 (Sept 2008), pp. 92-110.

Peirce, Kimberly (director), *Boys Don't Cry*, Hart-Sharp Entertainment/ Independent Film Channel/Killer Films, 1999.

Perkins, Pheme, *Resurrection: New Testament Witness and Contemporary Reflection* (London: Geoffrey Chapman, 1984).

Pinsky, Leonard, Robert P. Erickson and R. Neil Schimke, *Genetic Disorders of Human Sexual Development* [Oxford Monographs on Medical Genetics] (New York: Oxford University Press, 1999).

Preves, Sharon E., 'For the Sake of the Children: Destigmatizing Intersexuality', *Journal of Clinical Ethics* 9.4 (Winter 1998), pp. 411-20.

_____ 'Sexing the Intersexed: An Analysis of Sociocultural Responses to Intersexuality', *Signs* 27.2 (Winter 2001), pp. 523-56.

_____ *Intersex and Identity: The Contested Self* (New Brunswick, NJ and London: Rutgers University Press, 2003).

Prosser, Jay, *Second Skins: The Body Narratives of Transsexuality* (New York: Columbia University Press, 1998).

Quero, Martín Hugo Córdova, 'Friendship with Benefits: A Queer Reading of Aelred of Rievaulx and his Theology of Friendship', in Marcella Althaus-Reid and Lisa Isherwood (eds), *The Sexual Theologian: Essays on Sex, God and Politics* (London and New York: T&T Clark, 2004), pp. 26-46.

_____ 'This Body Trans/Forming Me: Indecencies in Transgender/Intersex Bodies, Body Fascism and the Doctrine of the Incarnation', in Marcella Althaus-Reid, and Lisa Isherwood (eds), *Controversies in Body Theology* (London: SCM Press, 2008), pp. 80-128.

Raphael, Melissa, *Thealogy and Embodiment: The Post-Patriarchal Reconstruction of Female Sacrality* (Sheffield: Sheffield Academic Press, 1996).

Rappmann, Susanne, 'The Disabled Body of Christ as a Critical Metaphor: Towards a Theory', *Journal of Religion, Disability and Health* 7.4 (2003), pp. 25-40.

Rees, Geoffrey, '"In the Sight of God": Gender Complementarity and the Male Homosocial Signification of Male-Female Marriage', *Theology & Sexuality* 9.1 (Sept 2002), pp. 19-47.

Reis, Elizabeth, 'Divergence or Disorder? The Politics of Naming Intersex', *Perspectives in Biology and Medicine* 50.4 (2007), pp. 535-43.

_____ 'What's in a Name? History, Medicine and Intersex', paper presented at Critical Sexology seminar, London South Bank University, 3 September 2008.

Robinson, Christopher, 'Developing an Identity Model for Transgender and Intersex Inclusion in Lesbian Communities', in Angela Pattatucci Aragón (ed.), *Challenging Lesbian Norms: Intersex, Transgender, Intersectional, and*

Queer Perspectives (Binghampton, NY: The Haworth Press, 2006), pp. 181–200.

Robinson, John A. T., *The Body: A Study in Pauline Theology* (London: SCM Press, 1952).

Roen, Katrina, '"But We Have To *Do Something*': Surgical "Correction" of Atypical Genitalia', *Body & Society* 14.1 (March 2008), pp. 47–66.

Rogers, Eugene F., *Sexuality and the Christian Body: Their Way Into the Triune God* (Oxford: Blackwell, 1999).

_____ (ed.), *Theology and Sexuality: Classic and Contemporary Readings* (Oxford: Blackwell, 2002).

Rolison, Victoria, 'Can Surgery Better Sex?', *Company Magazine* 34.7 (July 2008), pp. 102–103.

Rosario, Vernon A. (ed.), *Science and Homosexualities* (London and New York: Routledge, 1997).

Roscoe, Will, 'How to Become a Berdache: Toward a Unified Analysis of Gender Diversity', in Gilbert Herdt (ed.), *Third Sex, Third Gender: Beyond Cultural Dimorphism in Culture and History* (New York: Zone Books, 1994), pp. 329–72.

Roughgarden, Joan, *Evolution's Rainbow: Diversity, Gender and Sexuality in Nature and People* (Berkeley, Los Angeles, CA and London: University of California Press, 2004).

Rubin, Henry, *Self-Made Men: Identity and Embodiment among Transsexual Men* (Nashville, TN: Vanderbilt University Press, 2003).

Rudy, Kathy, '"Where Two or More are Gathered": Using Gay Communities as a Model for Christian Sexual Ethics', *Theology & Sexuality* 2.4 (March 1996), pp. 81–99.

_____ 'Subjectivity and Belief', in Gerard Loughlin (ed.), *Queer Theology: Rethinking the Western Body* (Oxford: Blackwell, 2007), pp. 37–49.

Ruether, Rosemary Radford, *Sexism and God-Talk: Towards a Feminist Theology* (London: SCM Press, 1983).

_____ 'Ecofeminism: Symbolic and Social Connections of the Oppression of Women and the Domination of Nature', in Carol J. Adams (ed.), *Ecofeminism and the Sacred* (New York: Continuum, 1993), pp. 13–23.

_____ *Introducing Redemption in Christian Feminism* (Sheffield: Sheffield Academic Press, 1998).

Sacks, Oliver, *The Man Who Mistook His Wife For a Hat* (London: Picador, 1985).

Salzman, Todd A. and Michael G. Lawler, 'Deconstructing and Reconstructing Complementarity as a Foundational Sexual Principle in Catholic Sexual Ethics: The (Im)Morality of Homosexual Acts', in Bernard Hoose, Julie Clague and Gerard Mannion (eds), *Moral Theology for the Twenty-First Century: Essays in Celebration of Kevin Kelly* (London and New York: T&T Clark, 2008), pp. 120–32.

Sax, Leonard, 'How Common is Intersex? A Response to Anne Fausto-Sterling', *Journal of Sex Research* 39 (Aug 2002), pp. 174–79.

Schneider, Laurel C., 'Yahwist Desires: Imagining Divinity Queerly', in Ken Stone (ed.), *Queer Commentary and the Hebrew Bible* (Sheffield: Sheffield Academic Press, 2001), pp. 210–27.

Schober, Justine Marut, 'A Surgeon's Response to the Intersex Controversy', *Journal of Clinical Ethics* 9.4 (Winter 1998), pp. 393–97.

Schüssler Fiorenza, Elisabeth, *In Memory of Her: A Feminist Theological Reconstruction of Christian Origins* (London: SCM, 1995).

Scully, Jackie Leach, 'When Embodiment Isn't Good', *Theology and Sexuality* 9 (Sept 1998), pp. 10–28.

Shaw, Jane, 'Reformed and Enlightened Church', in Gerard Loughlin (ed.), *Queer Theology: Rethinking the Western Body* (Oxford: Blackwell, 2007), pp. 215–29.

Sheridan, Vanessa, *Crossing Over: Liberating the Transgendered Christian* (Cleveland, OH: Pilgrim Press, 2001).

Simpson, Robert Hamilton, 'How to be Fashionably Queer: Reminding the Church of the Importance of Sexual Stories', *Theology & Sexuality* 11.2 (January 2005), pp. 97–108.

Sonderegger, Katherine, 'Barth and Feminism', in John Webster (ed.), *The Cambridge Companion to Karl Barth* (Cambridge: Cambridge University Press, 2000), pp. 258–73.

Soskice, Janet Martin, 'Turning the Symbols', in Daphne Hampson (ed.), *Swallowing a Fishbone? Feminist Theologians Debate Christianity* (London: SPCK, 1996), pp. 17–32.

Soskice, Janet Martin and Diana Lipton (eds), *Feminism & Theology* (Oxford: Oxford University Press, 2003).

Southgate, Christopher (ed.), *God, Humanity and the Cosmos*, (London: T&T Clark, 2003, 2nd edn).

_____ *The Groaning of Creation: God, Evolution, and the Problem of Evil* (Louisville, KY: Westminster John Knox Press, 2008).

Southgate, Christopher, Michael Robert Negus and Andrew Robinson 'Theology and Evolutionary Biology', in Christopher Southgate (ed.), *God, Humanity and the Cosmos* (London: T&T Clark, 2003, 2nd edn), pp. 154–92.

Spencer, Daniel T., 'A Gay Male Ethicist's Response to Queer Readings of the Bible', in Ken Stone (ed.), *Queer Commentary and the Hebrew Bible* (Sheffield: Sheffield Academic Press, 2001), pp. 193–209.

Stewart, David Tabb, 'Leviticus', in Deryn Guest, Robert E. Goss, Mona West and Thomas Bohache (eds), *The Queer Bible Commentary* (London: SCM Press, 2006), pp. 77–104.

Stone, Alison, *Luce Irigaray and the Philosophy of Sexual Difference* (Cambridge: Cambridge University Press, 2006).

Stone, Ken (ed.), *Queer Commentary and the Hebrew Bible* (Sheffield: Sheffield Academic Press, 2001a).

_____ 'Queer Commentary and Biblical Interpretation: An Introduction', in Ken Stone (ed.), *Queer Commentary and the Hebrew Bible* (Sheffield: Sheffield Academic Press, 2001b), pp. 11–34.

_____ *Practicing Safer Texts: Food, Sex and Bible in Queer Perspective* (London and New York: T&T Clark, 2005).

_____ '1 and 2 Samuel', in Deryn Guest, Robert E. Goss, Mona West and Thomas Bohache (eds), *The Queer Bible Commentary* (London: SCM Press, 2006), pp. 195–221.

Stone, Sandy (1991), 'The *Empire* Strikes Back: A Post-transsexual Manifesto', in Katie Conboy, Nadia Medina and Sarah Stanbury (eds), (1997), *Writing on the Body: Female Embodiment and Feminist Identity* (New York: Columbia University Press), pp. 337–59. ?Why 2 different dates?

Strain, L., J.C.S. Dean, M.P.R. Hamilton and D.T. Bonthron 'A True Hermaphrodite Chimera Resulting From Embryo Amalgamation After In Vitro Fertilization', *New England Journal of Medicine* 338, (1998), pp. 166 –69.

Stuart, Elizabeth, *Gay and Lesbian Theologies: Repetitions With Critical Difference* (Aldershot: Ashgate, 2003).

_____ 'Proverbs', in Deryn Guest, Robert E. Goss, Mona West and Thomas Bohache (eds), *The Queer Bible Commentary* (London: SCM Press, 2006), pp. 325–37.

Stuart, Elizabeth, 'Sacramental Flesh', in Gerard Loughlin (ed.), *Queer Theology: Rethinking the Western Body* (Oxford: Blackwell, 2007), pp. 65–75.

Sugirtharajah, R.S., *Postcolonial Reconfigurations: An Alternative Way of Reading the Bible and Doing Theology* (London: SCM Press, 2003).

Sweasey, Peter, *From Queer to Eternity: Spirituality in the Lives of Lesbian, Gay and Bisexual People* (London and Washington: Cassell, 1997).

Swinton, John, 'The Body of Christ has Down's Syndrome,' *Journal of Pastoral Theology* 13.2 (2003), pp. 66–78.

_____ (ed.), *Critical Reflections on Stanley Hauerwas' Theology of Disability: Disabling Society, Enabling Theology, Journal of Religion, Disability and Health* Special Issue, 8.3/4 (2004).

Sytsma, Sharon E. (ed.), *Ethics and Intersex* (Dordrecht: Springer, 2006a).

_____ 'The Ethics of Using Dexamethasone to Prevent Virilization of Female Fetuses', in Sharon E. Sytsma (ed.), *Ethics and Intersex* (Dordrecht: Springer, 2006b), pp. 241–58.

_____ 'Intersexuality, Cultural Influences, and Cultural Relativism,' in Sharon E. Sytsma, (ed.), *Ethics and Intersex* (Dordrecht: Springer, 2006c), pp. 259–70.

Talbott, Rick, 'Imagining the Matthean Eunuch Community: Kyriarchy on the Chopping Block', *Journal of Feminist Studies in Religion* 22.1 (Spring 2006), pp. 21–43.

Talley, Louis, personal communications (12 July 2005, 2 August 2005).

Tan, Amanda Shao, 'The Disabled Christ', *Transformation* 15.4 (1998), pp. 8–14.

Tanis, Justin, *Trans-Gendered: Theology, Ministry, and Communities of Faith* (Cleveland, OH: Pilgrim Press, 2003).

Tanis, Justin, 'Philippians', in Deryn Guest, Robert E. Goss, Mona West and Thomas Bohache (eds), *The Queer Bible Commentary* (London: SCM Press, 2006), pp. 639–55.

Thatcher, Adrian, 'Some Issues with "Some Issues in Human Sexuality"', *Theology & Sexuality* 11.3 (May 2005), pp. 9–29.

Thatcher, Adrian and Elizabeth Stuart (eds), *Christian Perspectives on Sexuality and Gender* (Leominster: Gracewing and Grand Rapids, MI: William B. Eerdmans, 1996).

Thistlethwaite, Susan Brooks, *Sex, Race and God: Christian Feminism in Black and White* (London: Geoffrey Chapman, 1990).

Toomey, Christine, 'The Worst of Both Worlds', *The Sunday Times Magazine*, 28 October 2001, pp. 34–40.

Triea, Kiira, 'Power, Orgasm and the Psychohormonal Research Unit', in Alice Domurat Dreger, *Intersex in the Age of Ethics* (Hagerstown, MD: University Publishing Group, 1999), pp. 140–44.

Turner, Stephanie S., 'Intersex Identities: Locating New Intersections of Sex and Gender', *Gender & Society* 13.4 (August 1999), pp. 457–79.

Turner Syndrome Society of the United States, http://www.turnersyndrome.org/

United Kingdom Intersex Association, http://www.ukia.co.uk/

Valantasis, Richard, *The Gospel of Thomas* (London and New York: Routledge, 1997).

van Huyssteen, Wessel (producer/director), *The 3rd Sex*, broadcast SABC (South Africa), November 2003.

Vannini, Phillip and Dennis D. Waskul, 'Body Ekstasis: Socio-Semiotic Reflections on Surpassing the Dualism of Body-Image', in Dennis Waskul and Phillip Vannini (eds), *Body/Embodiment: Symbolic Interaction and the Sociology of the Body* (Aldershot, Hampshire: Ashgate, 2006), pp. 183–200.

Vatican Congregation for the Doctrine of the Faith, 'Letter to the Bishops of the Catholic Church on the Collaboration of Men and Women in the Church and in the World', (2004), online at www.vatican.va/roman_curia/congregations/ cfaith/documents/rc_con_cfaith_doc_20040731_collaboration_en.html

Volf, Miroslav, 'The Trinity and Gender Identity', in Douglas A. Campbell (ed.), *Gospel and Gender: A Trinitarian Engagement with Being Male and Female in Christ* (London: T&T Clark, 2004), pp. 155–78.

Waetjen, Herman C., 'Same-Sex Sexual Relationships in Antiquity and Sexuality and Sexual Identity in Contemporary American Society', in Robert L. Brawley (ed.), *Biblical Ethics and Homosexuality: Listening to Scripture* (Louisville, KY: Westminster John Knox Press, 1996), pp. 103–16.

Ward, Graham, 'The Erotics of Redemption – After Karl Barth', *Theology & Sexuality* 8 (March 1998), pp. 52–72.

_____ *Cities of God* (London and New York: Routledge, 2000).

_____ 'On the Politics of Embodiment and the Mystery of All Flesh', in Marcella Althaus-Reid and Lisa Isherwood (eds), *The Sexual Theologian: Essays on Sex, God and Politics* (London and New York: T&T Clark, 2004), pp. 71–85.

_____ 'There Is No Sexual Difference', in Gerard Loughlin (ed.), *Queer Theology: Rethinking the Western Body* (Oxford: Blackwell, 2007), pp. 76–85.

Warne, Garry and Vijayalakshmi Bhatia, 'Intersex, East and West', in Sharon E. Sytsma, (ed.), *Ethics and Intersex* (Dordrecht: Springer, 2006), pp. 183–205.

Warner, Michael, 'Introduction: Fear of a Queer Planet', *Social Text* 29 (1991), pp. 3–17.

Warnke, Georgia, 'Intersexuality and the Categories of Sex', *Hypatia* 16.3 (Summer 2001), pp. 126–37.

Waskul, Dennis and Phillip Vannini (eds), *Body/Embodiment: Symbolic Interaction and the Sociology of the Body* (Aldershot, Hampshire: Ashgate, 2006).

Watts, Fraser, 'Transsexualism and the Church', *Theology & Sexuality* 9.1 (September 2002), pp. 63–85.

Webster, John (ed.), *The Cambridge Companion to Karl Barth* (Cambridge: Cambridge University Press, 2000).

_____ '"There is no Past in the Church, so there is no Past in Theology": Barth on the History of Modern Protestant Theology', in John C. McDowell and Mike Higton (eds), *Conversing With Barth* (Aldershot, Hampshire and Burlington, Vermont: Ashgate, 2004), pp. 14–39.

Weil, Elizabeth, 'What if it's (Sort of) a Boy and (Sort of) a Girl?', *The New York Times Magazine* 24 September 2006, online at www.nytimes.com/2006/09/24/magazine/24intersexkids.html?ex=1316750400&en=11174796a1323948&ei=5088&partner=rssnyt&emc=rss

Wendell, Susan, *The Rejected Body: Feminist Philosophical Reflections on Disability* (London and New York: Routledge, 1996).

West, Mona, 'Reading the Bible as Queer Americans: Social Location and the Hebrew Scriptures', *Theology & Sexuality* 10 (March 1999), pp. 28–42.

_____ 'Esther', in Deryn Guest, Robert E. Goss, Mona West and Thomas Bohache (eds), *The Queer Bible Commentary* (London: SCM Press, 2006), pp. 278–85.

Whittle, Stephen, *The Transgender Debate: The Crisis Surrounding Gender Identity* (Reading: South Street Press, 2000).

Wyschogrod, Edith, *Saints and Postmodernism: Revisioning Moral Philosophy* (Chicago, IL and London: University of Chicago Press, 1990).

Young, Frances M., *Face to Face: A Narrative Essay in the Theology of Suffering* (Edinburgh: T&T Clark, 1990).

General Index

INDEX OF SCRIPTURAL REFERENCES

Printed in Great Britain
by Amazon

77479958R00160